Research Series on the Chinese Dream and China's Development Path

Drawing on a large body of empirical studies done over the last two decades, this Series provides its readers with in-depth analyses of the past and present and forecasts for the future course of China's development. It contains the latest research results made by members of the Chinese Academy of Social Sciences. This series is an invaluable companion to every researcher who is trying to gain a deeper understanding of the development model, path and experience unique to China. Thanks to the adoption of Socialism with Chinese characteristics, and the implementation of comprehensive reform and opening-up, China has made tremendous achievements in areas such as political reform, economic development, and social construction, and is making great strides towards the realization of the Chinese dream of national rejuvenation. In addition to presenting a detailed account of many of these achievements, the authors also discuss what lessons other countries can learn from China's experience.

More information about this series at http://www.springer.com/series/13571

Fang Cai
Editor

China's Economic New Normal

Growth, Structure, and Momentum

SSAP

Springer

Editor
Fang Cai
Chinese Academy of Social Sciences
Beijing, China

Translated by
Fuyu Chen
Chongqing Jiaotong University
Chongqing, China

Published with financial support from the Innovation Project of the Chinese Academy of Social Sciences.

ISSN 2363-6866 ISSN 2363-6874 (electronic)
Research Series on the Chinese Dream and China's Development Path
ISBN 978-981-15-3226-9 ISBN 978-981-15-3227-6 (eBook)
https://doi.org/10.1007/978-981-15-3227-6

Jointly published with Social Sciences Academic Press
The print edition is not for sale in China Mainland. Customers from China Mainland please order the print book from Social Sciences Academic Press
ISBN of the Co-Publisher's edition: 978-7-5097-7097-9

This Springer imprint is published by the registered company Springer Nature Singapore Pte Ltd.
The registered company address is: 152 Beach Road, #21-01/04 Gateway East, Singapore 189721, Singapore

Foreword

In order to promote a comprehensive and profound understanding of the "new normal" theory put forward by Chinese President and General Secretary of the Communist Party of China's Central Committee, Xi Jinping, the Academic Division of Economics of the Chinese Academy of Social Sciences (CASS) organized an international symposium on China's economic development, entitled "China's New Normal: Growth, Structure, and Momentum," on December 17, 2014. At the conference, economists from home and abroad explored new directions in China's economic restructuring and new dynamics for China's economic growth, while also exchanging views and suggestions on the paradigm shift of China's macro-control.

Co-organized by the CASS Bureau of International Cooperation and the CASS Institute of Population and Labor Economics, the symposium was attended by over 20 renowned scholars from the US, the UK, the Republic of Korea, and China. Notable participants included Vice Minister Liu Shijin with the Development Research Center of China's State Council, Prof. Kwanho Shin with Korea University, Senior Economist Sun Tao with the International Monetary Fund, Senior Advisor Harry X. Wu with the Conference Board China Center for Economics and Business, Karlis Smits with the World Bank in China, Deputy Chief Economist Zhuang Juzhong with the Asian Development Bank, Chief Strategist Huang Haizhou with China International Capital Corporation Limited, Chief Economist Louis Kuijs with the Royal Bank of Scotland (China), Executive Dean Li Shi with the China Institute for Income Distribution at Beijing Normal University, Dean Gan Li with the Research Institute of Economics and Management at Southwestern (China) University of Finance and Economics, Deputy Dean Huang Yiping with the National School of Development at Peking University, CASS Vice President and Member Li Yang, CASS Vice President and Member Cai Fang, Director Wang Lei with the CASS Bureau of International Cooperation, CASS Members Zhang Zhuoyuan and Wang Tongsan, Deputy Dean Zhang Ping with the CASS Institute of Economics, Office Director Zhang Xiaojing with the CASS Academic Division of Economics, as well as Dean Zhang Juwei,

Research Fellow Du Yang, and Associate Research Fellow Lu Yang with the CASS Institute of Population and Labor Economics.

Utilizing relevant theories and previous global experiences with economic growth, these foreign and Chinese experts systematically and comprehensively summarized and analyzed both the manifestations of and implications for the new normal of both the Chinese and global economy. They also analyzed the foundations of both the real economy while also considering directions for future economic development, all in light of the predicted speed, structure, and momentum of future economic growth. Moreover, they provided enormous amounts of data and valuable guidance toward a more precise forecasting of China's economic trends, an overview for strategically implementing the CPC Central Committee maxim "to understand the new normal, adapt to the new normal, and lead the new normal," and in-depth research experience in their relevant fields.

This book is a selection from the symposium records. For a number of reasons, it was not possible to include herein every speech delivered at the conference. What's more, out of consideration for the book's structure, these texts do not strictly follow the order in which they were delivered. As it goes to press, we regret that we have been unable to fully recapture the grand event or make public all the academic achievements presented at the conference.

February, 2015

Yang Li
Director, Academic Division of Economics
The Chinese Academy of Social Sciences
Beijing, China

Series Preface

Since China's reformand opening began in 1978, the country has come a long way on the path of Socialism with Chinese characteristics, under the leadership of the Communist Party of China. Over 30 years of reform, efforts and sustained spectacular economic growth have turned China into the world's second largest economy, and wrought many profound changes in the Chinese society. These historically significant developments have been garnering increasing attention from scholars, governments, and the general public alike around the world since the 1990s, when the newest wave of China studies began to gather steam. Some of the hottest topics have included the so-called "China miracle", "Chinese phenomenon", "Chinese experience", "Chinese path", and the "Chinese model". Homegrown researchers have soon followed suit. Already hugely productive, this vibrant field is putting out a large number of books each year, with Social Sciences Academic Press alone having published hundreds of titles on a wide range of subjects.

Because most of these books have been written and published in Chinese, however, readership has been limited outside China—even among many who study China—for whom English is still the lingua franca. This language barrier has been an impediment to efforts by academia, business communities, and policy-makers in other countries to form a thorough understanding of contemporary China, of what is distinct about China's past and present may mean not only for her future but also for the future of the world. The need to remove such an impediment is both real and urgent, and the *Research Series on the Chinese Dream and China's Development Path* is my answer to the call.

This series features some of the most notable achievements from the last 20 years by scholars in China in a variety of research topics related to reform and opening. They include both theoretical explorations and empirical studies, and cover economy, society, politics, law, culture, and ecology, the six areas in which reform and opening policies have had the deepest impact and farthest-reaching consequences for the country. Authors for the series have also tried to articulate their visions of the "Chinese Dream" and how the country can realize it in these fields and beyond.

All of the editors and authors for the *Research Series on the Chinese Dream and China's Development Path* are both longtime students of reform and opening and recognized authorities in their respective academic fields. Their credentials and expertise lend credibility to these books, each of which having been subject to a rigorous peer review process for inclusion in the series. As part of the Reform and Development Program under the State Administration of Press, Publication, Radio, Film, and Television of the People's Republic of China, the series is published by Springer, a Germany-based academic publisher of international repute, and distributed overseas. I am confident that it will help fill a lacuna in studies of China in the era of reform and opening.

Xie Shouguang

Contents

Chapter 1
New Normal Brings New Opportunities

Fang Cai

Much discussed nowadays, China's "new normal" has to be traced, logically and virtually, back to the point at which its economic growth began to slow down. For more than ten quarters, China's growth rate has remained below the annual average of the past 35 years and is likely to decline further. Like it or not, economic deceleration has become the inevitable—and a major issue for discussion.

1 What Are the Causes of China's Economic Slowdown?

To understand the "new normal" of China's economy, we must first acquaint ourselves with its "deceleration" and, more specifically, the causes for its economic slowdown. Only with a clear understanding of its causes will we be able to seek opportunities amid the new normal, and to avoid making hasty or wrong decisions. There are currently two contrary views in this regard. Some people believe that the slowdown—which is periodic, rather than chronic—is caused by demand-side changes, and that the economy will return to its normal track and resume its speed of growth when new changes take place among certain periodic factors. Others deem it to be the result of supply-side changes.

In line with the view of demand-based deceleration are two methods commonly used to predict future economic growth. One is the traditional extrapolation method, which may not be applied toward specific predictions but has, more or less, an effect on our ways of thinking.

The other approach is the convergence method, a modification of the extrapolation method. Through convergence analysis, we conclude that developing countries still benefit from huge second-mover advantages, and that a country's respective stage of economic development is almost without exception related to its level of GDP per

F. Cai (✉)
Chinese Academy of Social Sciences, Beijing, China
e-mail: caifang@cass.org.cn

F. Cai (ed.), *China's Economic New Normal*, Research Series on the Chinese Dream and China's Development Path, https://doi.org/10.1007/978-981-15-3227-6_1

capita. For example, the GDP per capita in mainland China is, at present, only 21% of that of the US. According to our analysis, Japan hit that figure in around 1950, South Korea in 1977, Singapore in 1967, and Taiwan of China in 1974. Since then, these economies had invariably experienced 20 years of rapid economic growth, ranging from seven to nine percent annually. If we extrapolate on that basis, China must be able to sustain a relatively high speed of economic growth for another 20 years, with the new normal as the starting point. This is the conviction held by many.

Meanwhile, there is also a purely statistical method of forecasting China's economic performance. In light of international experiences, for example, the growth of GDP per capita is bound to slow down when it reaches a certain level. Once it does occur, its causes are always anxiously sought, even though they usually vary greatly from economy to economy. This is what Lawrence H. Summers called "regression to the mean" in one of his latest publications. In other words, high-speed economic growth will have to return to the mean eventually, which, in this case, is the global average. We are looking forward to his follow-up findings to explain reasons for both the deceleration and the regression to the mean.

On the other hand, if China's economic deceleration is caused by recent changes to the supply side—to those factors that have long been driving China's economic growth, like the disappearance of the demographic dividend—it would be more advisable to predict its economic prospects using the potential growth rate.

2 Further Demand Stimulation Is a Recipe for Disaster

Different justifications for the deceleration will lead to different policy responses, which will lead to different results. For example, if the slowdown is attributed to demand factors, a series of measures will naturally be taken to stimulate demand. This can sometimes be the exact wrong approach, however. As things now stand, if China is to overstimulate its domestic demand, it would be inviting the following consequences:

First of all, it will lead to a further softening of the budget constraints on enterprises. Stimulus policies will soften the budget constraints for both state-owned enterprises and private enterprises, and even some small- and medium-sized enterprises, which will result in declining competitiveness and, in extreme cases, turn them into zombie enterprises that are more dead than alive. This is what we have learned from the bitter precedent set by Japanese growth.

Secondly, it can further increase China's financial and debt risks. Many studies have revealed that China's leverage level is now very high, and in fact well beyond what might be imagined. Such risks are usually referred to as "controllable," but, we should never forget, one of the preconditions for their being controllable is the "existence" of such risks in the first place.

Thirdly, it will result in an overall overcapacity of both manufactured products and infrastructure facilities. China's manufacturing overcapacity is widely recognized. As for infrastructure facilities, further construction is not always preferable. If existing infrastructure is not being fully utilized, it will indeed represent a new form of overcapacity.

What's more, according to our research, over-stimulation will also bring risks to China's labor market. Stimulus policies seem to be doing great good for employment, but is it really a good thing to attract large numbers of semi-skilled and even unskilled laborers to industries related to infrastructure construction, especially when we know such industries are likely to be subjected to overcapacity and huge potential risks, or even be prone to bubbles? In doing so, we will have to take into account the cyclical unemployment of such laborers. This has been borne out by the European experience, wherein many Spanish workers no longer attended school or obtained skills, whose subsequent cyclical unemployment eventually turned into structural unemployment. The labor market in China looks extremely inspiring today, but would probably slip into a new stage if domestic demand were to be overstimulated.

Therefore, we should know better than to merely stimulate domestic demand. Overstimulation can only result in a series of serious consequences, turning the economic slowdown into stagnation and pushing China closer to the middle income trap.

3 Reform Toward a New Environment for Creative Destruction

Correctly understood and proactively dealt with, the new normal can offer new opportunities and thus extend the period of strategic opportunities for China's economic development. Specifically, this judgment is based on the following:

On the one hand, having an appropriate understanding of the new normal is conducive to sustaining China's economic growth through reform, one of the dividends of this reformation process. According to our studies, reforms in certain sectors have had an immediate effect in increasing the potential growth rate. This is something that traditional stimulus measures have failed to do. Stimulation, as previously mentioned, will only result in the increased softening of the budget constraints for enterprises. Under the circumstances of an extremely loose policy environment bolstered by government subsidies, an enterprise will lose interest in shifting from the input-driven model of growth to one driven by the increase of its total factor productivity. To increase total factor productivity and thus drive economic growth is beyond the reach of stimulus policies. Only through reform is such an outcome possible. A key step in this process, however, is to harden the budget constraints on Chinese enterprises.

On the other hand, the conversion from an input-driven model of growth to a new model driven by the increase of total factor productivity is essentially connected to industrial restructuring and upgrading. In conventional theories, industrial upgrading is the replacement of labor by capital as labor costs increase. Under rigid external conditions, it is quite reasonable for enterprises to replace labor with capital. But such replacement—labor by capital and man by machine—is very likely to go against the principle of comparative advantages under stimulus policies when the government has given considerable weight to the comparative advantages of enterprises in the years ahead. In fact, it will only decrease the return on capital in enterprises; in other words, it will inevitably lead to diminishing returns to capital. Therefore, the improvement of total factor productivity should always be the core of industrial restructuring and upgrading.

There are many ways for enterprises to improve their productivity. Macroscopically speaking, higher total factor productivity lies in the increase of resource allocation efficiency. Under the old normal conditions, improvement of total factor productivity was quite easy. For example, resource efficiency was improved when our labor force flowed from the primary industry to the secondary and tertiary industries, a shift from lower-productivity sectors to higher-productivity ones.

Even when resources enter the same industry, say, the secondary industry, opportunities for profit can vary from sector to sector. For example, real estate was the most favored sector under the old normal conditions, and many resources swamped it, which may be regarded as a reallocation of the resources from a macroscopic point of view. Under the new normal, however, such chances have been significantly reduced, and we have entered the third stage of resource allocation—reallocation of resources among different enterprises within the same sector. An enterprise of high productivity has a better chance of developing and expanding, and even taking advantage of the productive factors that belong to others. On the contrary, if an enterprise cannot improve its productivity so as to sustain its competitiveness, it is bound to be sidelined. Therefore, in order to improve total factor productivity, we need a new environment for creative destruction, which will be a normal demand of growth.

Under the new normal conditions, the government should no longer arbitrarily protect enterprises by means of traditional institutions, stimulus macroeconomic policies, or industrial policies. The only right thing to do is to create a better environment for competition, which is the key to the improvement of China's total factor productivity and the transformation of China's economic development from input-driven growth to productivity-driven growth. That is, reform must be regarded as integral to China's new normal.

Chapter 2
Understanding and Adapting to the New Normal

Yang Li

1 Introduction

The "new normal," as a concept, was formally written into China's national development strategy at the conclusion of the recent Central Economic Working Conference. A number of questions have arisen in response: How is this different from the old normal? How will the country shift from the old to the new normal?

In order to address such questions, we must first elucidate the following key points:

First of all, the "new normal" is to be understood in relation to the "old normal." Generally speaking, the "new normal" began with the recent global crisis. It has divided both international and Chinese development since the 1980s into two phases that are systematically different in terms of both economic performance and the economic system that supports such performances.

Secondly, the new normal is a regular state of affairs. That is, the new normal is neither intermittent nor transient, and unlike certain regulatory policies, it is highly unlikely to change anytime soon. In other words, there is a high probability that the old normal will never return. Therefore, we must quickly adapt to the new normal while simultaneously guiding its future development, which was one of the tasks proposed at the closing of the Central Economic Working Conference.

Thirdly, the new normal carries with it new momentum for development. The new momentum, however, is still more of a possibility than an actual state of affairs, and may not necessarily develop according to expectations. Therefore, we must steadfastly and unswervingly reform those development models that were taken for granted under the old normal. On the other hand, however, we must also enact a revolutionary adjustment to our existing economic structure, which has been distorted by the old normal. When we talk about China's entering the new normal, it will never be a pleasant shift to the new stage; rather, it marks the beginning of a new period

Y. Li (✉)
Chinese Academy of Social Sciences, Beijing, China
e-mail: liyang@cass.org.cn

F. Cai (ed.), *China's Economic New Normal*, Research Series on the Chinese Dream and China's Development Path, https://doi.org/10.1007/978-981-15-3227-6_2

when we must implement reform and structural adjustment with painstaking efforts. Only through reform can we fully reap the benefits of the new normal.

Finally, in the context of globalization, the new normal is also a universal or global phenomenon. Hence, to understand China's new normal, it is necessary to first understand the new normal as it pertains to global development overall—just as China's old normal required understanding within an international context. In other words, we have to view China's new normal from a global perspective.

After establishing that the new normal is not a periodic phenomenon, what, then, is the so-called crisis? Many people tend to associate China's new normal with the recent global financial crisis, as they happened to coincide within roughly the same period of time. Thus, we might begin by discussing what exactly a crisis is.

As I see it, a crisis indicates an aberration in the economy—that the economy has run off the rails. In that case, there can only be two ways out of the crisis. One is to adjust, return to the old track, and repeat the process over a period of years, forever repeating the financial cycle as defined by economists. The other is to move in a different direction and find a new path, rather than return to the old normal state, which necessitates overcoming the inertia of the old cycles. Why do we call it a "new" normal in today's China? The reason lies exactly in that it differs from the recession stage typical of normal economic cycles. Instead of regressing to the old track, it is blazing a new trail in a new direction. Hence, the new normal suggests a revolutionary transformation.

On a global scale, a new normal means supply-chain reengineering, the reshaping of global divisions, economic restructuring, reformation of the world's intellectual systems, and the reconstruction of existing power relationships. As a significant force on the global economic stage, China will certainly undergo and participate in the above-mentioned major changes. For China, however, the new normal is far more than that. It is also an opportunity for the rebirth of the Chinese economy—it is time that we break away from the old development models and shift to a new track of development; it is time that we thoroughly adjust the old economic structures and shift to a new economic structure; it is time that we completely do away with the old system of dynamics and seek new momentum for growth.

The above represent a number of preconditions for understanding China's new normal. Specifically, we must address two questions: Why the shift from the old to the new normal? And in what aspect(s) can we leap forward under the new normal? Both issues will be discussed, respectively, in the following pages.

2 Causes of the Shift Toward the New Normal

When it comes to the reasons for such a shift, we have to look back at why such a high rate of growth was sustainable in China over the past decades in the first place. Why is it no longer sustainable now? And why does the Chinese economy need to grow at low-to-medium rates? We will answer these questions through a contrastive analysis of the old with the new conditions.

2.1 *China's New Normal Is a Result of the Decreasing Efficiency of Resource Allocation*

In the first place, we must look at the old and new normal states from the perspective of resource allocation. Under the old normal, the allocation structure of the Chinese economy was reflected in a number of industrial resource transfers. Over the past three decades, there has been a steady and massive transfer of large amounts of resources, including human resources, from the primary sector (agriculture and plantation) to the secondary sector (mainly manufacturing). It has lasted for more than 30 years and, as a matter of fact, has corresponded to China's industrialization process, which saw tens of millions of laborers shifted annually from the primary industry to the secondary industry—equivalent to the population of a medium-sized European country.

What are we concerned about in this transfer process? Our focus is on the disparity in labor productivity between the two sectors, as well as the difference in the overall productivity caused by this transfer. Further analysis of this situation makes one thing quite visible: the labor productivity of China's primary sector (e.g., agriculture and plantation) has been fairly low, and the productivity of its manufacturing is roughly ten to fifteen, and even more, times that of its agriculture. Thus we can conclude that, over the past decades, the transfer of resources from China's primary industry to its secondary industry—that is, from agriculture to manufacturing—has been a process of improvement to China's overall labor productivity, which also means an acceleration of China's economic growth. This is our real-economic interpretation of China's old normal in light of resource allocation efficiency.

Further probing using the same analytical framework reveals, however, that the opposite is taking place. The labor force is, at present, already saturated in China's manufacturing sector and, together with other resources, started transferring toward the tertiary sector, against the background of China's national strategy to increase the proportion of its tertiary industry. Likewise, what if we make a comparison of the labor productivity of China's secondary sector—in particular its manufacturing—and that of its tertiary sector? China's tertiary industry is primarily service-oriented, which is typical of low labor productivity. In a manufacturing-oriented to service-oriented transition, almost all countries, including those with developed economies, have experienced a decline in labor productivity, as it is generally lower in services than in manufacturing sectors. This is especially true in China, where the majority of services remain at the lower end up till now.

As our study in Shanghai shows, the labor productivity of the city's service sectors is only 70% of that in its manufacturing sector. Relatively low labor productivity in the service sector seems inevitable in the ongoing transfer of both the labor force and other resources from manufacturing to services. What follows will be the inevitable decline of overall labor productivity and, as a result, we will have to accept a lower growth rate for the Chinese economy overall.

Secondly, we must look at the old and new normal states from the perspective of factor supply. This is because the economy is an outcome of the combination of labor input, capital formation, and technical progress. Labor input comes first. Under the old normal, tens of millions of idle and semi-idle laborers were introduced into China's manufacturing industry every year, which was, up until recently, the major factor supporting China's rapid economic growth. But now, significant changes have taken place within China's population structure, marking the end of the country's traditional, cheap-labor-based industry model. In other words, the demographic dividend has disappeared in China as labor costs rise. Therefore, under the new normal, all we see is a relative decline in China's labor input, which can no longer increase its economic growth rate.

What follows, then, is capital formation. China's high savings rate has long been a fact. On that basis, China has sustained a high rate of capital formation for more than 30 years. With the disappearance of its conventional demographic dividend, however, along with the termination of its traditional industrialization and a gradual increase in its spending power, and, in particular, with diminishing marginal returns to capital, non-inflationary capital input has started to decline. Only through calculations based on the flows-of-funds tables are we able to obtain an accurate rate of capital formation. The more convenient way is estimation by use of an approximate indicator—in this case, the growth rate of China's fixed investments. Under the old normal, the average annual growth rate of China's fixed investments was 26%. Under the new normal, however, the figure has been declining every year: below 20% in 2012, below 18% in 2013, and below 16% in 2014. We estimate it will have hit 14% or even lower in 2015. It is widely predicted by scholars that China's fixed investments will grow at an annual rate of around 10% during the 13th Five Year Plan period. This translates into a shrinking role of capital formation in boosting China's economic growth. When full consideration is given to the two aforementioned factors, we can only rely on technical progress for growth. It is a pity, therefore, that our technological growth is, even to this day, chronically slow.

Thirdly, we must consider both the old and new normal states from the perspective of the capacity for innovation. In China, at least as long as it continues to lag behind the innovative capacities of numerous foreign countries, innovation comprises a broad number of aspects. For example, the term may well be considered to include the introduction of technology and management skills that are more advanced than those we already have. Such "innovation" is still far from being world-leading in either the strict sense or in terms of independent intellectual property.

When we look at China's innovations in this broad sense, we can find that, under the old normal, we had indeed achieved perfection in terms of importing technologies which were not at all cutting edge and of which we had no independent intellectual property rights. For more than 30 years, China's technological innovation has been a process of learning from the rest of the world and narrowing the gap in between, which accords with a classical model of development economics. For a long while, it has been quite unnecessary, as it were, to develop new technologies of our own. The model has been: open the door and wave in foreign capital, and this would bring more advanced technology—enough for us to imitate and learn.

On the other hand, we have easily transferred our underemployed rural labor forces to export-oriented manufacturing sectors that are heavily dependent on imported technologies and, simultaneously, constantly increased our productivity. Over the past few decades, this strategy of "putting both ends of production on foreign markets" has been a huge success. At one time, China's total import and export value accounted for 70% of its GDP, an extremely high percentage resulting from this strategy of importing technology and exporting products. But now, the good old days are over. The once-underemployed rural labor forces are now depleted; manufacturing employment has begun falling from its peak; economic growth relies increasingly on service sectors that are significant in their low productivity; and the country's enormous stock of capital—what we have inherited from large-scale investments over the past decades—requires maintenance and the support of more savings. Everything seems to have run into a bottleneck overnight.

In summary, we have almost finished the race to catch up with the world's developed countries, so much so that there is very little left to learn from our foreign counterparts. Accordingly, we must turn to brand new, innovation-oriented models of economic development. This is exactly the reason why Xi Jinping, General Secretary of the CPC Central Committee, stressed that the direction of China's science and technological development is "innovation, innovation, and [more] innovation." His remarks have underlined the critical importance of innovation for China's future economic development.

Finally, we must look at the old and new normal states from the perspective of environmental and resource constraints. In the past, China's extensive method of economic development was typified by wasted resources. However, such a model of growth—based as it was on high resource consumption—is no longer sustainable in the 21st century, when the prices of the world's energy and other commodities soar and fluctuate wildly.

What's more, while it was once taken for granted as a "negligible" external factor, the environment has turned out to be a hard constraint on the traditional model of economic development, with haze obscuring our sky, excessive heavy metals poisoning our food, and our drinking water being seriously polluted. To cope with these environmental constraints, a series of response indicators have been designated among the many indices of economic growth. For example, there are currently four levels of responses (i.e., blue, yellow, orange, and green) for environmental factors, and once environmental degradation reaches a certain level, a designated number of factories and vehicles are suspended from running. Like it or not, environmental and resource constraints have already become a new negative consideration in China's economic growth, which is totally endogenous in the traditional model of development. Yet never before has it been so real—as large numbers of factories are shut down in neighboring areas when the Beijing smog hits hazardous levels. That is to say, the environment has indeed become a hard negative constraint.

By way of comparison and contrast, we have analyzed the inevitability of China's transition from the old normal to the new normal. During the transition period, we must primarily base our economic growth target on China's potential growth rates, which will likely continue to be the major foundation of our growth targets and macroeconomic policies under the new normal. A great number of studies have been done by many domestic and foreign research institutes on the potential growth rates of the Chinese economy. Table 1 is the prediction of the CASS Macroeconomic

Table 1 Potential growth rates of the Chinese economy

Period	α	1 − α	Potential growth (%)	Capital growth (%)	Labor growth (%)	Proportion of technical progress	Impact of energy saving and emission reduction
2011–2015	0.7	0.3	7.8–8.7	10–11	0.8	0.2	−1
2016–2020	0.6	0.4	5.7–6.6	9–10	−1	0.3	−1
2021–2030	0.5	0.5	5.4–6.3	8–9	−0.5	0.4	−0.5

Institution, which forecasts a steady decline in the potential growth rates of the Chinese economy by the year 2030.

The decline may make us feel uncomfortable, but if the slightly lower potential rate reflects highly effective economic growth, we should still take pride in such growth—and the fact that China is on its way to becoming a comprehensive world power. Under the new normal, economic growth is bound to slow down eventually, and from that alone, some people may assume that China's new normal equals a new recession and a hard landing for the Chinese economy. They think wrong. The statistics may not be as pretty as they were, but China's new normal indicates a new stage of higher-quality and more efficient growth for the overall economy, a new leap forward for China economically.

First of all, the new normal is conducive to "squeezing the water out" and ridding the Chinese economy of overdependence on investments and exports.

The so-called "water" problem herein refers to the underreporting, concealment, and misrepresentation of economic statistics by local governments across different levels. Why are we so concerned with "the water problem" in China's economic statistics? Over the past decades, a great deal of investment has failed to increase our production capacity, and even though some investment has succeeded in capacity expansion, much has turned out to be excess capacity—that is, "water." A glimpse of the Chinese economy tells us that the declining growth rate corresponds exactly with the declining growth of investment. Therefore, if we reduce or halt such investments as lead to ineffective or excess capacity from the very beginning, we will be able to rid the Chinese economy of an overdependence on investment. This is where we start to break away from the traditional model of economic development and where we start to squeeze the water out of the Chinese economy.

If the economic slowdown under the new normal is nothing but a process of "squeezing the water out," then we should all greet such deceleration with cheers. But we would also do well to probe further into the problem so as to find the real cause of the economic slowdown. According to statistical analysis, the declining economic growth results from declining investment. If investment is also part of the cause of our overcapacity, another obstinate problem in China's distorted economic structure, we must give a warmer welcome to such decline. To constantly "squeeze out the water" is not only a specific approach to quality and efficiency improvement and sustainable development, but also the only way to upgrade China into a developed economy. Isn't this what we have been desiring for more than a decade? It is time to stop being afraid of what we want.

Secondly, the new normal is conducive to the implementation of an innovation-driven development strategy.

Now that investment and exports are no longer reliable drivers of the economy, we have no choice but to shift to a new, innovation-driven model of development. Continual investment over the past years has pulled down the marginal returns to capital, and consequently, most investors are wary of further injection. On the other hand, the proportion of China's net exports in GDP has lingered below 3% for a couple of years, which is largely related to recent changes in both the international and domestic environments. In light of its contribution rate, there is no doubt that exports have ceased to be a major engine of the Chinese economy. What to count on then? Innovation is the only resort. Nevertheless, a practical problem for the time being is our weak institutional foundation for innovation. Accordingly, to boost innovation, we must establish positive incentive mechanisms and straighten out the price system. Furthermore, we should bring into play the decisive role of the market and, as needed, the government's role in resource allocation. Obviously, we are going to be faced with huge challenges in the transition from input-driven growth to innovation-driven growth.

Thirdly, the new normal is conducive to rationalizing the relationship between the government and the market.

One of the most prominent characteristics of the new normal is the weakening of the GDP-based appraisal mechanism. It will not only weaken local governments' impulse to invite or make more investments, but will also restrain them from habitual functional offside and absences, so that they can really shift their attention to issues concerning people's livelihood, such as increasing income, enhancing employment, improving social security, maintaining law and order, and environmental protection.

In the meantime, the new normal also requires us to strengthen the principal status of enterprises and their dominant role in resource allocation and maximize resource allocation according to the rules, prices, and competitions already extant on the market.

Fourthly, the new normal is conducive to the construction of an ecologically-mindful civilization.

Only under the terms of a relatively loose macro environment are we able to cope with such problems as resource wastefulness and the destruction of the environment, so as to substantially press forward with the construction of ecological civilization. To this end, we need to make changes to a series of our intuitions and mechanisms. For example, any input relevant to environmental governance is treated as a cost within the existing statistical framework, which views the issue from an input perspective. As a result, many enterprises involved in environmental violations (i.e., environmental violators) are unwilling to increase their input towards environmental protections. Can we just refine our statistical approach to change the present situation? In April 2003, the United States made a significant change to its statistical system, whereupon funds generated by research and development (R&D) and cultural industry royalties are counted towards output, both of which had been previously counted as costs.

The revision boosted US GDP by 3%. The main purpose of the US government was to encourage corporate innovation and boost the development of its cultural and creative industries. Such adjustment has proved enlightening for China, where—as I understand it—statistical adjustment is being considered by the relevant government departments.

When enterprise input towards environmental governance—such as in pollution control and in research and development—is invariably counted as output, greater numbers of enterprises will be motivated to increase investment in this field. That is the hope of our environmental recovery and ecological restoration, which will lay a solid foundation for further innovation.

Finally, the new normal is conducive to the promotion of social equity and justice.

For a long time, we have been relying too much on investment in pursuit of higher growth. Our excessive reliance on investment has rendered an unequal preeminence to capital owners in economic activities. Consequently, capital rules labor in production, while profits erode wages in distribution. This has resulted in a very small proportion of labor income in distribution, and may give rise to new obstacles to laborers' social mobility, as well as a series of other social problems. Should the current distributional inequality persist, it is bound to lead to further polarization, accompanied by the solidification of social strata and unequal interest patterns. In our view, the transition from reliance on investment to reliance on consumption will significantly contribute to weakening the dominance of capital over the economy and therefore to promoting social equity and justice in China.

The above-listed are five of the brightest aspects of China's new normal. Yet it should be noted that, at this time, most of them remain merely a possibility. More accurately, they not only represent opportunity, but also pressure and the impetus to act. To make them a reality, we must strengthen our national economic reforms.

In conclusion, we must fully understand the new normal and adapt to its new conditions. In the first place, the new normal has brought us new opportunities for development and endowed China's period of strategic opportunities with brand-new connotations. Secondly, we have to positively adjust our conceptualizations, mentality, strategy, and policy, so as to quickly adapt to the new normal—both new ways of life and new modes of production—and play a leading role in the new normal era. Finally, the new normal is already a global phenomenon, and, in response to its call for changes, reforms are already well under way in major countries, which marks the official kickoff of what can be considered a global competition in reform. To meet such challenges, the Third and Fourth Plenary Sessions of the 18th CPC Central Committee, respectively, have adopted certain decisions on several major issues concerning the comprehensive deepening of reformations and conclusions on major issues, comprehensively advancing the rule of law. It is our firm conviction that both decisions, like beacons, will lead the Chinese people to carry out a new round of reforms and bring about the Chinese dream of the great rejuvenation of the Chinese nation.

Chapter 3
The Inevitability of the New Normal

Shijin Liu

1 Where Is the Point of Equilibrium for Medium-to-High Growth?

The Chinese economy has entered a period of economic growth categorized as a "new normal," but we have not yet come up with a theory that adequately and convincingly elaborates this new normal, nor have we developed an internationally-accepted theoretical or analytical framework for it. In this respect, our economists seem to have thus far failed to meet their obligations.

A marked deceleration of economic growth is the first component of the new normal. During my leadership of a team under the Development Research Center of the State Council, we conducted a 2010 study on the historical experience of post-WWII industrialization. According to our findings, while a number of countries/economies have entered the period of industrialization, most have proven unsuccessful and have successively fallen into the middle income trap. Among those economies that have managed to avoid the middle income trap—such as Japan, South Korea, Singapore, and Hong Kong and Taiwan of China—our study has revealed something in common. That is, following 20–30 years of high-speed growth, their economies invariably experienced a slowdown once their GDP per capita reached USD 10,000.

Frankly, we were not bold enough to declare at that time that this was a regular feature across all economies, as we were still at an initial stage of research. Later on, however, we found that this was a repeating phenomenon—almost all economies are subject to certain changes in their economic structure, working-age population, and employment structure as soon as they hit that USD 10,000 point. What we did then was purely economic: we analyzed the Chinese course of development using three different methods. The first was a holistic approach to the Chinese economy. The second was a classificatory analysis that divided the 31 provincial divisions

S. Liu (✉)
Development Research Center of the State Council of China, Beijing, China
e-mail: wxu@drc.gov.cn

F. Cai (ed.), *China's Economic New Normal*, Research Series on the Chinese Dream and China's Development Path, https://doi.org/10.1007/978-981-15-3227-6_3

in mainland China into six groups of varying development levels. And the third was a quantitative analysis of several key indicators, such as power production, car ownership, steel quantity, etc. To our great surprise, our conclusions suggested that China's growth rate would start declining somewhere between 2013 and 2015. That is to say, China would also encounter economic slowdown when its GDP per capita reached USD 10,000.

We refer to such a slowdown as a phase transition for China's economic growth—from high-speed growth at around 10% to medium-to-high growth. This transition is not yet over, we believe, and that is why the downward pressure of the Chinese economy has been so strongly felt over the past years. When will it be over? Or rather, where is the so-called equilibrium point of this medium-to-high growth? It is well worthwhile to dig into the issue.

According to our most recent estimation, the annual growth rate of China's investment is likely to fall between 10 and 11% in the future. Specifically, its fixed investment will likely grow by about 13%, manufacturing investment by about 11%, and real estate investment by about 5%. What's more, its consumption (total retail sales of consumer goods) growth rate is predicted to be around 10%, and its export growth rate will likely fall somewhere between 5% and 10%. All these ultimately translate into a potential growth rate for China's GDP ranging from 6 to 6.5%—most probably around 6.4% in our estimates, which may turn out to be the equilibrium point of China's medium-to-high growth.

2 When Will We Reach the Equilibrium Point?

When, then, will the so-called equilibrium point arrive? This question demands further observation. In fact, China's economic growth is primarily based on its large investment, most of which has gone into infrastructure, real estate, and manufacturing, all of which add up to 80–85% of China's total investments. Moreover, its investment in manufacturing is heavily dependent on its infrastructure, real estate, and exports. In popular terms, we can only wait for the other shoe to drop—that is, only when infrastructure, exports, and real estate have all smoothly landed in succession can there be soft and safe landing for the Chinese economy overall. Up until now, we have basically finished with the "landing" of our infrastructure and exports, but real estate remains a major problem. There is still great uncertainty as to how our real estate is to land on its feet and whether we should settle the matter at one go or cope with it in a progressive, more gentle way. Once the country's medium-to-high growth reaches its equilibrium point, the new normal will stabilize for, in my opinion, about five years. Put plainly, we have a great opportunity to achieve our national developmental goals by 2020.

In recent years, there have been many studies on this topic, both at home and abroad. What we have done is indeed empirical, and therefore must not be taken as a foundational theoretical framework. The most basic convergence analysis is to compare China—or any of the later-developing countries in the broader sense—with the representative developed economies of the world (e.g., the US). For example, Japanese GDP was 21% that of the US in the early 1950s, and what followed was over 20 years of high-speed growth for the Japanese economy. At present, the Chinese GDP is also about 20% that of the US, so it is all-too-easy to assume that there would be another 20 years of high-speed growth for the Chinese economy. It sounds so reasonable that it is received wisdom. Yet it is wrong—logically. Suppose Japan was 21 years old and the United States was 100 when, in the early 1950s, the Japanese GDP accounted for 21% that of the US. As a 21-year-old young man, Japan was at the prime of his life and full of enough energy to run fast for another 20 years—until he was in his forties. Yes, he made it—the high-speed growth of the Japanese economy did not slow down until the early 1970s. It is true that the Chinese GDP is now about 20% that of the US, but how old is China now? So anthropomorphized, he is already in his 40s—equivalent to Japan in the early 1970s. How old is the United States then? No, it is no longer 100—it is 200 years old. Is it possible for the 40-year-old man to keep running fast for another 20 years, as he has been doing over the last 20 years? The answer is, unequivocally, no. Japan was in his 40s when its economic growth decelerated in the early 1970s—when its GDP per capita amounted to around USD 10,000. What happened to Japan now is happening again—the Chinese growth will begin to slow down when its GDP per capita reaches USD 10,000. There seems to be something in common among the later-developing countries—each has the chance of high-speed growth for a certain period of time. The difference lies only in where they are on the developmental timeline.

3 Nonnegligible Peak Demand

What follows is something that no Chinese or foreign economist should ignore as a core component of their theoretical frameworks. Traditional development economics usually focuses on the so-called economic take-off, or the commencement of industrialization, of a traditional developing country. Yet little has been done theoretically as to how long it will be able to persist after taking off or when it ought to touch down, and we are still in need of a mature theory in this regard. Lawrence Summers has begun to address this question, and so has Lionel W. McKenzie, who put forward similar questions in his South Korea studies two years ago. It has been touched here and there in many relevant studies across the world, but we still lack a theoretical framework that adequately elaborates the deceleration of economic growth. In fact, the much discussed trend today is no more than a conclusion of economic observations, and thus remains far removed from stating an overarching, comprehensive analytical framework. Our analytical framework gives priority to demand—we primarily take into consideration long-term demands, rather than short-term demands, and in particular structural changes in demands. On the other hand, supply is certainly important, too, and we do not neglect its role. In my eyes, further research must be done on both demand and supply, both of which are indispensable for growth, and focus attention on a number of key issues.

In our analysis, we have particularly stressed the concept of "peak demand." What does it mean, then? In the process of industrialization and urbanization, "peak demand" refers to the highest demand that has occurred over a specified time period, or a historically high point of the aggregate demand for some product. It can also refer to the highest point of demand growth in some cases. The peak demand does indeed exist. For example, China's real estate and infrastructure investment and industrial growth are slowing down because we have already reached the peak demand for houses, infrastructure facilities, and industrial products. This is also empirical of course. While many people have taken demand for granted as a short-term issue, we deem it necessary to pay more attention to medium- and long-term demands or, rather, the structural changes in demands.

Take for example the demand for housing. What is the peak demand for residential housing? An average of 30 m^2 would be large enough for an urban resident. What is bad about an average of 60 or 90 m^2? And why do people in many countries cease to pursue larger houses when they have an average of 30 m^2? Cleaning, for example, would be the first problem for a big house in the short term. In the long run, people's demand for houses is predetermined by their technological levels. It depends on a series of technology—not merely construction technology, but also transportation technology, food technology, health technology, and agricultural technology. Everyone has to strike a balance among different demands and decide according to individual likes and dislikes.

4 Questions to Be Answered

Another key issue at stake is supply. According to Cai Fang, noted demographer and economist, China has reached the Lewis Turning Point, or at least has shown some signs of it. This is quite controversial in foreign countries. If his judgment proves to be correct, the Lewis Turning Point and the peak demand—the highest point of supply and the highest point of demand—must have arrived almost simultaneously in China. Why, then, have they arrived together? And how are they related to each other? These questions have long been perplexing.

As a matter of fact, the transformation of power is a long-term process that will never be settled by means of a short-term stimulus. Historically, for example, Japan used massive stimulus policies, but they actually turned out to be the culprit behind its economic bubbles and mired the country in recession for a long time. On the other hand, some countries have been quite successful in utilizing short-term stimulus policies. South Korea is a good example. In response to the 1998 financial crisis, South Korea implemented dramatic structural reforms and gave birth to a cluster of technology-based companies spearheaded by Samsung. Even though Samsung has recently shown signs of internal and market strife, there is no denial that it overtook many Japanese electronics giants almost overnight. For China, it is worthwhile to learn from the success of our neighbor here in terms of economic transformation.

Finally, macroeconomic policies are certainly very important. If an economy slumps, something must have gone wrong. Take, for example, the ongoing issue of deflation in China. Is it a short-term problem or not? Sometimes short-term problems can be mixed up with long-term issues, but does that mean a short-term therapy should be applied to a chronic disease? This is another question worthy of careful deliberation.

5 Reforms and an Increase in the Potential Growth Rate

Many people now believe that we can reform with the goal of a higher potential growth rate. I doubt this view, and in fact think it quite questionable. What is wrong with it? Is reform bound to increase our potential growth rate? Let me give some examples.

The first goal is the anti-corruption campaign that is ongoing in China. Is anti-corruption part of our reform? I would say yes, because its ultimate goal is to establish a mechanism that addresses both the symptoms and causes of corruption. In fact, much of our reform has been political or institutional and will continue to be so in the coming years. It is true that many restaurants have closed down due to decreased demand, which will absolutely have a negative effect on our economic growth. For example, there used to be endless banquets held by officials during their training periods in the party school, events which left everyone exhausted. That was an institutional problem. Since the CPC Central Committee introduced its eight-point austerity rules, both teachers and students have felt much less burdened by the necessity of banqueting at the party school. The so-called demand for such banquets is indeed an extravagance. Therefore, it is totally unnecessary to regret the decline of such a demand, which is in fact a good thing, even though it negatively impacts our GDP.

The second is China's investment in infrastructure construction. We should not only be concerned about China's real estate bubble, but must also recognize that infrastructure facility and production capacity can turn into bubbles when they are overrepresented. A big part of China's overcapacity is rooted in administrative factors. I insist on a relatively low growth rate, because, in most cases, breakneck growth is extremely risky. Why do we have to make new investment when demand is not yet strong enough? Without sufficient demand, infrastructure construction would offer no return on investment, to say nothing of its ability to bring about any long-term social benefit. Once our reform takes place, this kind of ineffective and wasteful investment will be reduced and, ultimately, brought to an end. Again, this is likely to slow down our economic growth in the short run. Yet we have a package of measures in place to improve our productivity, which will ultimately produce a positive effect in the long run. For sure, the majority of our reform measures are designed to have such a positive effect.

It should be noted, however, that not all of our reform measures will boost China's economic growth. Therefore it is obligatory for us to carefully examine the relationship between reform and economic growth. The ultimate goal of reform is to improve efficiency, but that does not necessarily correlate with economic growth. We have to look at our reform measures on a case-by-case basis.

A third example is about the improvement of productivity. In the past, we *did* improve our productivity considerably by way of cross-sectoral transference of production factors, in particular from agricultural sectors to non-agricultural sectors. In the future, when both our productivity and production factors are predicted to decline, any further increase of productivity will have to rely primarily on our production divisions, and economic growth will depend more heavily on our factor production. Personally, I am confident in China's huge potential for factor transference from agricultural to non-agricultural sectors. For example, Chinese agricultural products—especially its major farm products—are currently far more expensive (usually priced 20–100% higher) than those on the international markets. This illustrates well the lack of competitiveness of Chinese agriculture, as well as the fairly low productivity of China's agricultural sectors. The recently-concluded Central Economic Working Conference proposed to transform the development models of China's agricultural economy. To transform is to reform, in effect. Statistics show that 30% of China's labor force remains in its agricultural sectors. I feel that this percentage is much too high, because our agricultural output now accounts for only 10% of our GDP. Proportionally, our agricultural labor force far outweighs our agricultural output. Hence, it is feasible to transfer more of our rural labor force through steady improvements in our agricultural productivity, so as to further unleash our potential for growth. On the other hand, we also have great potential in the cross-sectoral allocation of production factors, especially in our basic industries. In general, the service industry is indeed less efficient than our manufacturing sector, but a considerable part of the production services industry remains rather efficient, which is exactly what China needs most at present. Producer services not only serve our producers but also our manufacturers. Therefore, we should never give up our manufacturing; on the contrary, we must attach greater importance to its development. In the future, a key orientation of China's service industry is bound to be production services for the transformation and upgrading of the manufacturing industry.

The last example I will provide is about the internet. For any further transformation or upgrading of the Chinese economy, we must prioritize the in-depth integration of the internet and the real economy, which up until now has only been vaguely alluded to. From an economic point of view, the internet has solved a core economic problem, that is, information asymmetry. I frequently use this example of how the internet saves resources: many women love shopping for clothes. In the past, they had to comparison shop between at least five stores, and even then couldn't ultimately be sure of making the best decision. In order to make returns, a shopper had to travel between her home and the shopping mall at least once—and likely up to five times. So to bring home what they wanted, ten women had to go out a minimum of ten times and a maximum of 50 times in total. But now, with the rise of the internet, things are different. Without leaving home, they have access to more than 5,000 stores and the chance to compare them online. When they have placed their orders, one courier would be enough to deliver all that is ordered from the warehouse to the neighborhood, which saves significant energy consumption on the road. What used to require ten to 50 trips by each of these ten persons—by bus or by taxi—is now effected by a single run of one person. Therefore, we should never ignore the internet's role in saving energy. This is a typical example of how the internet has solved the economic problem of information asymmetry. What happens in our consumption sectors is just the beginning. In the future, we are going to carry out a comprehensive transformation of our production sectors as well. It is thus important that we pay closer attention to the internet economy in future research.

Chapter 4
Global Economic Outlook in the Era of China's New Normal

Haizhou Huang

In order to analyze the new normal, we need to pay close attention to both the demand and supply sides, though at present it is more necessary to focus on the latter. What follows are some of our viewpoints on global economic prospects under the new normal, focusing primarily on the supply side.

Since the economic crisis of 2008, significant changes have taken place to the world economy as a whole. In order to facilitate analysis, we have divided this issue into three economic areas, namely, the US, Europe (the eurozone), and emerging economies, all of which have undergone profound changes since 2008.

In regards to the US economy, what we know is that over a period of six years, the US has completed its financial sector deleveraging and largely completed its household deleveraging. To some degree, the US has almost finished those structural reforms centered around financial sector deleveraging as the core task. Given certain additional problems with its economic structure, the US is now better positioned for a phase of recovery growth. We call this the pull-up phase after taking off.

If the economic crisis of 2008 was, as many people consider it to be, a once-in-a-century occurrence, then the US was faced with one of three possible choices going forward. The first is a free-fall deleverage, as it did during the Great Depression. From 1929 to 1933, 9,000 US banks went broke, the Standard and Poor's 500 Index plummeted by five-sixths, the US GDP slumped by half, and unemployment soared to 25%. That was the most drastic and painful adjustment in US history, indistinguishable from what might be termed a "self-mutilation." The second option is a Japanese model of restructuring, which could take ten, 20, or even 30 years.

The US has chosen neither this time. Rather, it has turned to an orderly deleveraging and a soft landing for the economy. It has been doing well so far—it has achieved both objectives mainly through two big moves. One is fiscal pump-priming to help

H. Huang (✉)
China International Capital Corporation Limited, Beijing, China
e-mail: Haizhou.Huang@cicc.com.cn

F. Cai (ed.), *China's Economic New Normal*, Research Series on the Chinese Dream and China's Development Path, https://doi.org/10.1007/978-981-15-3227-6_4

troubled banks back on to their feet, and the other is three rounds of quantitative easing (QE) to boost the orderly recovery of its capital market and the orderly growth of its economy.

Thanks to the aforementioned measures, the US economy has shown definite signs of recovery over the past years, and is likely to continue doing so in the years to come. Our forecast is that US economic growth will increase from 2 to 2.2% of this year to 3 to 3.3% in the next. As far as I am concerned, it is capable of sustaining a 3% annual growth for at least a couple of years. The major uncertainty surrounding US growth prospects is speculation about when (or if) the Federal Reserve will begin raising interest rates. Personally, I expect Fed rate hikes to be much slower and milder than market expectations.

In terms of the eurozone, what we know is that the leverage ratio of EU banks was much higher than their US counterparts during the crisis. What is worse, corporate debt-to-GDP ratio was much higher in the EU (140%) than in the US (60%). Even after the worst of the crisis abated, Europe has long been dragging its feet in financial sector deleveraging. Over the last year, however, we have seen EU banks speeding up their deleveraging.

There are two ways of deleveraging. One is through orderly reform, while the other is through disorderly transformation. The former is intended to effectively restructure the economy while ensuring steady growth, while the latter is nothing other than the aforementioned "self-mutilation." Without steady economic growth, what can banks do to deleverage? They can do nothing but reclaim loans and liquidate assets. That is why so many EU banks are under tremendous pressure. For a long time, EU banks have been providing 50% of the world's trade financing, but recently the figure is closer to zero. We are not ruling out the possibility that crisis may still occur among some EU banks in 2015, however, as major European countries—including Germany, France, and Italy—are now heading toward deflation, while some European countries are already stuck in it.

Moving on to addressing the emerging market economies, we know quite a number of them have been leveraging since 2008. Generally, the leverage ratio of emerging market countries has been pushed high in recent years. From 2014 on, though, differentiation started to grow among the emerging market economies. In terms of stock market returns, two countries are believed to be most worth investing in—the first being China, followed by India. As for the other emerging market countries, there are all kinds of problems with their economies, including some quite serious issues.

In light of economic dynamics, China is now experiencing a certain amount of downward pressure on both its growth and inflation, with the result that it is likely to be faced with deflation risks in 2015.

Another contributing factor is that there was a considerable drop in the oil price in 2014. According to an IMF estimate, on the base price of USD 120 per barrel, a 20% decrease in the oil price may result in a 0.5% increase in China's GDP.

I am not completely in favor of the IMF estimate, because the oil price mechanism in China is still conventional and thus more complex than the IMF assumes. In fact, the price of oil products in China never declines as rapidly as that seen with crude oil. Nevertheless, generally speaking, a lower oil price would be fairly favorable to China's GDP growth.

A significant concern for global investors is the risks posed to China's financial system. For China, the systematic financial risk is distributive rather than cumulative. With a high savings rate, China has accumulated foreign exchange reserves of up to USD 4 trillion. The problem lies in its distribution. If China optimizes its foreign exchange portfolio, it will be able to greatly reduce its systematic financial risk.

We have to view the Chinese economy in a global light and pay close attention to the structural characteristics of the Chinese economy, as well as those characteristics that define China as a global power. China is the second largest economy in the world. According to a World Bank estimate based on purchasing power parity (PPP), however, China might have actually become the world's largest economy recently. Should the 6–7% annual growth of China's GDP persist for another ten years, how much will China contribute to global GDP growth in the years between 2013 and 2023? According to the same IMF estimate, besides China, only two countries are capable of a double-digit contribution to global GDP growth over this period, with one of them being the United States with a contribution rate of 10%. Western Europe is estimated to contribute around 7.2%, and Eastern Europe, the Middle East, Africa, and Latin America will weigh in at 6.2%, 4.1%, 5.7%, and 6.9%, respectively. By contrast, China's contribution to global GDP growth may reach as high as 25%, because China is close to the US in economic size but is growing more than twice as quickly as the latter. The EU is a large economy, but it grows too slowly. Eastern Europe is both small and slow. And the other economies are either too small, too slow, or a combination of both. That is why we must pay more attention to the big powers when discussing structural issues. As a rising power, China has displayed many significant characteristics that are well worth studying from a global perspective.

Since the 2008 financial crisis, people have come to realize that it is difficult for smaller countries to run huge financial institutions—only the big powers are capable of doing so. In the future, the world's largest financial institutions are very likely to concentrate in the big powers, that is, the US and China. Likewise, it would also be difficult for smaller countries to operate huge companies. China is a fertile breeding ground for companies such as Alibaba and Tencent—their long-term survival would be called into question in small countries, the best example of such being Nokia. The Chinese market, on the other hand, is capable of nurturing giant corporations. Not only because of the large size of the Chinese economy and the huge potential for corporate growth, but also because of the huge dividends brought about by China's reform and opening-up and the Chinese propensity for innovation, which should never be underestimated.

In light of economic dynamics, India is on an upward trend of economic growth, with its growth rate up from 5 to 6% annually, while its inflation is in decline from 10 to 7% annually. It is better off now than it was in the recent past. Not only has its inflation rate dropped from the annual average of 10–7%, its economic growth has also accelerated to an annual rate of 6% from the 4 to 5% over the past years.

Everything seems favorable to India at present. Yet high inflation rates and current account deficits are two obstinate problems that continue to vex the Indian economy, which is dependent on imports for 90% of its oil consumption. Now that the price of oil has dropped from USD 120 to USD 60 per barrel, India is better positioned to cope with its inflation and deficit problems—it has not only brought down its inflation from 10 to 7% but also measured the significant growth of its GDP.

The other emerging market economies can be roughly divided into two types. The first type is made up of raw material exporters, such as Brazil and Russia. These countries currently face significant economic difficulties. For example, Brazil has just experienced a sharp decline in its GDP growth rate, from 2.5% in 2013 to 0.5% in 2014, while Russia is currently faced with a looming financial crisis due to the precipitous decline in the value of the ruble. On the base price of USD 120 per barrel, a 20-dollar decrease in the price of oil equals a 0.7% decrease in Russia's GDP. The other category of emergent market economies is made up of those beneficiaries of China's economic growth (e.g., Southeast Asian countries) and the US economic growth (e.g., Mexico). For such countries, their economic problems are relatively minor.

In view of the global economic development, we can say that the US is at its apex, Europe is still dreaming of a better future, China is demonstrating its potential, and India is on a good roll.

In the future, we expect global economic growth to further differentiate disparate markets, market fluctuations to further aggravate affected economies, and global inflation to continue to decline. Global inflation was at 4.5% in 2011, 3.2% in 2012, and 3.1% in 2013. We estimate it will be 2.8 or 2.9% in 2014 and 2.8% in 2015. In other words, there is unlikely to be any sign of significant global inflation in the coming two or three years.

Touching back on Federal Reserve rate hikes, my judgment is that they will come much later and more slowly than market expectations, an analysis which is based on the following reasons:

The first reason is the low inflation level of the US. On what grounds shall the Federal Reserve raise interest rates when inflation lingers at 2%? The US CPI (Consumer Price Index) is anticipated to be 2% next year and even the year after. Such anticipatory levels do not support a Fed rate hike. The Federal Reserve has set an inflation target of 2.5% and may adjust it to around 3.5% when the US economy resumes growth. Yet a 3.5% inflation rate would be almost impossible for the US over the next three years.

The second reason is the employment rate. The US economy added 352,000 new jobs in October 2014. The latest number has convinced market participants, including the chief economists of several investment banks, of a quick Fed rate hike. But I disagree with this assessment. At present, the unemployment rate of the US is around 5.8%. It should be noted, however, that the labor force participation rate (LFPR) has declined greatly in the US since the 2008 financial crisis. During the most prosperous period of the US economy the LFPR reached as high as 70%, but it now makes up no more than 62%—with an evident 8% gap between the figures. It remains controversial whether this 8% is due to structural or cyclical unemployment.

Let us suppose that a fairly significant portion of the 8% is due to cyclical unemployment (say, 6%) and the rest structural. When the economy grows well, the cyclically unemployed will be reemployed. In other words, to further reduce its unemployment rate, what the US has to do is far more than just bring unemployment percentages down to 4% from 5.8%—it has to first add the cyclical unemployment (6%) to the current unemployment rate (5.8%). That is to say, the US has to decrease its real unemployment rate from approximately 12 to 4%. This would be impossible in fewer than two or three years.

The third reason lies in the fact that the US experienced two years of recession following the 2008 economic crisis, during which it suffered negative GDP growth at an annual rate of −6% for several quarters. There is a gap of some eight percentage points between its current growth rate and its GDP trendline in those two years. Will the US give them up forever, or will it be able to make them up in the years ahead? In my view, many Americans—including their statesmen—would hope to fill that gap by means of a relatively high rate of economic growth over a longer period of time.

Finally, the fourth reason I find an immediate Fed rate hike unlikely is due to the exchange rate. Both the EUR-USD (Euro to US Dollar) and JPY-USD (Japanese Yen to US Dollar) exchange rates tumbled in 2014. If the US is to raise its interest rates, how much higher should the US dollar shoot up? It will have no benefit for the US economy, but *will* do harm to the rest of the world.

Chapter 5
Global Competition in Reform Under the New Normal

Xiaojing Zhang

My topic today is the global economy's new normal and the reforms that are to be carried out in response to it. I have here summarized the new normal into a single sentence that may not be very accurate or generally agreed upon: that is, the Chinese economy's new normal is marked mainly by structural deceleration, while that of the global economy—in particular developed economies—is marked more by long-term stagnation.

1 The New Normal of Developed Economies: Long-term Stagnation

First of all, I would like to say a few words about China's new normal, which many experts have already comprehensively analyzed in their speeches. What I want to mention is limited to the causes for China's structural deceleration. This is not only a result of the declining efficiency of our resource allocation, factor supply, and technological learning, it is also a result of increasing resource and environmental constraints as well as intensifying external competitive pressures. Of the nine characteristics of China's new normal summarized at the Central Economic Working Conference, I consider the most important one to be the structural deceleration of the economy, while the other characteristics are more or less related to this central issue.

Next, I will focus on the new normal of developed economies. Some experts—such as Huang Haizhou and Sun Tao—shared their predictions for the global economy. But how on earth is the global economy going? And what will become of it in the medium- and long-term? What really matters, I think, is not how we view it, but how our counterparts from developed economies view it.

X. Zhang (✉)
CASS Academic Division of Economics, Beijing, China
e-mail: xjzhang@neri.org.cn

F. Cai (ed.), *China's Economic New Normal*, Research Series on the Chinese Dream and China's Development Path, https://doi.org/10.1007/978-981-15-3227-6_5

At the end of 2013, former US Treasury Secretary Lawrence H. Summers warned of the "secular stagnation" of the US and other major global economies. Why did he raise that notion of "secular stagnation," an old idea originally put forth by US economist Alvin Hansen during the 1930s' Great Depression? By using this term, Summers has expressed his pessimism about the medium-to-long term growth of developed economies. As soon as it was publicized, his view received wide support among mainstream economists, including Joseph E. Stiglitz, Paul R. Krugman, and Olivier J. Blanchard. Why are there so many echoes of his concern? This shows a common recognition among these economists of the obstinate diseases of developed economies—in particular those problems accumulated during the Great Moderation that has been ongoing since the 1980s—that would take a very long time to resolve.

There are many reasons for secular stagnation. We prefer to analyze the real economic factors, instead of other factors, such as demand and policy. We have therefore focused on three major factors: the slowdown of technological advancement, problems with the population and the labor market, and the deterioration of income distribution.

First and foremost are changes in technology. We take the US as a typical example in this respect. It is a global leader both in the economy and in innovation. Nonetheless, its total factor productivity (TFP) has been on the decline for the past dozen years (see Fig. 1).

Why has technological advancement slowed? We can explore the reasons from various perspectives, including institutional structures, cultures, values, etc. In Gordon's view, many of today's technological innovations—such as the Internet, iPhones, and other personal electronic devices—have a far smaller effect in terms of promoting output efficiency, compared with those inventions made during the second Industrial Revolution a century ago, such as electricity, combustion engines, and piped water systems. According to his studies, the second Industrial Revolution and its fruits brought about a period of sustained growth lasting over 80 years. By contrast, the so-called Internet-based economic growth has already sailed into choppy waters without

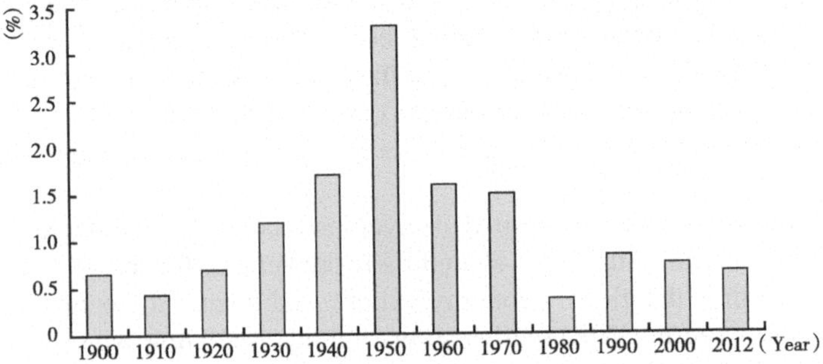

Fig. 1 Annual Growth of the US Total Factor Productivity *Note* Each rectangular bar represents the average annual growth rate of the US TFP over the past decade. *Source* Quoted from Robert J. Gordon, "a new method of estimating potential real GDP growth: implications for the labor market and the Debt/GDP ratio," NBER working paper no. 20423 (2014): 13

even having persisted for long—and Gordon is extremely pessimistic about it. On the other hand, he strongly disapproves of big data, which he reckons is no more than a zero-sum game so far. For example, while big data enables an airline company or online seller to foresee the likes and dislikes of their customers and focus on the true designated delivery of their products, the success of one enterprise using big data nevertheless means a failure for others, because people's income growth is relatively slow and their spending power is limited. Enterprises using big data are merely getting a bigger slice of the cake. This is how Gordon views big data. Of course, big data can benefit us in various ways. Yet one thing is clear—he has reminded us not to sing the praises of the advantages of big data and the Internet—on the contrary, we must stay cool-minded however hot they may appear to be.

What follows is growing pressure from the population and the labor market. One indicator alone is enough to reveal the extremely serious aging problem endemic to developed economies. Table 1 shows the "support ratios" of some developed economies, a concept that refers to the ratio of producers to effective consumers in a society. Producers are generally considered to be the working-age population, while effective consumers mainly consist of the aged. Therefore, a declining support ratio indicates a shrinking youth population and an expanding aged population. Without exception, the support ratios of the developed economies in Table 1 are predicted to fall in the upcoming decades, indicating the increasing severity of the aging problem. Closely related is the decline of the growth rates of the workforce. These obviously pose a threat to the future growth of developed economies.

Finally, there is the problem of income distribution. What has turned *Capital in the Twenty-First Century* into a best seller? It is the deterioration of income distribution in developed economies. It is for the same reason that the Occupy Wall Street movement was launched by the 99% against the 1%, and the reason for which so many people are now concerned about income distribution. As a social problem, income inequality can also drag developed economies into growth stagnation, so to speak.

Table 1 Support ratios of developed economies

Year	1950	1970	1990	2010	2030	2050	2100
US	0.79	0.71	0.78	0.80	0.72	0.70	0.65
Japan	0.66	0.78	0.83	0.76	0.67	0.58	0.57
Germany	0.84	0.76	0.84	0.81	0.68	0.62	0.59
UK	0.82	0.74	0.77	0.77	0.70	0.67	0.62
France	0.85	0.77	0.83	0.83	0.74	0.72	0.67
Italy	0.70	0.71	0.74	0.77	0.67	0.60	0.59
Sweden	0.98	0.91	0.91	0.91	0.83	0.80	0.73
Canada	0.71	0.67	0.78	0.82	0.73	0.69	0.65
Australia	0.80	0.74	0.80	0.80	0.73	0.70	0.64

Source National transfer accounts. Quoted from Charles Goodhart and Philipp Erfurth, "demography and economics: look past the past," *VOX, CEPR policy portal* (November 2014)

2 Global Competition in Reform

How, then, should we cope with such growth stagnation? In fact, China and developed economies share a common feature known as "institutional inertia." That is, they make changes only when they have to. On the other hand, different institutions and systems vary in elasticity and response to pressures, hardships, and external shocks. For example, why has the US recovered more quickly than other developed economies following the 2008 global recession? Why is Europe still in the depths of stagnation? And why have Japan's endeavors proven ineffective up till this point? These questions are well worth further consideration.

Since the 2008 financial crisis, the whole world has been busy restructuring, rebalancing, and reforming the economy, but the point here is that different economies have seen very different results. Yet we must pay close attention to the global competition that is ongoing amongst economic reform.

2.1 New Connotations in the Period of Strategic Opportunity for China's Development Under the New Normal

The secular stagnation of developed economies not only means new pressures, but also new opportunities for China's development.

1. Secular stagnation will force developed economies to seek new growth points by all means possible, which is bound to impact China's development. The first thing many developed economies are doing is instigating an internal technological revolution, despite knowing this may cause difficulties in the immediate future. For example, the US and Germany have implemented projects known as the third Industrial Revolution and Industry 4.0, respectively, with additional industrial innovations well under way in other developed economies, including the formulation of plans for as-yet unrealized technological revolutions. Meanwhile, they have not forgotten the use of policy measures, such as quantitative easing and the strategy of inflation. For example, the current inflation rate for the US is around 2%, but some economists now argue for an inflation target of 4%. Inflation *does* work—it is particularly effective in bringing down a high debt ratio. Quantitative easing, inflation as a strategy, and the third Industrial Revolution—these will all have a significant impact on China's development, but will also provide the country with new opportunities.
2. The public investment priorities of developed economies offer a golden chance for Chinese overseas investment. Currently, interest rates are relatively low, even sometimes negative, in developed economies, and therefore the associated costs of public investment are also fairly low in these countries. According to an analysis by the Organization for Economic Cooperation and Development (OECD), global demand for investment in infrastructure development will add up to USD

53 trillion from 2010 to 2030. For China, this translates into a rare opportunity. What's more, the Belt and Road Initiative and the development of other economies have also opened up tremendous opportunities for China's overseas investment while also providing a new chance for China to ease its overcapacity.

2.2 *Global Reform Competition*

Developed economies employ both domestic and international strategies. While implementing structural reforms domestically, they also seek to make new rules internationally.

2.2.1 The Domestic Reforms of Developed Economies

1. In 2009, the United States issued *A Strategy for American Innovation Securing Our Economic Growth and Prosperity*, which was updated in 2011. *The Strategy* has three core components that focus on: one, investing in the building blocks of American innovation, namely, the workforce, science, and infrastructure; two, promoting market-based innovation to facilitate the formation of an ecosystem that encourages innovation and entrepreneurship, drives US economic growth, and secures the global leadership of the US; and three, catalyzing breakthroughs in areas considered national priorities, including alternative energy development, the application of health IT towards the reduction of healthcare costs while increasing the quality of care, the advanced development of educational technologies, and advances in biotechnology and nanotechnology to ensure US leadership in an expanding number of fields. As a steadfast advocate for Keynesian economics and demand expansion, even Summers admits that demand-side support for the economy is far from enough. The only solution to secular stagnation is to bring about bolder reforms by encouraging innovation and entrepreneurship, promoting education, increasing labor market flexibility, raising the retirement age, improving both the country's immigration policy and the corporate tax system, etc.
2. In 2010, the European Commission proposed the Europe 2020 strategy. It sets targets for the growth of the European Union (EU), which are broken down into the following initiatives:

    (1) to enhance the quality of Europe's education, to invest more in R&D and adjust key fields of R&D input, to improve the business environment for private R&D investment, and to strengthen the development of new products based on R&D achievements;
    (2) to shift toward a low-carbon economy and improve energy efficiency by increasing the share of renewables in final energy consumption, as well as

capital input in cleaner technologies, so as to protect the environment, combat climate change, create new business and job opportunities, and realize the sustainable growth of the economy;

(3) to increase labor market flexibility in order to raise both the labor force participation rate and employment rate, e.g., to raise the employment rate for those aged 20–64 from 69 to 75%, to increase the employment rate of women and older workers, and to better integrate legal migrants into the EU labor market;

(4) to reduce the number of Europeans living below national poverty lines by 25%, lifting 20 million people out of poverty; and to promote social inclusion.

As European Central Bank (ECB) President Mario Draghi remarked, "The risks of doing too little are bigger than the risks of doing too much and this applies to structural reforms as well."

3. In Japan, a reform-dominated growth strategy constitutes "the third new policy arrow" of Abenomics (the other two being a quantitative-easing-based monetary policy and a fiscal stimulus policy). The strategy consists of an industrial rebirth plan, a plan for strategic new market development, and an internationalization promotion plan, all of which boil down to four aspects. The first is to rebuild the competitiveness of Japanese industry: to expand the equipment investment of private enterprises through tax reform; to boost online banking and venture capital investment in order to encourage entrepreneurship, increase the opening rate, and accelerate the mergers and acquisitions of enterprises; to implement substantial deregulation in order to improve the competitiveness and vitality of Japan's information technology, healthcare, energy, tourism, trade, agriculture, forestry, and fisheries; and to open up new areas of industry. The second is to improve the level of human capital in Japan: to improve Japan's workforce competitiveness by allowing for greater labor mobility, raising the employment rate for both young and elderly workers (women workers in particular), enhancing Japan's higher education standards, and attracting high-level overseas talent to work in Japan. The third is to strengthen Japan's regional competitive advantage: to establish national strategic special zones in Tokyo, Osaka, and Aichi that are supported by deregulations; to significantly improve the socioeconomic environment and living conditions of foreigners; to establish the world's most favorable investment climate; and to attract more foreign investment. The last is to re-establish global trade patterns: to facilitate the implementation of the Trans-Pacific Partnership Agreement (TPP), the China-Japan-Korea Free Trade Agreement (CJKFTA), and the EU-Japan Economic Partnership Agreement (EJEPA); to raise the proportion of FTA-based volume in Japan's overall international trade from 20% to around 70% within three years; to expand overseas business (in particular large-sized public works projects), and more.

In summary, the reform measures of major developed economies (the US, EU, and Japan) mainly encourage innovation and entrepreneurship, promote educational development, increase labor market flexibility, raise the retirement age, and improve both migration policies and corporate tax policies.

2.2.2 International Strategies of Developed Economies

Since the outbreak of the global financial crisis, developed economies have by and large completed the global strategic layout undertaken in order to rearrange global governance architecture for their establishment and the dominance of a new global economic order in the future. Take, for example, some new frameworks for trade and investment, such as the Trans-Pacific Partnership Agreement (TPP), the Transatlantic Trade and Investment Partnership (TTIP), and the Trade in Services Agreement (TiSA). Compared with the World Trade Organization (WTO), they have adopted higher standards and are thus more effective. These new frameworks are distinguished from conventional ones by the following characteristics. The first is a shift in focus from merchandise trade to service trade and investment. The second is the priority of border over rules, a deviation from the traditional preference for trade over border, which means foreign investors will have to face more restrictions in trade rules, such as enterprise transparency, governance structure, and accounting principles. The third is the dominance of developed countries and the absence of major emerging countries. The last is the introduction of competitive neutrality and state capitalism, a move presumably targeting China.

To meet the challenges of global competition amongst economic reform, the Third and Fourth Plenary Sessions of the 18th CPC Central Committee have fully committed to deepening reform and promoting the rule of law in China. We should not only realize the importance of getting a head start on the competition, but also be aware that reform is a marathon—a long race requiring persistent efforts. Only with such awareness can we stay confident and rest easy in our strategic arrangement, shake off the constraints of the currently-slipping growth rate, and free ourselves from the impulse for a stimulated higher growth. As the saying goes, "better late than never." What matters most is not whether China grows at 7 or 6% annually, but whether it is able to sustain its growth. For more than one hundred years, the United States has grown at an average annual rate of 3% and remained the largest and strongest national economy in the world. If China's growth rate persists, surpassing the United States in terms of economic size is just a matter of time. Therefore, it is essential that we have the long-term picture in mind and press ahead with our reforms with keen determination.

Chapter 6
Structural Adjustments Under the New Normal

Tao Sun

I work with the International Monetary Fund (IMF). A significant portion of what the IMF does is to assess the potential economic growth and associated risks of certain countries and to subsequently judge their policy orientations through a lens of international comparison. The theme of my speech today is "Structural Adjustments Under the New Normal." While much of it is based on the results of many researchers at the IMF, I would add to it some of my personal judgments, which should be taken as representative of my personal views only.

My speech will consist of three parts:

Part one: the new normal. In a general sense, the "new normal" is what people predict for the future. In China, however, the new normal has turned out to be more of a process of passive acceptance of reality. What we have to accept, I have concluded, is that high growth can no longer be achieved without increased risk. In other words, to realize higher growth, we have to take higher risks and, vice versa, in order to lower our risks, we have no choice but to accept lower growth. This is my fundamental judgment. In simple terms, what we now call the new normal has proven a result of natural selection, and we have to accept it.

Part two: the risks. We are now faced with many potential challenges. What are the ways out? How can we find them?

Part three: my conclusions.

In part one, I approach the issue from three perspectives. The first is to analyze the changes in both the real and potential growth rates of several select countries and regions—including China—from the IMF's comparison of these economies. The second is to assess the fundamental risks to China and other Asian economies from a global perspective in order to see whether they are increasing or decreasing. The third is to explore the major constraints on China's growth from a macroscopic perspective.

T. Sun (✉)
International Monetary Fund (IMF), Washington, USA
e-mail: TSUN@imf.org

F. Cai (ed.), *China's Economic New Normal*, Research Series on the Chinese Dream and China's Development Path, https://doi.org/10.1007/978-981-15-3227-6_6

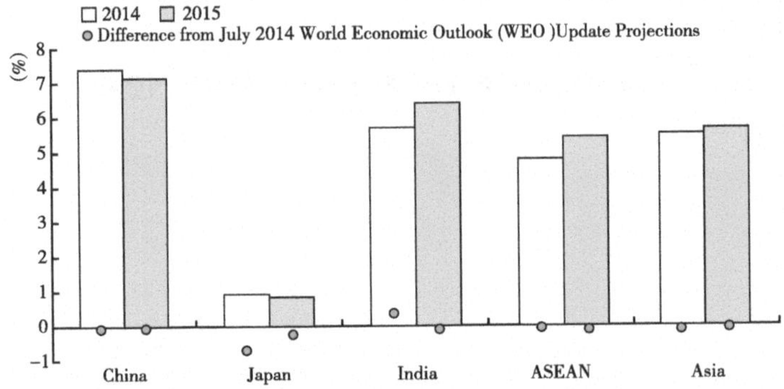

Fig. 1 Changes in projected growth rates

1 The New Normal: A Result of Natural Selection Featuring Lower Growth and Higher Risks

1.1 China: A Declining Growth Rate

Figure 1 is our most recent comparison of the major economies in Asia, wherein China is the left-most. Of the rectangular bars for each economy, one represents the estimated growth rate for 2014 (left) and the other for 2015 (right). According to our comparison, China's growth rate will decrease slightly over these years, while the growth estimates for some Asian economies, such as India, will increase. Changing conditions typically cause the IMF to revise its economic growth projections, reflecting the fact that the IMF's existing research and judgment of China's economic growth continue to be generally in line with reality. In the past, the Chinese economy usually grew beyond all expectations, especially given all the problems referred to in the IMF's analysis. Yet both China and the IMF now agree that the country's growth rate has started to decline.

1.2 Decline in the Potential Growth Rate and the Contribution of Total Factor Productivity

Figure 2 shows the potential growth rates of major economies in Asia, including China, India, the Republic of Korea, and ASEAN. As can be seen in Fig. 2, their potential growth rates have been marginally declining in recent years, indicating a generally downward trend in Asia. The same is true, in fact, of major economies throughout the world. In other words, our projections of economic growth for each of the coming years will be lower than the real growth rates of the previous year.

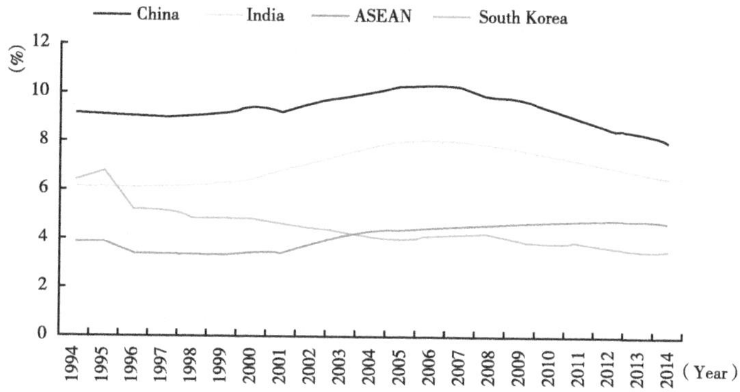

Fig. 2 Changes in potential growth rates. *Source* IMF staff calculations

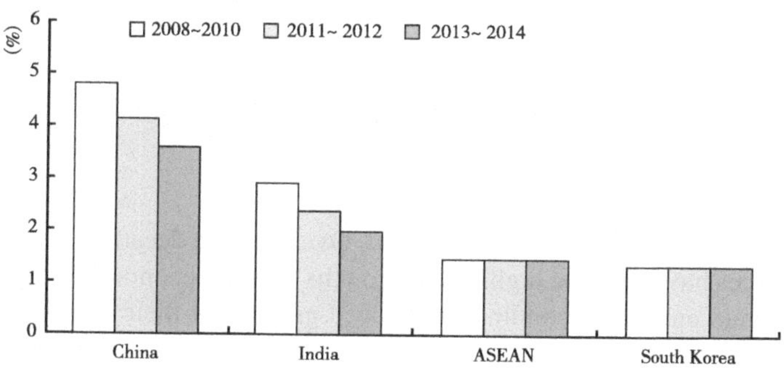

Fig. 3 Changes in TFP contribution to potential growth rates. *Source* IMF staff calculations

Figure 3 reflects the growth rates of total factor productivity (TFP), where we can see a decline of TFP contributions to China's potential growth rate. This coincides with the decline of its real growth rate. We thus conclude that there is an ongoing decline in both China's real growth rate and the TFP contribution to its potential growth rate.

1.3 China: A Positive Credit-to-GDP Gap Versus a Negative Output Gap

Figure 4 is another comparison by the IMF that reflects the correlation between economic growth and credit. What we can learn from it is that there is a positive credit-to-GDP gap and a negative output gap in China. That is to say, while China's real GDP growth rate is declining, its credit-to-GDP contribution has increased. By contrast, the credit-to-GDP contribution of Japan and the Republic of Korea has dropped alongside their downward real GDP growth rates.

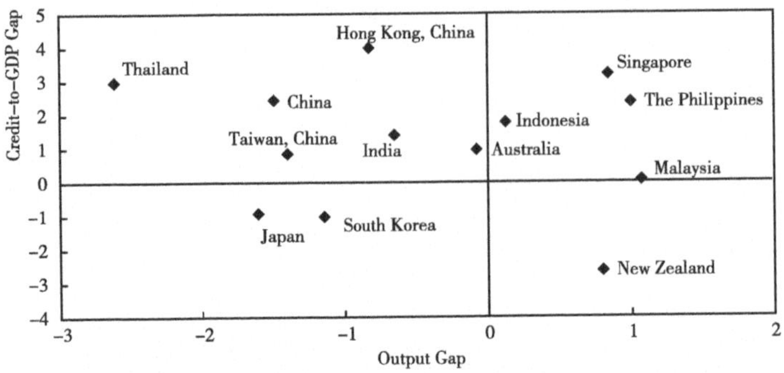

Fig. 4 Latest credit-to-GDP and output gaps compared. *Source* CEIC Data Company Ltd.; IMF, *World Economic Outlook*; and IMF staff calculations. *Notes* Credit-to-GDP as of May 2014 or latest available. Credit gap is calculated as a percent deviation from the trend credit-to-GDP ratio (approximated using the H-P filter over the period 2000–2012). Output gap is based on country estimates for 2014

1.4 A Downward Trend in External Demand After the Financial Crisis

Figure 5 reflects changes in external demand. Over the past decade, China and many Asian countries have realized high-speed growths for their economies. Yet they have failed to sustain any corresponding high-speed growth for their exports, which are largely dependent on external demand drivers. If we extend the trendline of Asia's export growth before the crisis, we can find a widening gap between potential and real export growth. What follows is that our exports of goods and services are now growing far more slowly than before.

Figure 6 reflects the correlation between exports and global demand. The ratio of export growth to global demand growth used to be slightly more than two, but it has declined slightly in recent years. From a global perspective, the expanding capacity

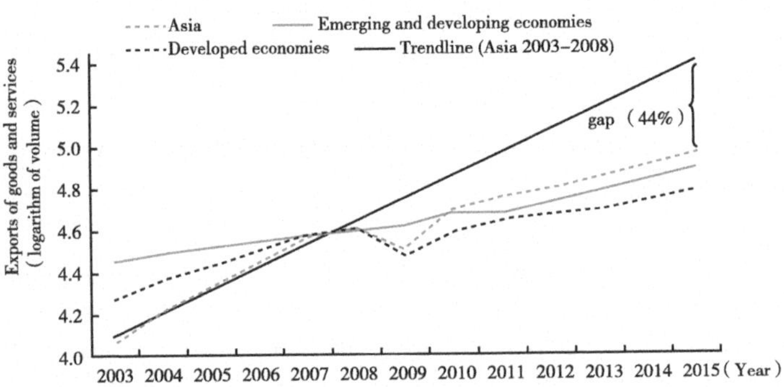

Fig. 5 Exports of goods and services

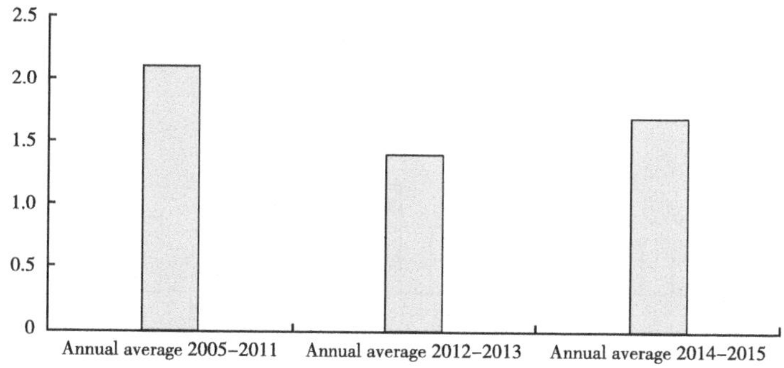

Fig. 6 Ratio of export (goods and services) growth to global demand growth. *Note* Excluding 2009 due to the effects of the global financial crisis

for exports is generally weaker than before, which will have a significant negative effect on export-oriented economies.

1.5 China: Credit's Weakening Role in Driving GDP Growth and the Decline in Investment Growth

Meanwhile, credit expansion can no longer be counted on to boost GDP growth. As can be seen in Fig. 7, credit's capacity for boosting economic growth has weakened in many countries and regions over the past years.

What can also be seen in Fig. 8 is a slight decline in China's real investment growth over the same period of time. Now that China finds itself faced with a decline in both its credit's contribution to GDP and its real investment growth, the new normal can

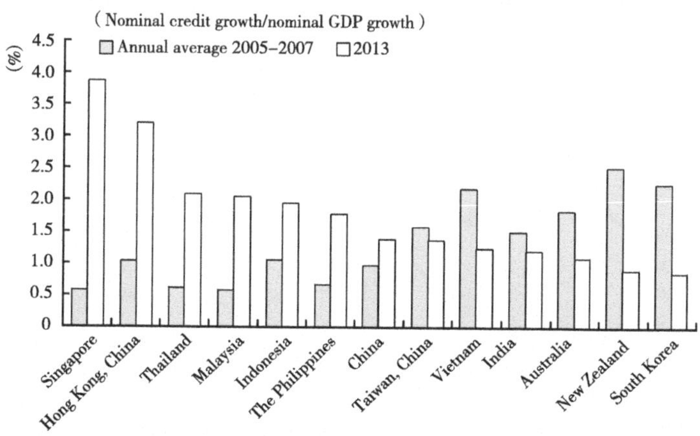

Fig. 7 Credit expansions for GDP growth

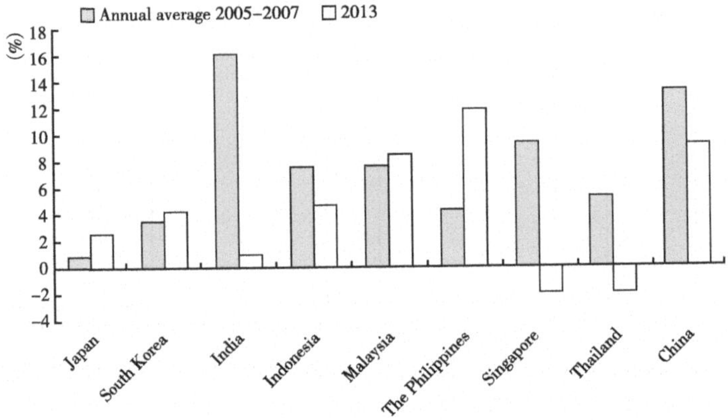

Fig. 8 Real investment growth

be interpreted as a result of the natural trend towards accepting a lower economic growth rate.

1.6 China: Credit Expansion and Deviation from Equilibrium

Figures 9 and 10 reflect China's credit expansion and its deviation from equilibrium. Presented in Fig. 9 are the ratios of financial institutional credit to GDP of six Asian countries. In the top right corner, the second trendline represents China and reads 163%—second only to Thailand. Nonetheless, it is much smaller than China's overall debt to GDP ratio (250%), because "overall debt" covers a wider scope than financial institutional credit. Clearly, the trendline of China has been on the rise in recent years.

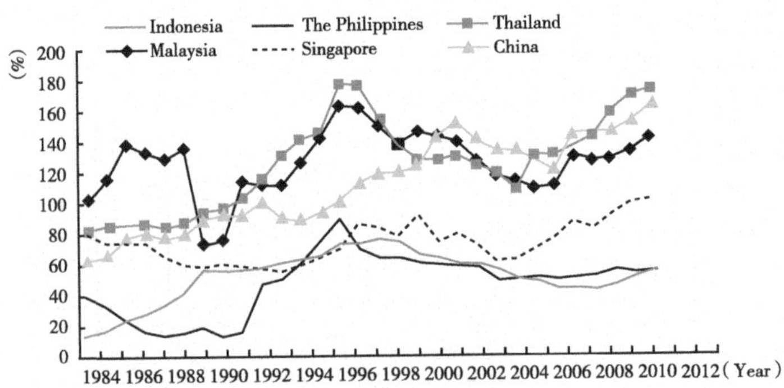

Fig. 9 Ratios of financial institutional credit to GDP of Asian countries

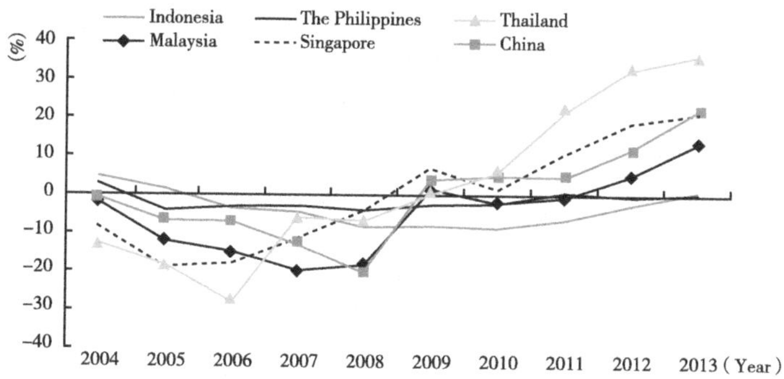

Fig. 10 Ratios of credit's deviation from equilibrium to GDP of Asian countries

Figure 10 is frequently used by IMF researchers to describe national economic vulnerability, that is, deviation from equilibrium. Similar to Fig. 9, China is the second highest in this regard. Such deviation implies certain risks derived from our credit expansion, which should draw our attention. Yet this is not a problem limited to China only—other Asian countries are also faced with similar challenges.

1.7 China: Increases in Credit Risk, Macroeconomic Risk, and Market Liquidity Risk

Figure 11 reflects global financial stability. Figure 12 reflects China's financial stability; based on the latest statistics, we can see an increase in credit risk, macroeconomic risk, and market liquidity risk.

1.8 Uncertainty About the Timing and Degree of US and Japanese Rate Hikes

Figure 13 is our forecast of interest rate trends, from which we conclude that there is significant uncertainty about interest rates in the future. We have to consider two questions: When will the US and Japan raise their interest rates? At what pace will they hike their rates? The Federal Reserve may raise interest rates more slowly than previously expected and, before that, smokescreens can be set up. If this is the process undertaken, there would be significant room for financial imbalances to pile up. That is one of our biggest concerns at present.

In Fig. 14, we predict the possible effects that the US hiking its interest rates and tightening its monetary policy would have on major Asian economies. The gray bars indicate the effects of slower US rate hikes, and the white ones of faster rate hikes. In our calculation, rapid US rate hikes are likely to result in a 0.79% point decrease in China's economic growth.

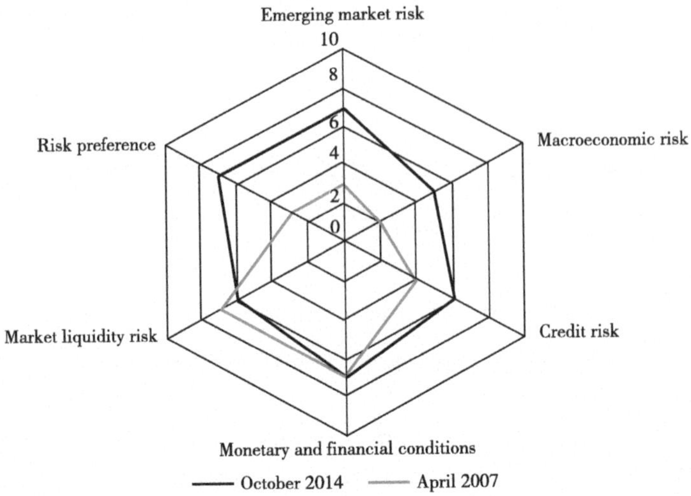

Fig. 11 Global financial stability. *Note* The farther away from the center, the higher the risk/the less stable the monetary and financial conditions or the higher the risk preference

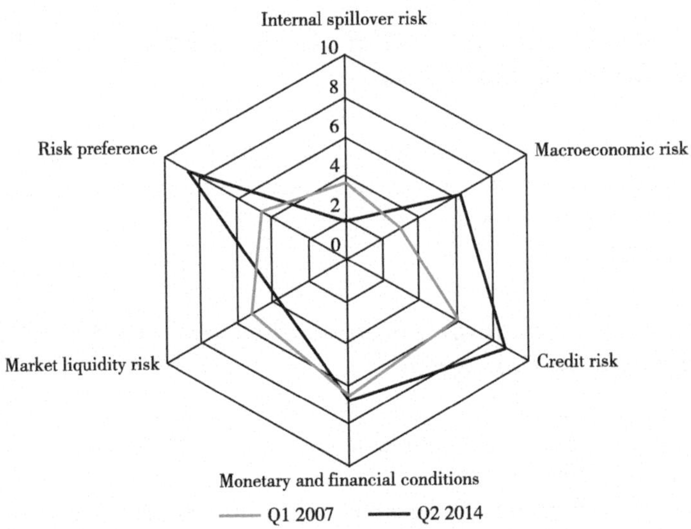

Fig. 12 China's financial stability. *Note* The farther away from the center, the higher the risk/the less stable the monetary and financial conditions or the higher the risk preference

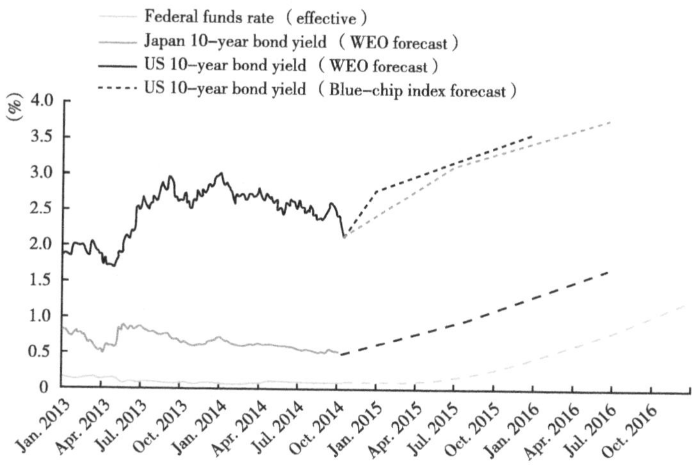

Fig. 13 Selected interest rates and forecasts

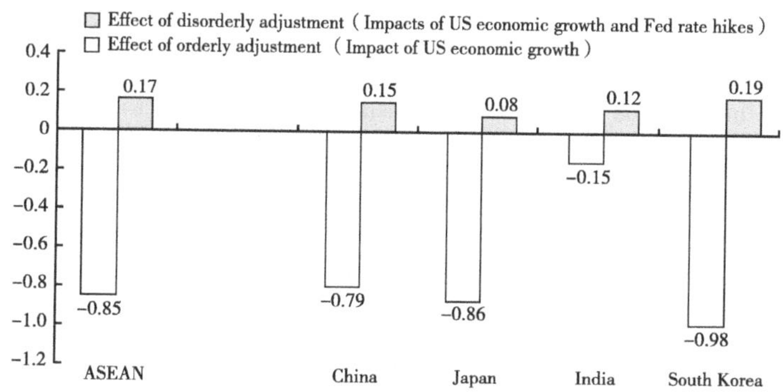

Fig. 14 Effects of US monetary policy adjustment on economic growth rates

1.9 Reversion of Arbitrage Trading Returns and the Rising Pressure of Domestic Currency Depreciation

In recent years, the exchange rates of emerging market countries have been noticeably volatile and have been accompanied by massive capital flows. Figure 15 reflects the changes in arbitrage trading and the exchange rate of the US dollar, where the light gray trendline represents the Asia Arbitrage Returns Index, and the dark gray trendline represents the Nominal US Dollar Index.

As Fig. 15 shows, following the appreciation of the US dollar, the light gray line has started declining in recent years. That is to say, changes in the interest margin and exchange rates have brought down the return of Asia arbitrage trading and even pulled it into negative territory, a result that is already reflected in recent market volatility.

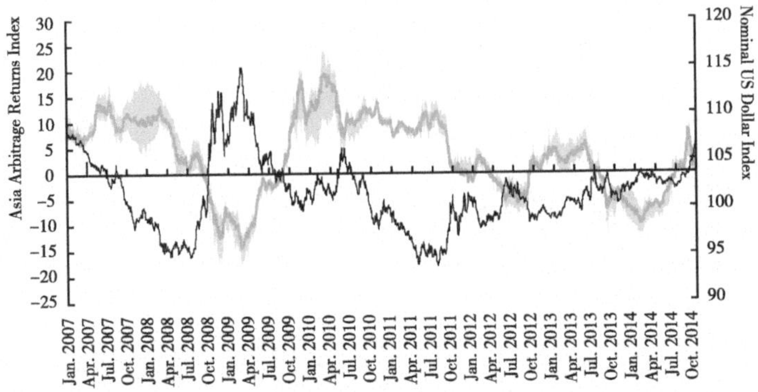

Fig. 15 Asia arbitrage returns index and nominal US dollar index

1.10 China: Risks of Shrinking Real Estate Investment and Further Decline of the Economic Growth Rate

As shown in Fig. 16, if China's real estate investment slips further or beyond our given assumptions, its GDP growth rate would also fall below our current estimates. The dotted line tells us that its GDP growth can be lowered to around 5%. This adequately proves the significant role of real estate in China's economic growth.

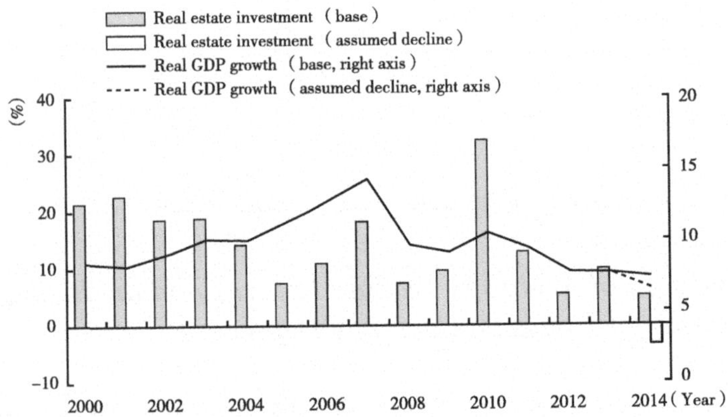

Fig. 16 Assumption of China's real estate investment and GDP growth

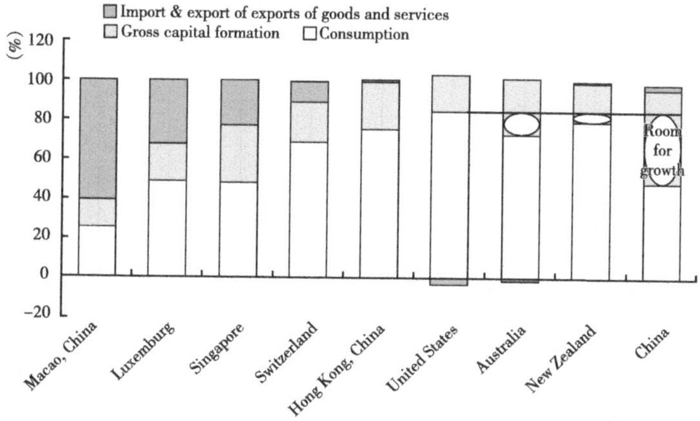

Fig. 17 Proportions of consumption, investment, and import and export in GDP

2 Ways Out: Enormous Room for Structural Adjustments Toward Sustainable Growth

With so many internal threats and external pressures, what shall we do to cope with such challenges?

2.1 *Room for the Expansion of China's Consumption*

Figure 17 shows the proportions of consumption, investment, and import and export in GDP. We draw a line to compare China and the US and a small ellipse to indicate the room still remaining for China's expansion. Now that consumption comprises 84% of US GDP, we can see what enormous room China will have to expand its consumption before it reaches the same level.

2.2 *Room for the Expansion of China's Services*

Figure 18 shows the proportions of services, industry, and agriculture in GDP. We have also used an ellipse to indicate the room still remaining for China to expand its services before it reaches the US level. That is to say, China still has extensive room for industrial restructuring.

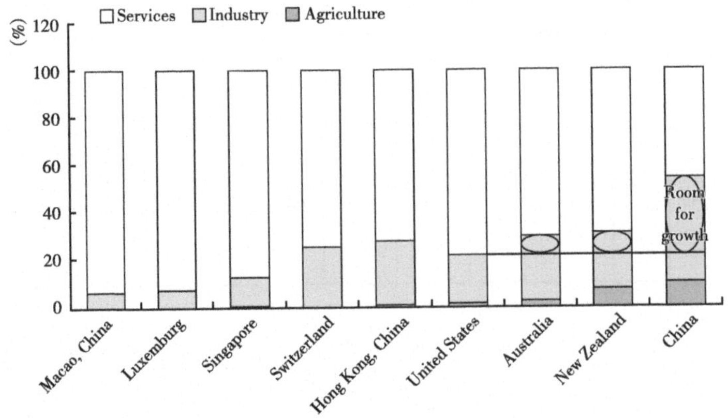

Fig. 18 Proportion of services, industry, and agriculture in GDP (by value added)

2.3 *Room for Improvement in China's Trade Integration*

With its tremendous import and export volumes, is China doing better than other countries in trade integration? The answer is no. Figures 19, 20, 21 and 22 shows the composition of exports calculated by value added rather than volume of trade. The value added of trade is calculated by subtracting the import value from the export value. For example, if China imports ten dollars' worth of goods and exports them for 15 dollars, the value added of this trade is five dollars. The white bar in the graphs below represents intermediate products. The higher the white bar, the larger the proportion of intermediate products and the more a country participates in trade integration. Over the past two decades, intermediate products have stabilized at around 50% of all US exports. The same is true for Japan and Thailand. By contrast, intermediate products have accounted for only about 37% of China's exports and stabilized below 40% over the same period. As one of the world's largest traders,

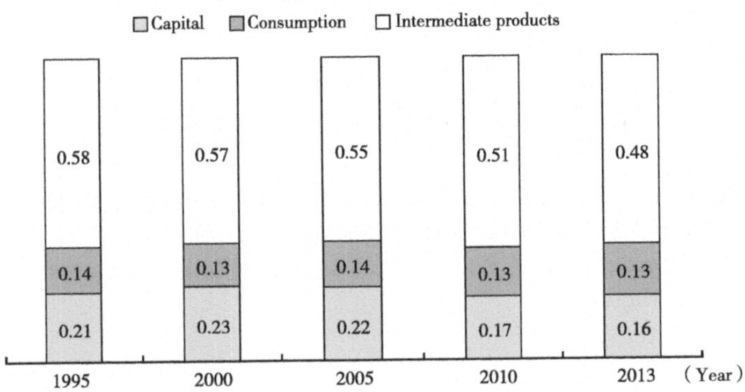

Fig. 19 Composition of US exports

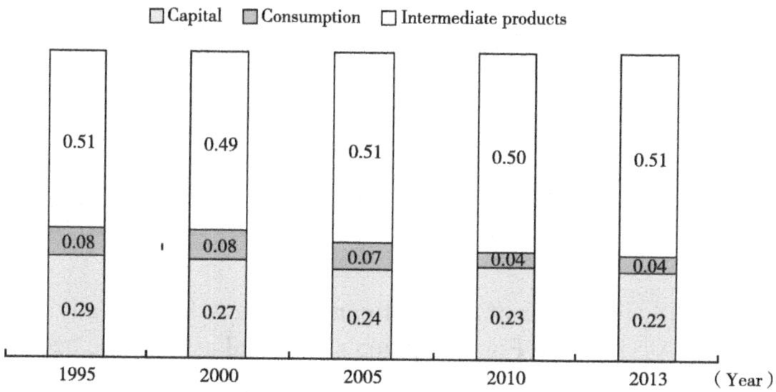

Fig. 20 Composition of Japan's exports

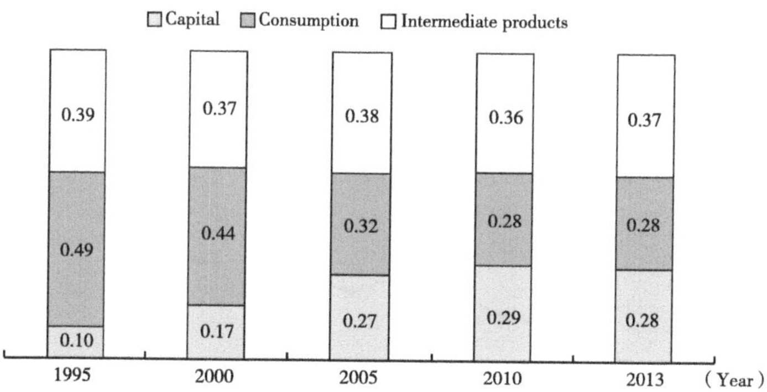

Fig. 21 Composition of China's exports

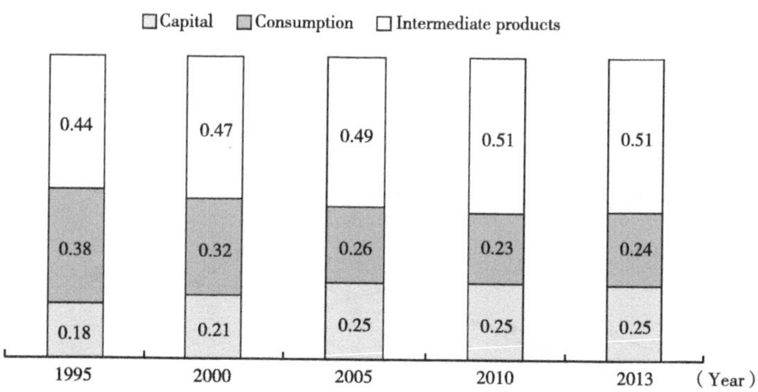

Fig. 22 Composition of Thailand's exports

China is in a weaker position than the US, Japan, and even Thailand in terms of industrial chain division. In other words, there is indeed still significant room for China to develop its trade integration.

2.4 *Room for the Expansion of China's Financial Market*

By the end of 2013, the value of global financial assets had already amounted to USD 250 trillion. As shown in Fig. 23, China's financial assets have been increasing rapidly over the past several years and in 2013 reached USD 37 trillion—larger than that of Japan but still far smaller than that of the US (USD 75 trillion).

Figure 24 reflects the proportions of financial assets in GDP of some countries. In 2013, financial assets accounted for 374% of China's GDP—close to the global average of 378%. Compared with more developed countries, however, there is still significant room for China to expand its financial sector.

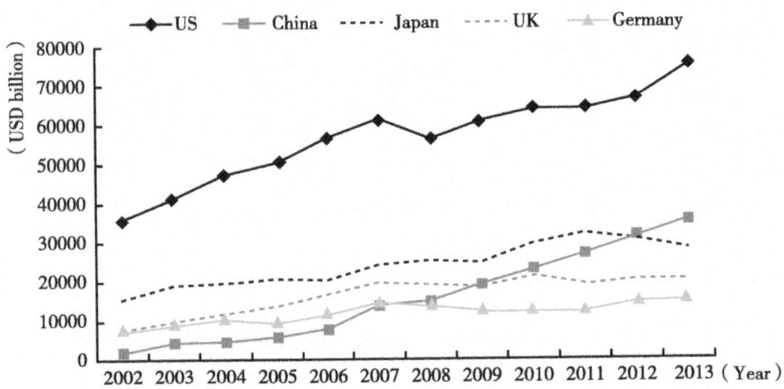

Fig. 23 Financial assets of key economies

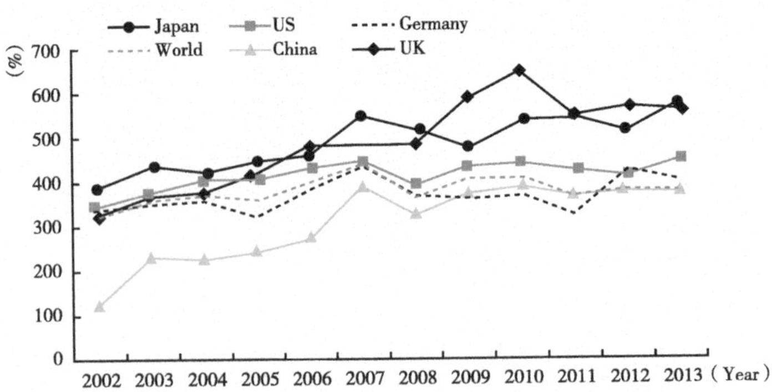

Fig. 24 Proportions of financial assets in GDP

2.5 Room for the Restructuring of China's Financial Market

Figure 25 reflects the constant increase in China's proportion of the global financial assets.

Figure 26 reveals a structural issue with financial assets. China's financial assets (in the ellipse below) are mainly comprised of bank assets. For years we have been emphasizing the importance of converting indirect finance into direct finance but, according to current statistics, these discussions have brought little change to China's financial asset structure. Compared with the US (left-most) in terms of financial asset composition, there is still enormous room for China to develop its stock and bond markets.

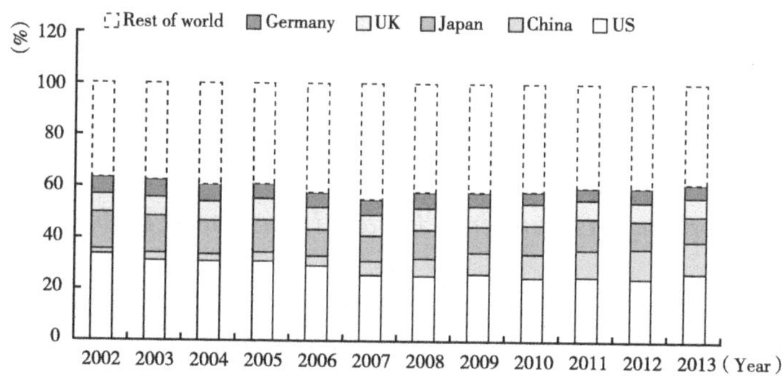

Fig. 25 National proportions of global financial assets

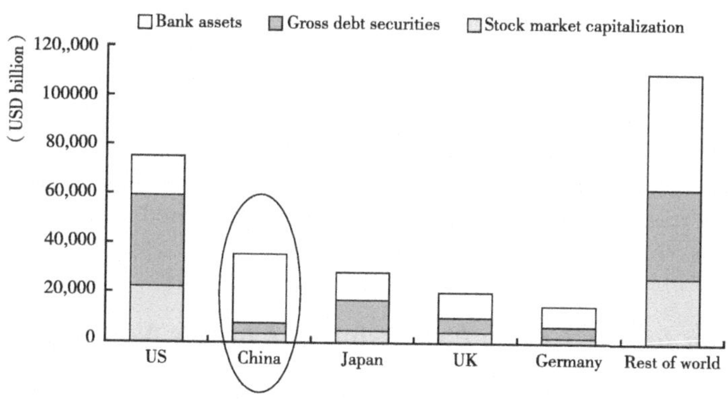

Fig. 26 Size of financial markets (as of 2013)

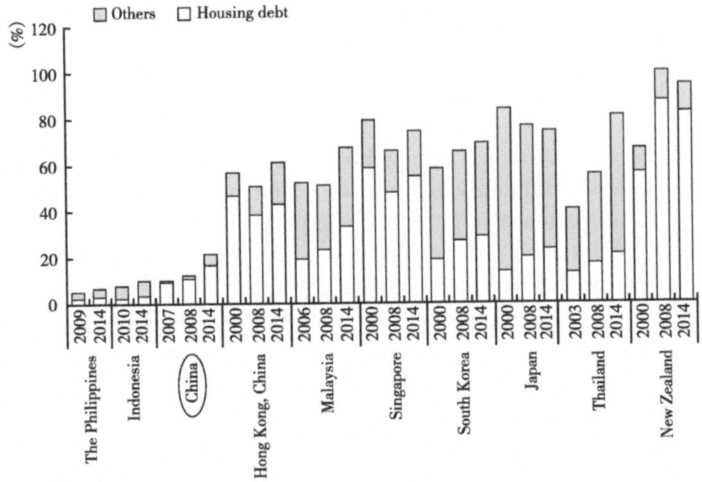

Fig. 27 Household debt-to-GDP for major Asian economies

2.6 *Room for an Increase in China's Household Debt*

Figure 27 shows China's debt level. Much talked about in our discussions, household debt is closely related to real estate prices. This leads to the question of whether or not China's household debt is too high. If its debt-to-GDP ratio is too high, the country's economic growth will be subject to a strong negative impact once housing prices fall.

As Fig. 27 shows, household debt-to-GDP has remained at a relatively low level in China over the past years, averaging between 20 and 30%. At the same time, many Asian economies have been agonizing over a high debt-to-GDP ratio. It is worth mentioning that they vary in debt composition. For example, most debts in China are real estate loans, while the opposite is true for some countries, such as Thailand, where most debts are in non-real estate sectors. Specifically, household debt has increased significantly in China alongside its real estate development, but it has not yet reached a particularly high level when compared with other countries.

2.7 *Room for the Equity Expansion of China's Non-financial Enterprises*

Figure 28 reflects the debt-to-equity ratio of China's non-financial enterprises in 2007 (the white bar) and 2013 (the gray bar). Despite the decline over this period (as we can see in the ellipse below), China still ranks higher than many countries in non-financial corporate debts. The solution lies partially in the potential for the expansion of China's stock market. If we increase the equity weight of such enterprises, the debt-to-equity ratio will be brought down further.

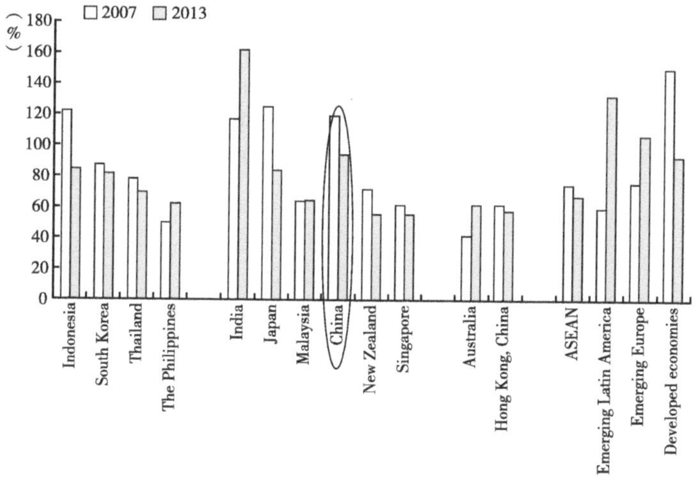

Fig. 28 Debt-to-equity ratios of non-financial enterprises

3 Conclusions

It is a fact that China's growth has slowed down. Deciding what policy measures should be adopted to cope with deceleration now, therefore, poses a serious challenge. Mere stimulation for demand growth will only cause more serious problems to pile up, because fiscal and monetary expansion and other stimulus measures will impede deleveraging and balance sheet adjustment. It would be akin to drinking poison to quench one's thirst.

From a global perspective, I would never expect any country to implement any real-sense structural reform—it is so difficult that it has become an almost impossible task, even though they know that they are going to suffer when the next crisis arrives. This is the first issue under consideration.

At the operational level, China has carried out a series of policies that will more or less support its GDP growth, including the current interest rate policy (downward interest rates), a deficit financing fiscal policy, a local government's policy to prevent housing price depreciation, the regulatory authority's policy to prevent further increase of nominal non-performing loans, etc. Despite all these efforts, the problems persist—and will continue to exist until sometime in the future when we can no longer sweep them under the rug. This is another concern of ours.

The most likely factor to bring such problems into the light will be a sharp rise in global interest rates. Once that happens, it is bound to bring significant changes to China's economic growth. According to statistics provided by the Bank for International Settlements (BIS), foreign capital flowing into China by way of bank loans and bond issuance has amounted to over USD 1 trillion so far, indicating huge sums of external funding in China's banks, enterprises, and shadow banking system. Massive capital outflow can occur when there are changes in world interest rates, all of which will significantly affect China's exchange rates, financial system liquidity, and real economic development. Therefore, it is necessary to ask whether China is really going to make any big moves in its reform. If we do not make substantial reforms until we are faced with unavoidably enormous impacts, we will then be confronted with much greater internal and external pressures than those on the US and Europe at present.

Chapter 7
China's New Normal and Deceleration Governance

Ping Zhang

It is now common knowledge that the Central Economic Working Conference has concluded that China's new normal is characterized by nine specific features. As such, I would like to talk about the substantive meanings of the new normal from four different perspectives: the various definitions of China's new normal, the impacts and superimposed effects of deceleration, the decline in total factor productivity and resource allocation efficiency, and the institutional reasons for lower efficiency and the governance of growth deceleration.

1 The New Normal of the Chinese Economy

As the name suggests, the "new normal" is a term used to imply that something that was previously abnormal has become commonplace. In this case, China's ongoing deceleration and adjustment must be recognized as a state of new normalcy relative to the country's more conventional high-speed growth. Such deceleration and adjustment marks the end of China's period of high-speed growth and the start of what may be characterized as a transition toward a new period of growth. Therefore, it is a typical transitional period characterized by distinct directional, temporal, durational, and structural attributes, as well as institutional, policy, and mechanistic reforms.

In fact, the new normal has already been defined very clearly by Western economists. Put simply, it is a process of rebalancing. As opposed to a standard normal state, it represents a transition from high-speed growth to highly efficient and balanced growth—changes that take place alongside a series of inevitable structural reforms and institutional adjustments.

In 2011, the term "new normal" appeared 700 times per month in print and online. Internationally, it is defined by an increasing number of scholars as a transitional

P. Zhang (✉)
CASS Institute of Economics, Beijing, China
e-mail: zhangping@cass.org.cn

F. Cai (ed.), *China's Economic New Normal*, Research Series on the Chinese Dream and China's Development Path, https://doi.org/10.1007/978-981-15-3227-6_7

period in the context of long-term global economic slowdown and sluggish economic recovery. During this period, global economic and trade growth remains at a low level, a new framework for global governance has not yet come into being, and the whole world suffers from constant trade friction and rising trade protectionism. In the meantime, economic stimulus and deleveraging are simultaneously exercised, while governments continue to adjust their policies within an extremely limited space. During this period of adjustment, the world's major economies differ in economic and policy cycles—while the US and the UK withdraw from their stimulus policy of quantitative easing, the rest of Europe and Japan have resorted to strengthened stimuli by means of a larger scale of quantitative easing. This has intensified economic frictions extant among different economies. The coexistence of a prosperous financial market and a weak real economy, mass unemployment, and growing income gaps are all important parts of the new transitional period.

1.1 Characteristics of China's New Normal

1. The deceleration of China's economic growth is distinctly structural. That is, those factors that structurally accelerated the country's economic growth during its catching-up process—such as the demographic dividend, the cheap workforce under the dual-sector model of the economy, and the effect of "learning-by-doing" for technical progress during industrialization—have now turned into decelerators. In other words, the positive factors—for example, the growing demands of global prosperity—are gradually fading away. From 2001 to 2011, China's economic growth averaged 10.4% annually. From early 2012 to early 2014, however, its GDP growth lingered somewhere between 7 and 8% for a good number of consecutive quarters, which is a distinct characteristic of a transitional period.
2. Economic restructuring persists. It is no longer what we knew as the proportional adjustment among the primary, secondary, and tertiary industries, but an adjustment of the economic structure in a broader sense. The significance of China's economic restructuring lies in the following five specific aspects. First of all, economic restructuring will boost domestic demand and drive China's economic growth. Secondly, it will adjust China's income distribution in order to increase the proportion of consumption in domestic demand. Thirdly, it will constantly improve China's industrial efficiency by way of industrial restructuring, transformation, and upgrading. Fourthly, it will realize a new normal state characterized by a more balanced regional development through the adjustment of China's regional economic structure. Finally, it will reform the mechanisms for primary distribution and the redistribution of factor prices.
3. The simultaneous practices of macroeconomic policies, micro stimulus measures, and financial risk prevention are part of China's new normal, the purpose of which is to reduce the country's high leverage ratio and those local government debts resulting from past overstimulation. In order to ensure steady economic growth, China has been resorting to micro stimulus measures, but these

measures, by their very nature, will increase leverage. Limited to a very narrow policy space, the government must make such moves more frequently.

4. High-cost factor supply characterizes China's new normal. The low-cost industrial age is gone, and so, too, are the low-cost lands, workforce, environmental protections, and taxation. China's unique advantage—based as it was on distorted land, labor, and environmental costs—is also slipping away. Going forward, China's economic growth will have to count on an increase in its total factor productivity and human capital. To reverse China's factor supply, however, we must change existing mechanisms outlining the supply and allocation of various factors. That is to say, we must carry out market-oriented reforms, which are the only way to improve the supply side, effectively increase labor productivity, and boost technological progress.
5. Comprehensively deepening reforms—which are oriented to market-based resource allocation—has become an important component of China's new normal. Overly dependent on the government during the country's catching-up process, the traditional model of resource allocation must give way to market-oriented resource allocation. We must cross the "red line" and put an end to government interference in China's reforms, such as factor price formulation, state-owned enterprise reformation, the market-oriented reformation of interest and exchange rates, government administrative reform, the function-based reformation of public institutions, rural land reform, the reformation of the urban household registration system, and fiscal and taxation system reform. As an indispensable element of China's new normal, such reforms will play a decisive role in boosting China's high-efficiency development and transformation in the years ahead.

1.2 The New Normal as Transition to Efficient Equilibrium

In this transitional period, the direction and duration of transition, as well as maintaining sustained reform, are of primary importance. The only direction open to us is a shift from structural catching-up and surpassing to efficient and balanced growth, which necessitates the following aspects.

1. Conversion of the dual sectors of the economy into modern economic sectors. This will not only achieve consistency in the work efficiency of both agricultural and modern sectors, but also realize market-based economic restructuring (e.g., market clearing) without government interference in allocation. In terms of value added, China has by and large completed the modernization of its industrial structure, but it has not yet updated its configuration of employment. Large numbers of rural laborers have finished their career transition and are now working in cities, but they do not yet belong to these cities simply because their identity conversion has not yet been fully accomplished. As a matter of fact, at present,

work efficiency is still not high enough in China's industrial sectors, while the dual economy is still undergoing further transformation.

2. A market economy has been preliminarily established, but we have not yet accomplished the directive "to give play to the decisive role of the market in resource allocation" proposed at the Third Plenary Session of the 18th CPC Central Committee. On the other hand, there is still a long way to go in terms of our reformation of state-owned enterprises, public institutions, regulatory departments, and government administration.
3. China's economic growth must rely on an increase in its total factor productivity and human capital, rather than ever-increasing input, and follow the principle of endogenous growth. The biggest problem with our growth for the time being is a constantly-decreasing TFP contribution, which was previously expected to rise. Should we fail to bring the roles of technological progress and human capital into play, we will be unlikely to accomplish any kind of transformation of our mode of production. It will take quite some time to complete the current transition, and deceleration will be a new normal state before we arrive at what is forecast to be the new equilibrium. In this process, reforms, structural adjustments, and policy incentives will be essential to China's new normal.

Personally, I would rather view China's new normal as a test—that is, a procedure for self-regulation and self-cultivation. As long as we perform well, we will be able to transit to a period of efficient equilibrium. If, unfortunately, we mess it up, we will be forced to accept a different outcome. This procedure begins with the catching-up period of steady economic growth so characteristic of the country's recent past, and will last until we arrive at the new, more efficient equilibrium. By reference to the East Asian model, medium-to-high growth falls exactly within an adjustment phase. If we manage to avoid the middle income trap by adjusting our medium-to-high growth, we will enter a period of efficient and balanced growth. If we are unable to do so, we will likely fall into the trap.

2 The Impacts and Superimposed Effects of Deceleration

At present, the most pressing problem with the Chinese economy is the various impacts and superimposed effects of deceleration. Significant changes have affected those factors that contributed to the structural acceleration of the Chinese economy, with many of them even turning into economic brakes under the current state of affairs. Considered in light of the current industrial structure, China is already a modernized economy, one in which agriculture only accounts for 10% of the economy in constant prices and 7% in current prices.

2.1 Impact 1: Inverted U-Shaped Capital Growth

Following its structural evolution from industry- to service-dominated economic growth, China will soon witness a decline in its rapid investment growth and investment rate. A theoretical explanation may go something like this: during the industrial age, return on investment (ROI) in industrial sectors was higher than in agricultural and service sectors, a fact that must be attributed to economies of scale and standardized production. For developing countries, investment-driven growth was a marked characteristic of their economy during the catching-up process, when their investment and capital kept increasing. Upon the completion of their industrialization periods—and particularly as focus shifted to urbanization—the proportion of services was likely to rise, whereas investment and capital growth would decline.

2.2 Impact 2: Inverted U-Shaped Workforce Growth

China's urbanization corresponded with its demographic dividend, or, differently interpreted, a demographic window of opportunity. With rapid changes to its demographic structure, the growth of China's working-age population has declined.

According to statistics from the World Development Indicators (WDI) Database, the growth of China's working-age population reached a turning point in 2009. If we break up GDP growth into two parts—one resulting from an increase in labor productivity and one resulting from the growth of the working-age population, respectively—the contribution of the demographic dividend (i.e. growth of the working-age population) to China's overall GDP growth has dropped from 29% in the 1980s to 17% in the 1990s (a percentage that persisted from 2000 to 2008), and below 10% since 2009. Given the intrinsic trend of China's demographic transition, a demographic dividend contribution falling below 10%—or even a negative value—may be a long-term trend.

2.3 Impact 3: Decrease in the Learning-by-Doing Effect

To a great extent, China's large-scale urbanization and relevant improvements towards efficiency can be attributed to the role of learning-by-doing. On the one hand, technological availability has been fairly high for China during its catching-up period, which had long lagged behind internationally-advanced technology. On the other hand, the effect of learning-by-imitation was conducive to the constant improvement of China's efficiency. Nonetheless, with the completion of its industrialization—in particular its heavy industry—foreign technology has become less and less available, and the country is heading toward the top of an S-shaped learning curve. At the same time, both its investments and its overall efficiency have begun to slow.

2.4 Other Factors Superimposed on Deceleration

This includes the reversion of factor elasticity, the conflict between standardized industrial production and changes to the structure of consumption, constrains on resources and environmental constraints, and restrictions of the global business climate.

3 The Decline in Total Factor Productivity and Resource Allocation Efficiency

3.1 Capital Mismatch and TFP Decline

Through a reference to Ge (2012), we have here divided the Chinese economy into such sectors as Economic Infrastructure, Social Infrastructure, Real Estate, Industry, and Other Services. Figure 1 shows changes in the proportion of investment over the past decades by sector, wherein capital mismatch by sector is evident.

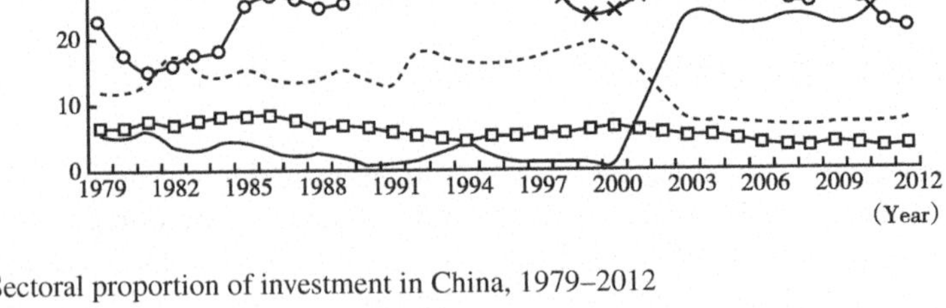

Fig. 1 Sectoral proportion of investment in China, 1979–2012

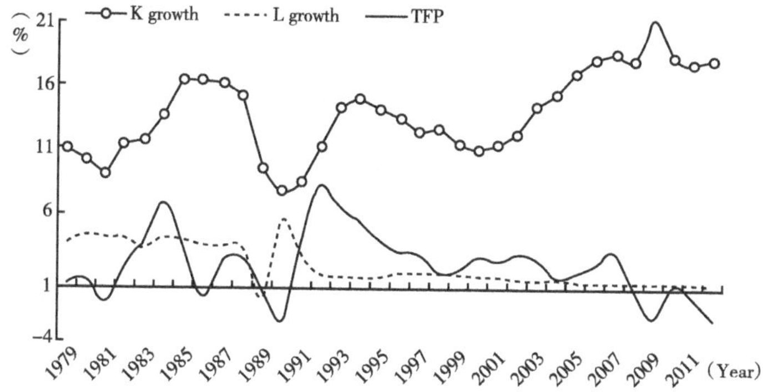

Fig. 2 Factor trends in China's growth, 1979–2012

3.2 Estimates of China's TFP Growth

3.2.1 Capital Stock Estimates

We first categorize the above sectors into Major Sectors K (real estate, economic infrastructure, and social infrastructure) and L (industry and other services). We then set their rates of depreciation as 2 and 7% and their base values of capital stock as RMB 145.13 billion and RMB 312.20 billion, respectively. Finally, we calculate the aggregate capital stock of the two major sectors (see Fig. 2).

3.2.2 Sluggish Human Capital Growth

We use the average number of years of schooling to measure the human capital levels of China and other countries. Primary amongst our conclusions is that China not only lags behind developed countries on this metric but also a number of developing ones, such as Indonesia and Thailand (see Table 1).

Moreover, in terms of the average number of years of schooling, China is lower than most countries possessing a higher GDP per capita, as well as many countries with a lower GDP per capita (see Fig. 3).

3.2.3 Human Capital Mismatch

To begin with, China is behind Russia, ten European countries, and the US in terms of human capital (see Fig. 4).

Secondly, even at a relatively low level of human capital, China has a serious problem with human capital mismatch among its economic sectors (see Fig. 5).

Table 1 Average number of years of schooling for population over age fifteen

Year	1970	1975	1980	1985	1990	1995	2000	2005	2010
US	10.8	11.5	12.0	12.1	12.2	12.6	12.6	12.9	13.2
Japan	7.8	8.4	9.1	9.6	9.8	10.5	10.9	11.3	11.6
9 Lain American countries	4.0	4.2	4.6	5.3	6.0	6.7	7.3	8.0	8.5
Indonesia	2.8	3.2	3.6	3.9	4.2	4.6	5.2	6.4	7.6
Malaysia	4.2	4.8	5.8	6.7	7.0	8.4	9.1	9.7	10.4
Philippines	4.7	5.5	6.2	6.6	7.1	7.6	7.9	8.2	8.4
Thailand	2.5	3.0	3.6	4.2	4.9	5.5	5.7	7.0	8.0
India	1.6	2.0	2.3	2.9	3.5	4.1	5.0	5.6	6.2
China	3.6	4.1	4.9	5.3	5.6	6.3	6.9	7.3	7.5

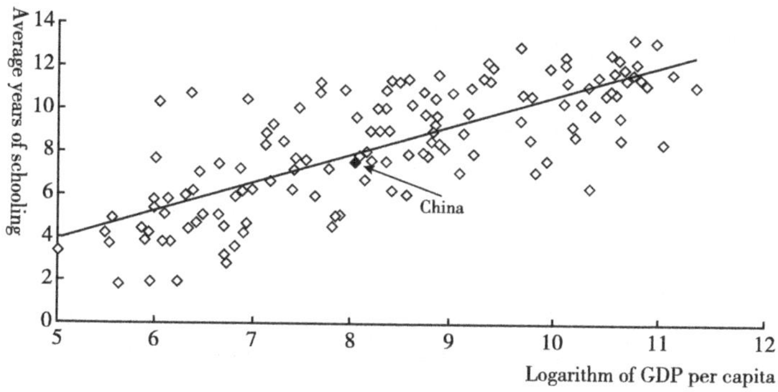

Fig. 3 Scatterplot for 145 countries by GDP per capita and average number of years of schooling

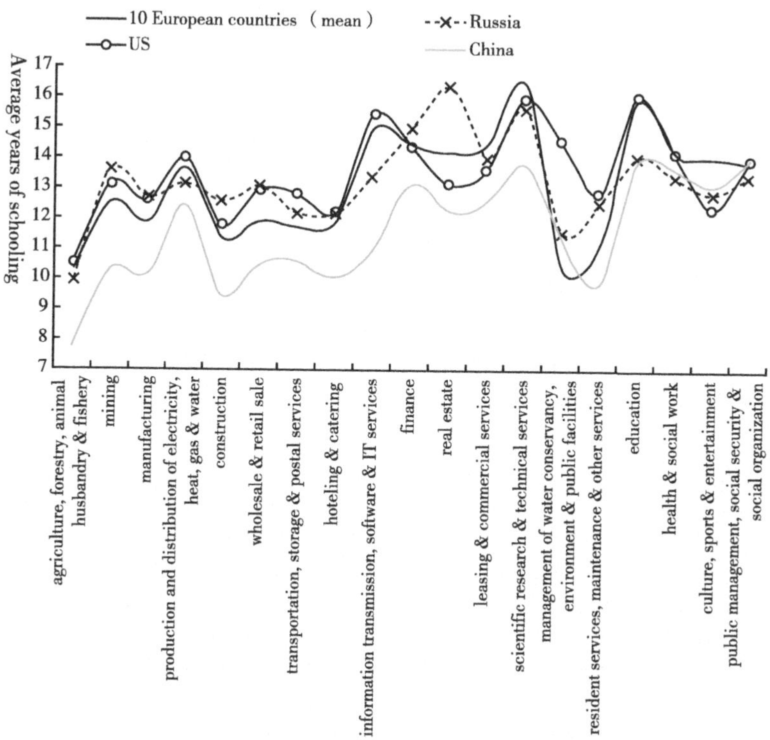

Fig. 4 Average number of years of schooling for laborers by sector (2012)

Ultimately, compared with other countries, China is more unbalanced in terms of the distribution of its human capital strength across sectors, with the biggest concentrations in its institutional and regulatory sectors (see Table 2).

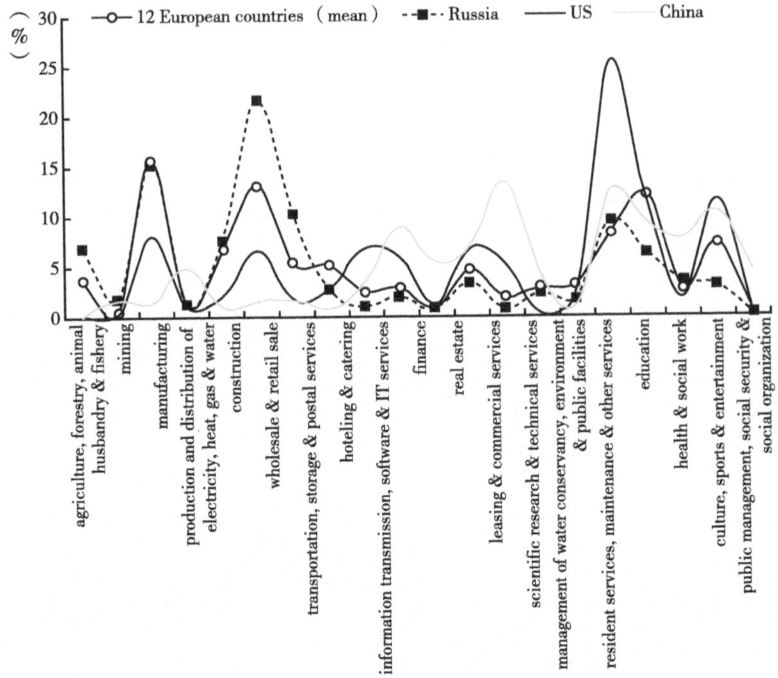

Fig. 5 Sectoral distribution of laborers with bachelor's degree or higher (2012)

3.3 Institutional Explanations for Low Efficiency and the Governance of Growth Deceleration

First of all, under the condition of vertical or top-down resource allocation under government interference, the government must render sufficient support to those enterprises liable to scale up, and separate from the market system such industrial services sectors as science, education, culture, and health.

Secondly, the existence of implicit government subsidies and differentiated labor markets has led to marked differences among the economic sectors in terms of both their objectives and operating mechanisms, as well as in their responses to market demand.

Last but not least, in the course of overall growth deceleration, different types of enterprises differ significantly in terms of their resource allocations due to varying degrees of government support. On the one hand, instead of being weeded out, well-supported, large-sized "zombie enterprises" continue chewing through their existing resources and pass the costs of their losses on to those unsupported by the government. On the other hand, innovative enterprises are usually burdened with high costs, but without the associated expectation of being able to obtain further resources.

Table 2 International comparison of by-sector human capital strength (2012)

Sector	China	France	Italy	UK	US
Agriculture, forestry, animal husbandry, and fishery	0.004	2.777	3.696	2.070	0.176
Manufacturing	0.040	1.465	1.206	1.222	0.661
Production and distribution of electricity, heat, gas, and water	2.235	0.595	0.651	0.435	0.502
Construction	0.125	1.401	1.098	1.307	0.563
Wholesale and retail sales	0.304	1.140	1.282	1.452	0.580
Transportation, storage, and postal services	0.817	1.264	0.633	1.269	0.553
Hoteling and catering	0.080	1.561	2.701	2.473	0.900
Information transmission, software, and IT services	1.651	0.322	0.362	0.439	1.031
Finance	1.700	0.690	0.388	0.426	0.945
Real estate	0.944	0.073	0.006	0.093	0.084
Leasing and commercial services	3.449	0.363	1.120	0.314	2.808
Scientific research and technical services	9.197	1.351	0.113	1.697	0.556
Resident services, maintenance, and associated services	0.594	3.026	0.785	1.091	1.102
Education	4.129	1.364	1.675	1.648	23.647
Health and social work	5.794	0.976	1.503	1.757	1.469
Culture, sports, and entertainment	12.230	1.304	2.737	1.535	1.654
Public management, social security, and social organization	2.772	1.048	1.114	1.395	0.878

4 Conclusions

Without an effective mechanism in place for the elimination of "zombie enterprises," backward production capacity has been rendered a reality in China, even as it is backed by government support. As China's human capital is concentrated primarily on nonmarket sectors, the market sectors—the principal drivers of innovation—are restricted by high costs, lack of financial support, and a workforce characterized by high volume and low skills, while at the same time being faced with an increase in innovation difficulties and a decrease in motivating forces for innovation.

4.1 *Deceleration Governance*

1. The basic principle of China's deceleration governance is to strengthen the mechanisms supporting competition and turn deceleration into a "cleaning" process for the Chinese economy.

2. Replace the "vertical division" characteristic of the central governmental departments with the market's horizontal allocation of resources so as to inspire and encourage innovation.
3. Terminate the selective support of the central and local governments while reducing their roles in resource allocation and ceding primacy to market-based allocation.
4. Reform such nonmarket sectors as science, education, culture, and health, and leave room for the further development of China's modern services.

4.2 *Structural Adjustment of Capital Stocks*

1. Press forward with the reformation of China's local government debt.
2. Encourage the renewal and transformation of capital stock in China's manufacturing sector by means of tax incentives and other policies.
3. Break down the existing institutional barriers standing in the way of rational capital allocation.
4. Improve China's human capital level by way of training and reallocate its human capital stocks for more rational utilization.
5. Expand existing space for the development of China's services through institutional reform.

Reference

Ge, J. (2012). The estimation of China's infrastructure capital stock. *Economic Research Journal*, 4, 4–8.

Chapter 8
Aspects of the Middle Income Trap

Zhizhong Yao

In 2007, the World Bank published the report, "An East Asian Renaissance: Ideas for Economic Growth," and raised the issue of "a middle income trap" for the first time. In "China 2030: Building a Modern, Harmonious, and Creative Society," released in 2012 by the World Bank and the Development Research Center of the State Council of the People's Republic of China, it was estimated that out of 101 middle-income economies in 1960, only 13 became high-income by 2008, namely, Greece, Ireland, Portugal, Spain, Japan, the Republic of Korea, Singapore, Hong Kong SAR (China), Israel, Puerto Rico, Equatorial Guinea, Mauritius, and Taiwan of China. That is to say, the other 88 middle-income economies have either remained there or been reduced to low-income economies over the past half century. In other words, 87% of the aforementioned economies had been trapped in middle-income status for some 50 years without achieving the transition into high-income status. Having so many countries and regions remain defined by their middle income for such a long time constitutes a serious warning for the rest of the world.

Nonetheless, very few people have ever noticed that, to move from the middle-income stage and exceed the high-income threshold within 50 years, a low-income economy must sustain a 5% or higher annual growth of Gross National Income (GNI) per capita for half a century. Historically, very few of today's high-income countries have sustained a 5% annual growth of per capita income over a span of 50 years—even the UK, the US, and Japan failed to achieve such goal during their golden ages. Thus, it seems quite typical for the vast majority of middle-income countries to be unable to make the transition into high-income status within 50 years. Besides, there are indeed cases of middle-income economies that have experienced the decline and stagnation of their economic growth—or even a reversal of their per capita income—following a period of high-speed growth. That being said, is there really a middle income trap? What is a middle income trap? What are the main causes of the middle income trap? How can a middle-income economy avoid the trap? These are extremely

Z. Yao (✉)
CASS Institute of World Economy and Politics, Beijing, China
e-mail: yaozz@cass.org.cn

F. Cai (ed.), *China's Economic New Normal*, Research Series on the Chinese Dream and China's Development Path, https://doi.org/10.1007/978-981-15-3227-6_8

important questions for China in its transition from middle income to high income.[1] Yet for all the discussion over these questions so far, significant confusion about the very definition and formation of the middle-income trap remains, which corresponds with a shortage of adequate and effective policy suggestions. How can one judge whether or not an economy is stuck in the middle income trap? With this question serving as the basis for our research, we will attempt to provide a clear definition of the middle income trap, evaluate the degree to which middle-income countries are stuck in the trap, explore the similarities and differences between low-income and high-income countries, and estimate the likelihood for middle-income countries of falling into the trap. By doing so, we hope to theoretically clarify the mechanisms underpinning the trap's formation, as well as lay an empirical foundation for more effective policy-making to avoid the middle income trap altogether.

1 The Inevitable Deceleration of Growth

In March 2011, economists Barry Eichengreen, Donghyun Park, and Kwanho Shin released an interesting working paper titled, "When Fast Growing Economies Slow Down: International Evidence and Implications for China." As the title suggests, at the time of writing, the authors have assumed that rapidly growing economies are bound to slow down. They cited the Canadian singer Nelly Furtado's "All Good Things Come to an End" to explain why periods of high growth would not last forever. They went on to elaborate upon what they identified as the four primary reasons for this: (1) eventually the pool of underemployed rural labor is drained; (2) the share of employment in manufacturing peaks and growth subsequently comes to depend more heavily on the more difficult process of raising productivity in the service sector; (3) a larger capital stock means more depreciation, requiring more savings to make up for it; and finally (4) as the economy approaches the technological frontier, it must transition from relying on imported technology to native innovation. Theoretically, all other things being equal, any of the above conditions would lead to a growth slowdown. In reality, they are all bound to occur in the normal course of development for a given economy. Therefore, that rapidly growing economies must slow down is not only commonsense but also a precondition for Barry Eichengreen and his colleagues, a fact borne out by their empirical analysis.

Now that all the aforementioned four changes have already taken place in China, there seems to be a high degree of consensus as to the inevitability of an economic slowdown for the country. Unless new variables are found that can accelerate growth, deceleration is inevitable for the Chinese economy.

Over a period of 35 years of reform and opening-up, China has sustained an average annual GDP growth rate of around 10%. Almost no one expects China to

[1] By the World Bank's definition, China was "low income" before 1997, "lower-middle income" in 1997, "low income" again in 1998, and "lower-middle income" between 1999 and 2009, while being considered "upper-middle income" since 2010.

continue to grow at such a high speed in the years ahead. At the same time, very few people believe that the Chinese economy will stagnate in the next ten or even 20 years. Most forecasters maintain that China's economic growth is likely to slow over the next ten to 20 years, but there is a world of difference between them as to the degree of China's slowdown. Estimated in the "China 2030: Building a Modern, Harmonious, and Creative Society" report—a product of the collaboration between of the World Bank and the Development Research Center of the State Council of the People's Republic of China—the potential annual growth rate of China's GDP would be 8.6% from 2011 to 2015, 7.0% from 2016 to 2020, 5.9% from 2021 to 2025, and 5.0% from 2026 to 2030. The US National Intelligence Council (NIC) predicted in *Global Trend 2030: Alternative Worlds* that the average annual growth rate of China's GDP would range between 5.0 and 6.7% from 2010 to 2030. In 2012, the Research Group on China's Economic Growth under the CASS Institute of Economics predicted that the potential annual growth rate of China's GDP would range between 7.8 and 8.7% from 2011 to 2015, between 5.7 and 6.6% from 2016 to 2020, and between 5.4 and 6.3% from 2021 to 2030.[2] In the same year, Lu Yang, working with the CASS Institute of Population and Labor Economics, forecast that the potential annual growth rate of China's GDP would be 7.8% from 2011 to 2015 and 6.3% from 2016 to 2020.[3] And Wang Xiaolu, Fan Gang, and Liu Peng estimated that the average annual growth rate of China's GDP would be 6.7% from 2008 to 2020, with the potential for it to rise even higher if advances in substantial reforms could be accomplished in the country's political institutions, educational arena, and social security.[4]

Even among the most pessimistic of the above estimates, China is forecast to be able to sustain a 5% or higher annual growth of its GDP up until 2030. At this rate, China is bound to develop into a high-income country. Therefore, it is totally unnecessary to worry about China falling into the middle income trap.

Internationally, countless economies have suffered a rapid drop in growth rate upon reaching middle-income levels and, consequently, are unable to further narrow the income gap with developed economies. Those that have succeeded both in catching up and growing into high-income economies themselves are few and far between. We are all aware that China's growth rate will also decline rapidly when it reaches middle-income status, so why, then, do we deem it unnecessary to worry about the middle income trap? This is primarily because China will remain at a relatively high level of growth after such a decline, which will be enough for China to gradually narrow the income gap with the US and other developed economies and ultimately evolve into a high-income country. It therefore follows that, although slowdowns are inevitable for fast-growing economies, this does not mean that they are wholly unable to raise their per capita income, to narrow the income gap with the US and other developed economies, and to achieve high-income status.

---

[2]Research Group on China's Economic Growth and CASS Institute of Economics (2012).

[3]Lu Yang, "The Potential Growth Rate of China's Output and Predictions," in *Reports on China's Population and Labor No. 13*, ed. Cai Fang (Beijing: Social Sciences Academic Press), 98–110.

[4]Xiaolu et al. (2009).

Given the above, we cannot ascertain whether a middle-income economy will be stuck in the middle income trap even when its growth has slowed down. On what ground, then, can we evaluate whether an economy has already fallen into the trap?

2 The Paradox of the Middle Income Trap

To understand the middle income trap, we need to first have a clear view of what constitutes "middle-income countries." In the existing literature, there are two primary methods by which to classify middle-income countries: using absolute and/or relative thresholds. The absolute threshold defines a range of per capita income and classifies countries that are within this range as middle income trapped countries. The relative threshold defines a certain proportional range relative to the per capita income of high-income countries, and classifies those within this range as middle-income countries, those above it as high-income, and those below it as low-income.

In order to identify providers and recipients of economic aid, the World Bank began classification of its member countries shortly after its establishment. At the beginning, all the member countries were divided into three categories: financial aid providers, eligible aid recipients, and other economies. At that time, this classification schema emphasized the political status of its member economies and considered national income only for reference, rather than as the sole indicator for classification. For example, at that time, Japan was classified as a financial aid provider despite being fairly low in GNI per capita. In order to modify such deviations within its classifications, the World Bank began to introduce more explicit indicators and, in time, came to consider GNI per capita as the best measure of economic progress. In the early 1980s, it adopted income groupings based on GNI per capita only. Following this methodology, the World Bank defined the ranges of GNI per capita for operational lending policies and other favorable terms as well as a per capita income threshold of ineligibility for preferential lending ("the graduation threshold") in each fiscal year, yet did not determine the operational thresholds of middle-income economies until much later. Such groupings are introduced in order to determine a member economy's eligibility for World Bank loans and corresponding operational policy, and are thus known as operational classifications. To date, they are still revised and released annually by the World Bank.

Meanwhile, the World Bank also uses analytical classifications for evaluating economies according to its World Development Indicators (WDI) and World Development Reports (WDR). In the 1978 World Development Indicators, all World Bank member economies were classified into three groupings: developing economies, industrial market economies, and capital surplus oil exporters. This classification was not income-based. Oil exporting countries were easily defined, for they were distinctly different from others; industrial economies consisted of members of the Organization for Economic Co-operation and Development (OECD, excluding Greece, Portugal, and Turkey); and developing economies were defined as the rest of World Bank member economies not fitting the profile of either oil exporters or industrial economies. Developing economies were further divided into low income and middle income in 1978. Low-income economies were defined as those with a GNI per capita of USD 250 or less, and middle-income economies were those with a GNI per capita of more than USD 250. This was the first-ever explicit criterion introduced by the World Bank to define middle-income economies, yet there are obvious flaws with it. For example, the USD 250 threshold was quite arbitrary. In addition, the line between developing economies and industrial economies was not clear enough, and some economies that were higher than many industrial countries in GNI per capita were then classified as middle-income, such as Israel and Singapore.

To make up for such deficiencies, the World Bank revised its member classifications in 1989 and established an analytical classification of economies based solely on GNI per capita estimates. Using 1987 as the base year, it defined high-income economies as those with a GNI per capita of USD 6,000 or more, low-income as those with a GNI per capita of USD 480 or less, and middle-income as those with a GNI per capita between USD 480 and USD 6,000. Middle-income economies were further divided into lower middle-income and upper middle-income by a threshold of USD 1,940. Generally speaking, low-income and middle-income economies are regarded as developing economies. Since 1987, the World Bank has been adjusting its income group thresholds using the GDP deflator and changes to the exchange rate.[5] In other words, the World Bank's income group thresholds do not change with the world's overall real income. For example, the middle-income and high-income thresholds of 2013 (USD 1,045 and USD 12,745, respectively) were equivalent to those of 1987 (USD 480 and USD 6,000, respectively) when adjusted for both inflation and exchange rate fluctuations. Such is typical of absolute thresholds that remain constant over time when measured by real income. Why did the World Bank establish the benchmark for middle-income economies between USD 480 and USD 6,000 in 1987 prices? In 1987, the world's global per capita income was USD 3,222. This figure was then doubled and rounded down to the nearest USD 1,000. That was how the 6,000-dollar high-income threshold came into being. Meanwhile, it was simultaneously determined that the high-income threshold should be 12.5 times the middle-income threshold, which was USD 480 in 1987 prices. It is hard to say whether such groupings were adequately grounded. Yet the World Bank classification has been considered fairly official and is still in use even now—and more importantly, it continues to serve as an analytical classification for economies. Today, the World

[5]The World Bank has adopted the *Atlas* conversion factor to reduce the impact of exchange rate fluctuations on international comparisons of GNI. The *Atlas* conversion factor for any given year is the average of a country's exchange rate for that year and its exchange rates for the two preceding years, with an adjustment for the difference between the rate of inflation in the country and international inflation. A country's inflation rate is measured by the change in its GDP deflator, and international inflation is measured using the change in a deflator based on the International Monetary Fund's special drawing rights, known as the "SDR deflator."

Bank's thresholds have become the major criteria used for defining low-, middle-, and high-income economies.[6]

Based on the aforementioned thresholds, we have observed the changes in per capita income of 192 countries and regions from 1991 to 2011[7] and come up with the following findings: The 39 high-income economies extant in 1991 remained high-income in 2011. Of the 54 low-income economies in 1991, only one achieved a high income, 21 became middle-income, and 32 remained low-income in 2011. Of the 99 middle-income economies in 1991, 19 achieved a high income, three declined to low-income, and 77 remained middle-income in 2011. That is to say, 40% of the low-income economies succeeded in transitioning to a higher-income stage from 1991 to 2011, while fewer than 20% of the middle-income economies achieved a high income over those same twenty years. Crossover at the low-income stage seems easier than doing so at the middle-income stage.

80% of the middle-income economies that existed 20 years ago either remained in the middle-income stage or had declined to low income by 2011. It is so difficult to cross over the middle-income stage that a middle income trap appears to be an inevitable reality. Not necessarily so. As previously mentioned, the ratio between the high- and middle-income thresholds has been determined to be 12.5. For an economy that has just crossed the threshold of middle income, this means a 12.5-time increase of its GNI per capita before it reaches high-income status. In order to achieve that goal within 20 years, this translates into an average annual growth of 13.5%. As far as we know, no country or region in human history has ever sustained such a high-speed growth for such a long period. Even if it is to finish the middle- to high-income transition in 50 years, it must still sustain an average annual growth of its real GNI per capita of at least 5.2%. In terms of GDP per capita, only five countries have sustained an average annual growth of 5.2% or higher over the past half century, namely, China (6.7%), Botswana (6.0%), Singapore (5.6%), the Republic of Korea (5.5%), and Equatorial Guinea (5.5%).[8] It is thus quite normal for most middle-income economies to have failed to sustain an annual growth in GDP per capita of 5.2% or higher. Clearly, it is anything but easy to transition from middle income to high income as defined by the World Bank's analytical classification thresholds. For middle-income countries, failure to cross over the middle-income stage within 50 years is very common, and those that have succeeded must be regarded as miraculous, rather than the norm.

As stated previously, only 13 out of 101 middle-income economies have grown into high-income ones in some 50 years, according to the World Bank's report titled,

---

[6] Cited from The World Bank at www.worldbank.org and Lynge Nielsen, "Classification of Countries Based on Their Level of Development: How It Is Done and How It Could Be Done." IMF Working Paper WP/11/31 (February, 2011).

[7] While the World Bank started its groupings in 1987, our observation starts with 1991 to obtain a larger number of samples.

[8] The figures in brackets are average annual growth rates of GDP per capita from 1961 to 2011, when Singapore, the Republic of Korea, and Equatorial Guinea had grown into high-income countries, while China and Botswana only grew from low-income to upper-middle-income due to their extremely low per capita income in 1961.

"China 2030: Building a Modern, Harmonious, and Creative Society." This conclusion, however, is not based on the Bank's analytical classification thresholds. Rather, it defines middle-income economies using per capita incomes relative to the US. It is a pity that the report has not established a clear range of proportions relative to the per capita income of the US as benchmarks of middle-income economies. In the report's core finding, which is that "few countries escape the middle income trap," two countries roughly denote the per capita income benchmarks. One is China. It is classified as a middle-income economy in terms of its 1960 per capita income relative to the US and is placed very close to the lower threshold for middle income on the chart. In 1960, China's per capita income was only about 2% of that of the US.[9] The other is Portugal. It is classified as a high-income economy in terms of its 2008 per capita income relative to the US and is placed close to the lower threshold for high income on the chart. In 2008, its per capita income was about 45% that of the US. We thus infer from the figure that the range defining middle income is roughly between 2 and 45% of US per capita income. In 2008, 2–45% of US per capita income ranged between USD 958 and USD 21,551. Compared with the World Bank's analytical classification, this report has almost doubled the upper threshold for defining middle-income—already ridiculously high—from USD 11,905 to USD 21,551. No wonder only 13 middle-income economies have attained a "high income" in over 50 years. It is therefore our view that such conflicting thresholds provide little support for the existence of a middle income trap.

Fortunately, another World Bank report has more accurately analyzed the middle income trap by studying the changes across relative income groups against the US.[10] Groups 2 through 4 are, respectively, defined as lower-middle, middle-middle, and upper-middle income, and are collectively referred to as middle-income countries. Likewise, Group 1 is comprised of low-income countries, and Group 5 high-income countries. Following the Markov transition matrix approach, the report estimates the ten-year probability of transition across different income groups between 1950 and 2008. The authors identified the probability of moving to a higher income group after a decade as: Group 1 (low-income) 5%, Group 2 (lower-middle) 18%, Group 3 (middle-middle) 35%, and Group 4 (upper-middle) 34%, which proves that the "upgrade" probability of GNI per capita does not drop significantly with the rise of a country's income level. Based on these findings, the report concludes that evidence is still inadequate to support the existence of a middle income trap. On the other hand, we maintain that such income grouping is not rigorous enough as a methodology. For example, it has ignored the difference in raising per capita income from 1 to 15% and from 30 to 45% of that of the US. As a matter of fact, there is a world of difference in the growth rates required to realize these two disparate goals. The former means a growth of 15 times, but the latter only 1.5 times—to say nothing of the fact that per capita income continues growing in the US even as it grows elsewhere.

[9]Since the World Bank per capita income data was not released until 1962, we hereby make an approximate substitution using the 1962 ratio between China and US in per capita income.

[10]Fernando Gabriel Im and David Rosenblatt, "Middle Income Traps: A Conceptual and Empirical Survey." World Bank Policy Research Working Paper 6594 (September, 2013).

For consistency across relative income intervals, the report adopts a different relative income classification for comparison, which sorts the countries into five groups by thresholds of 1/16, 1/8, 1/4, and 1/2 of US income, but comes to the same conclusion: the existence of a middle income trap lacks sufficient support. Judging by these thresholds, a middle-income country has to double its per capita income relative to the US to move to a higher income group in a decade. In other words, the average annual growth of its per capita income must be 7.2% points higher than that of the US over the same ten-year period. Now that the long-term growth rate of US per capita income is around 2.1%, a middle-income country will have to sustain a 9.3% average annual growth to upgrade within a decade. What follows from this is that it does not really mean much whether a country upgrades to a higher income group within ten years. Besides, given the higher upgrade probability for middle-income countries than for low-income ones, this should not be understood as a denial of the existence of a middle income trap—rather, it simply recognizes the unlikelihood of such a trap.

In a word, when we boil down all the arguments about the middle income trap—the various definitions and all sorts of evidence as to its existence or nonexistence—we find none of them are truly convincing.

3 Defining the Middle Income Trap

As discussed above, the confusion here primarily stems from the absence of a strict definition of the middle income trap, which is the core concept in this case. Yet any further serious analysis of the middle income trap and relevant issues necessitates a clear and rigorous definition of the term as hand, as well as a practical method of identification.

As there are absolute and relative thresholds defining middle-income economies, the middle income trap may well be defined using both absolute and relative criteria.

In absolute terms, an economy may be identified as being stuck in the middle income trap when it winds up stagnating in a given middle-income range, unable to move to high income, over a long period of time. Here some questions arise: How broad is the "given middle-income range?" And how long is that "period of time?" As we have previously pointed out, failure to accomplish the 12.5-time transition from middle to high income within 50 years—a period defined by the World Bank—does not necessarily equal falling into the trap. How about a longer span of stagnation in middle income, then? Presumably, if the middle-income range does not change over time, a country is bound to cross over the middle-income stage sooner or later, as long as its per capita income keeps growing—no matter how slow it grows. For example, it will take 64 years to achieve the 12.5-time upgrade from middle to high income if a country keeps growing at 4% annually, 85 years at 3%, 127 years at 2%, and 253 years at 1%. That is, using a given growth rate, we are able to calculate the time span needed to cross over the middle-income stage. Likewise, within a given time span, we are also able to calculate the average growth rate required to that end. Therefore, when we consider whether a country is stuck in the middle income trap, we may either base this evaluation on how long it has been sitting within the middle-income range or how slowly its per capita income has been growing—both work.

As previously mentioned, a country is bound to cross over a given income range and reach higher income eventually as long as it sustains positive growth—thus this is not guaranteed if it slips into stagnation or negative growth. As such, one reasonable definition of the middle income trap is stagnation or negative growth during the middle-income stage. History has provided us with plenty of examples of middle-income economies suffering from economic stagnation and negative growth—like Russia and many countries in both Latin America and Central and Eastern Europe in the late 20th century—which serve to alert us to the risk of the growth trap.

The other method of defining the middle income trap is by determining a certain level of low but positive real growth of per capita income as the benchmark and subsequently identifying those below this level as being stuck in the trap. The key to this method is to determine the growth rate benchmark. A feasible option for this is to use the growth rate of several representative high-income countries or the average of all high-income countries. This is because a middle-income country will never narrow the income gap if its per capita income does not grow faster than that of high-income countries. Judging by this relative criterion, it will linger on in middle income and even decline until it can be classified as low income. Thus it is logical to define such a state as the middle income trap.

From the above analysis, we can see that the middle income trap is indeed a growth trap, one which can be defined in two ways. In an absolute sense, a middle-income country must be recognized as being stuck in the middle income trap when it agonizes over economic stagnation or negative growth. In a relative sense, this is also true when its per capita income grows more slowly than that of high-income countries. Neither of our definitions emphasizes the threshold or range of middle income.

When we define the middle income trap using the absolute standard, we find that stagnation or negative growth can be either transient or chronic in middle-income countries. Therefore, the real question is: what length of stagnation or negative growth justifies identifying a country as having fallen into the middle income trap? Loosely speaking, a country can be recognized as having fallen into the trap once stagnation or negative growth occurs. Yet it is possible for a country to fall into the trap one year, get out of it the next, and fall into it again the year after. When a country suffers from periodic stagnation or negative growth, there are usually more and/or bigger traps in the course of its growth. Meanwhile, for some countries, stagnation or negative growth results from their normal economic cycle, and thus the average growth rate over the economic cycle would be a better measure. That is, a country must be plainly recognized as being stuck in the trap when its average growth rate over an economic cycle is at or below zero.

Similarly, when using the relative standard, we find that some middle-income countries may be either temporarily or constantly lower than high-income ones in terms of growth rate. Loosely speaking, we can identify a country as having fallen into the trap once its growth rate drops below that of high-income countries. Again, we may also base our judgment on its average growth rate over an economic cycle.

The above methods are not only applicable to identifying whether or not a middle-income economy has fallen into the trap, but also explain similar problems of low- and even high-income economies. Moreover, they can also be used to compare such traps across different income stages as well as the probabilities of falling into such traps.

4 The Probability of Falling into the Middle Income Trap

For middle-income countries, the risk of the middle income trap as a whole may be best expressed in the probability of falling into it in the first place. By the absolute standard of the trap previously introduced, this probability refers to the likelihood of a middle-income country sliding into negative growth. By relative standards, this denotes the chance of a middle-income country growing more slowly than high-income countries in terms of per capita income.

The analytical classifications used by the World Bank group middle-income economies within absolute thresholds, and are therefore applicable to our estimation of the probability of sliding into negative growth and thus falling into the middle income trap. Of the 92 middle-income economies in the Bank's 1991 classification, only eight (8.7%) had a negative annual average growth rate of GDP per capita over the two decades following their initial classification, while the vast majority achieved the positive growth rate of their GDP per capita during this same period (see Fig. 1). In other words, only 8.7% of the 92 middle-income economies fell into the middle income trap between 1991 and 2011, as measured by the World Bank's absolute thresholds.

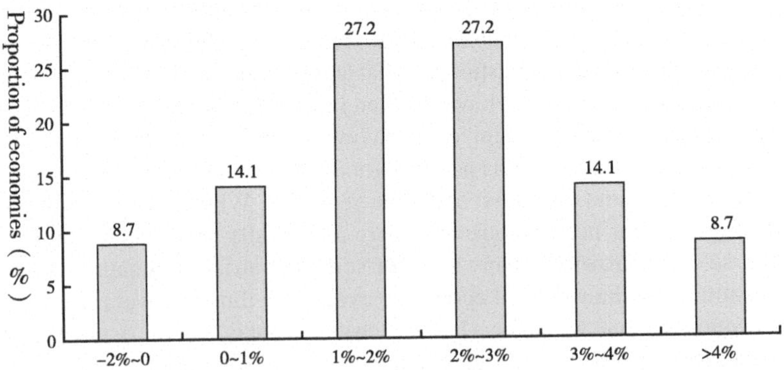

Fig. 1 Distribution of middle-income economies by growth rates of GDP per capita, 1991–2011. *Note* With the exclusion of seven middle-income economies that are incomplete in terms of GDP data from a total of 99 in the World Bank's 1991 classification. *Source* WDI Database, recalculated

A typical example of the middle income trap is the much-reviled Argentina. From 1991 to 2007, it had sustained a 2.3% annual average growth of GDP per capita,[11] and therefore cannot be recognized as having been stuck in the trap during this period. Nonetheless, Argentina *did* experience negative growth from 1980 to 1990, when its growth of GDP per capita averaged −3.3% annually. Thus, it is likely that we will miss some historical cases of the middle income trap if we estimate the probability of falling into it over a very short period of time, as proven by what has happened to Argentina.

For a more rigorous analysis of the likelihood of measuring the middle income trap using absolute thresholds, we now leave aside the World Bank's classifications and resort to GNI per capita and the growth rates of GDP per capita from 1960 to 2013. We first establish seven income groups with the thresholds of USD 1,000, USD 2,000, USD 4,000, USD 8,000, USD 16,000, and USD 32,000, respectively, in 2005 prices. Next, we calculate the seven-year moving average growth rate of GDP per capita of all the economies under consideration using a compound annual growth rate, because the economic cycles measurable between 1960 and 2013 typically lasted for about seven years. Finally, we observe the moving average growth rate of GDP per capita of each economy over each seven-year cycle as well as its GNI per capita in the first year of the cycle (paired together as an observed value), and place the value into a corresponding income group. By now, we are able to estimate the probability of negative growth in each of the income groups, which is the ratio of negative growth occurrences to the total number of observed values.

As we can see in Fig. 2, the different income groups fall into four ranges of probability for negative growth: 27% for economies with a GDP per capita of less than USD 1,000; 16–20% for those between USD 1,000 and USD 8,000; 7% for those between USD 8,000 and USD 32,000; and 12% for those with a GDP per capita of more than USD 32,000. Such distribution reflects three characteristics that are well

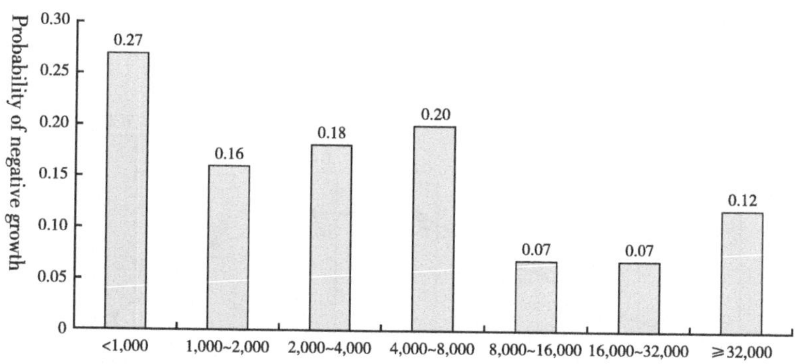

Fig. 2 Probabilities of negative growth of GDP per capita for different income groups, 1960–2013. *Note* Growth rates by seven-year moving averages. GDP per capita in US dollars in 2005 prices. *Source* WDI Database, recalculated

[11] The WDI Database only provides real growth rates of Argentina's GNI per capita up to 2007.

worth mentioning. First, the highest probability of negative growth is found in neither middle-income nor high-income economies, but in those low-income countries with a GDP per capita of less than USD 1,000. In other words, the probability of the low income trap is larger than that of the middle income trap, yet it is easier for low-income economies to escape the poverty trap. Second, the probability of being trapped is neither directly nor inversely proportional to income level. Rather, with the increase of per capita income, it declines first and then rises in a stepwise manner. Finally, the middle income trap does indeed exist, and its likelihood should not be ignored. For example, economies with a GDP per capita between USD 1,000 and USD 8,000 are estimated to have a 20% chance of negative growth in terms of seven-year moving average growth rates. That being said, this phenomenon is not so ubiquitous as the World Bank has previously reported.

On the other hand, we have also estimated the probability of the middle income trap using relative thresholds as based on the statistics of GNI per capita and growth rates of GDP per capita from 1960 to 2013. Again, we first divide all the economies into seven income groups using the thresholds of 2, 4, 8, 16, 32, and 64% of US per capita income, calculated using the World Bank *Atlas* method. We then observe the moving average growth rate of GDP per capita for each economy over each seven-year cycle along with the ratio of its GNI per capita to that of the US (paired together as an observed value), and place the value into a corresponding income group. Finally, we calculate the proportion of those economies that grow more slowly than the US in per capita income in each group and take that as the probability of falling into the growth trap. Figure 3 shows the results of our estimations.

Using the relative thresholds, we have concluded the following characteristics of the growth traps.

In the first place, across all income groups, the probability of falling into a growth trap by the relative thresholds is higher than that by the absolute thresholds. For

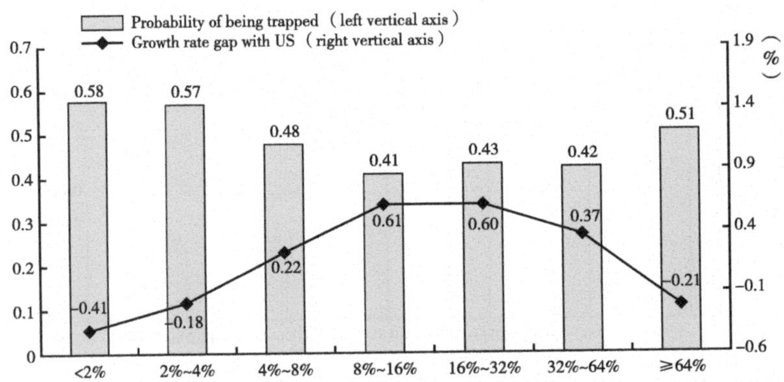

Fig. 3 Probabilities of being trapped and growth rate gaps with US among different income groups. *Note* Income grouping is based on GNI per capita relative to the US, calculated using the World Bank *Atlas* method. Probabilities of being trapped are defined as the likelihood of being lower than the US in a seven-year average growth rate of GDP per capita. *Source* WDI Database, recalculated

example, economies with a GDP per capita of less than 2% of that of the US have a 58% chance of falling behind the US in terms of the average growth rate, but only 27% of sliding into negative growth.

Second, the probability of being trapped initially declines with the increase of per capita income, and then rises as per capita income continues to increase. Yet it is less likely to be trapped in middle income than in either a low or high income during this course of development. That is, middle-income economies have a larger chance of exceeding the US in terms of growth rates than do low- and high-income ones.

Third, relatively low amongst all income groups, the probability of falling into the middle income trap is estimated to be as high as 40% or even higher. In other words, middle-income economies have at least a 40% chance of growing more slowly than the US. It makes sense to understand the demonstrated probability in this way. For more than 40% of a long period of heading towards a high income, a middle-income economy will be unable to narrow the income gap with the US but, rather, will only witness a further widening of the gap. With such a high probability, this is admittedly a huge trap.

Fourth, as soon as an economy reaches 4% of the US per capita income, the probability of it falling into the growth trap decreases significantly, and its GDP per capita is expected to grow faster—although only slightly faster—than that of the US. On average, it takes 320 years to transition from 4 to 8% of the US per capita income, 115 years from 8 to 16%, and another 115 years from 16 to 32%. Therefore, even if some economies have managed to avoid the middle income trap, they will have no way of escaping being "trapped" in the lengthy process of catching-up.

Finally, for middle-income economies, the most effective way to rapidly achieve high income—perhaps even catching up with the US—is to avoid the growth trap. For example, an economy with a GDP per capita between 4 and 8% of that of the US is estimated to have a 48% chance of being caught in the trap, or, at the very least, to grow more slowly than the US in terms of per capita income for 48% of the catching-up process. Consequently, it will only be 0.22% points higher than the US in terms of long-term average growth rate. Yet if it is able to avoid such a trap and ensure a generally faster growth than the US across every economic cycle, it will be 2.8% points higher than the US when measuring its long-term average growth rate. Accordingly, the time needed for it to transition from 4 to 8% of the US per capita income will decline precipitously, from 321 years to only 25 years. This also applies to the other income groups: an upgrade from 8 to 16% or from 16 to 32% of the US per capita income will decrease to only 28 years. Obviously, the most effective approach to any kind of rapid upgrade in a country's income status is to maintain steady economic development while also avoiding economic turmoil.

5 Conclusions

The middle income trap is, in essence, a growth trap. As there are both absolute thresholds and relative thresholds for defining middle income, there are also absolute and relative standards outlining the middle income trap. In the absolute sense, it refers to the stagnation or negative growth of a middle-income economy. In the relative sense, it denotes the situation in which a middle-income economy grows more slowly than a high-income economy or a representative of high-income economies. In addition to the middle income trap, there are also growth traps endemic to both the low-income and high-income stages of economic growth. In terms of the probabilities of falling into such traps, the middle income trap is lower than the low income and high income traps, but is still quite high. Relatively speaking, middle-income economies have at least a 40% chance of growing more slowly than the US in GDP per capita. It will take centuries for a middle-income country to upgrade to a high-income one if it cannot manage to avoid this trap. On the other hand, if it succeeds in avoiding the middle income trap, a country is likely to transition from being characterized by low income to high income in merely decades.

References

Research Group on China's Economic Growth, & CASS Institute of Economics. (2012). China's long-term growth: Path, efficiency, and potential growth rate. *Economic Research Journal, 12*, 4–17, 75.

Xiaolu, W., Gang, F., & Peng, L. (2009). China's economic growth: Modal transformation and sustainability. *Economic Research Journal, 1*, 4–16.

Chapter 9
Positive Changes in China's Economic Structure

Yiping Huang

I would like to talk here about economic structure. In my contact with the market, I have noticed that many people are rather pessimistic about the current economic structure, even as stock prices are shooting up. Very often I have discussions with others about why China's stock market has not been doing so well, and I have thereby come to the conclusion that it is because our economy has not been good enough. Now our own stock is actually on the upswing, but the reason remains the same: a lot of money has flown into the stock market because our economy is not good enough. This is a bit cheeky, but it does, nevertheless, convey profound messages.

I would like to discuss the issue from two perspectives. On the one hand, despite the current sense of pessimism about China's economic prospects and the great difficulty its economic growth currently faces, positive changes are taking place within the Chinese economy and must not be dismissed lightly. Fluctuation is likely to occur in the short run, but the long-term picture is rosy. On the other hand, for all the positive changes extant in the economic structure, further reform is a must to complete our transformation, the core of which is effective resource allocation. Of all the mechanisms available for resource allocation, I am more concerned about that of financial resource allocation, because I deem financial reform to be central to China's overall economic reform. To that end, the central task of our financial reform is to improve resource allocation and implement the market-based reformation of interest rates.

In my eyes, there are two feasible approaches to market-based interest rates. One is good, and the other not so good. For example, "shadow banking" is a form of spontaneous marketization of the interest rates in China, but it just proves that we have not done well enough in previous market-based reforms of interest rates. If we decompose China's GDP using the expenditure method, we will find three key drivers for its economic growth: exports, investment, and consumption. Over the

Y. Huang (✉)
National School of Development, Peking University, Beijing, China
e-mail: yhuang@nsd.pku.edu.cn

F. Cai (ed.), *China's Economic New Normal*, Research Series on the Chinese Dream and China's Development Path, https://doi.org/10.1007/978-981-15-3227-6_9

past decades, China's economic growth has mainly relied on exports and investment, while the share of consumption in its GDP has been shrinking.

Consumption accounted for only 22% of China's GDP in 2000 and rose to 44% in 2010. Structurally, this reflects the relative underdevelopment of China's services. As a manufacturing power, it is still weak in its development of services. This is a distinct characteristic of China's economic structure.

Moreover, China is also marked by its huge consumption of bulk commodities. Over the past 20 years, China has been a major engine for the commodities super cycle in the global market and is similarly responsible for strongly supporting many bulk commodities exporters. China accounts for only 10% of global GDP, but up to 1/3 of the world's consumption of commodities and resources. It has therefore touched off some degree of controversy. To many scholars, if it does not change its model of growth, China will not be able to sustain its economic expansion given limited global resources. To others, China is still far behind the US in terms of the absolute level of its resource consumption (e.g., per capita consumption of steel), and therefore there is enough room for the further expansion of our consumption. We had better look at it from a global perspective.

Should China catch up with the US in both per capita income and steel consumption, there would not be enough steel for these two largest global consumers. This view is backed up by a funny anecdote about Rio Tinto. As the world's second-largest mining corporation, Rio Tinto has an advisory committee in China, whose members often share their views on the Chinese economy with me. A few years ago, I mentioned the possibility of a structural transformation in China and pointed out that, if true, this would weaken China's demand for bulk commodities because it is bound to slow China's economic growth and pull down its investment rate. It was in 2010 when I said so. Those in the mining industry more or less agreed with me, but they felt it unlikely to occur. I told the Rio Tinto CEO then, "If China does not change its model of growth, there would not be enough steel in the world to support its growth." He responded quickly, saying, "Just fix your eyes on the economy and leave the supply to me." Now we know what has happened to Australia: an extremely serious problem of iron ore overcapacity.

For China, the question of sustainability will pose a problem if it does not improve its structure, and that is why it needs transformation. We have already seen a historic change in its growth rate, which has fallen from around 10% to around 7.5% and is likely to be lower still in 2014. Internationally or historically, a growth of over 7% is not too poor, only a little bit lower than before. Some of my former colleagues, back from overseas, come to the conclusion that the Chinese economy has collapsed because they hardly see any promising industry, and they refuse to believe in the 7% growth of China's GDP. Why do they have such a different impression? The macroscopic indicators are all right—not so the microscopic ones. Many people, especially foreign investors, would guess that China's growth rate might not be so high, and certainly not the 7.3% it is in actuality, or even anything above 7%. There is so far no denial of such guessing. Meanwhile, there is also no denying that the Chinese economy is still growing as a whole. Microscopically, there is indeed little room for optimism, especially at a time of economic downturn. As I see it, there are two big problems here.

One is the huge overcapacity of our heavy industry and capital goods industry. We used to count on investment for economic growth, but now our investment and growth have both slowed down, a direct consequence of which is enormous overcapacity in such industries. According to estimates, the average overcapacity in these industries has increased from 25% in 2007 to 35% at present. Thus, it is easy to understand why some people feel they can hardly afford a slowdown, especially in the construction materials sectors, such as steel and cement. Undoubtedly, this is a challenge to the conventional model of growth.

Over the past decades, labor-intensive manufacturing has also played a significant role in China's economic growth because it boosts exports. Yet export-oriented enterprises, in particular those in the Yangtze River and Pearl River Deltas, are also now in hot water. The reason is quite obvious and may be best illustrated by an example. A necktie maker once took pride in the fact that he was able to offer a tie for every gentleman in China, but now the time for such a boast is over. In 2004, the salary of a worker in Ningbo averaged RMB 1,200 per month. Today, it is almost impossible to retain a worker with even RMB 5,000 per month, whereas there has been almost no change in the price of a tie. Important as they were to China's economic miracle over the past three decades, such factories can no longer get by anymore.

There is a term in economics known as "the middle income trap." China's GDP per capita was USD 200 at the beginning of its reform and opening-up, and it has increased to USD 7,000 by this point. A direct consequence of China's economic success is rising costs, which have, in turn, resulted in enormous competitive pressures in those sectors or producers that once enjoyed a competitive edge in the market. On the one hand, many large enterprises, which used to play a major part in China's investment growth, are stuck in the midst of serious overcapacity; on the other hand, the country's once extremely active private enterprises, especially small- and medium-sized ones and export-oriented enterprises in the Yangtze River and Pearl River Deltas, are finding it hard to pull through nowadays. Therefore, it is normal for there to be some degree of pessimism.

Is the situation really as gloomy as all that, though? I think not. My point here is that we should give weight to the positive changes that also exist in China's economic structure. If we take a closer look, we will notice many positive changes that are taking place, and we must correlate them with the macroeconomic changes.

A good example is Alibaba, one of the country's most eye-catching companies and the envy of the world. But how has it achieved such a significant success in such a short time? The only answer is innovation, in both the technological and organizational senses. Alibaba is but a representative of numerous Internet companies in China, where online sales account for over 10% of the final retail sales of consumer goods—a figure that is increasing by 30–40% annually. Whether we take it into account or not, online shopping is obviously a central support structure for improving China's growth efficiency and the well-being of its people.

We can find many such examples in other fields. We can also see rapid innovation and great progress—mainly in those fields with relatively loose government regulation. The hard fact is that too much regulation only poses difficulty to further industrial development. The less control the government imposes, the faster a sector grows. Of course, there are bound to be risks if we relax regulations completely, for no policy is immune to problems.

Above all is our policy choice in the past. What we implemented during the global financial crisis had a great effect on our economic growth, but some of our policies were overdone and caused a series of unforeseen consequences. For example, the serious overcapacity currently in our capital goods industry undoubtedly has something to do with government stimulus in those years. A second problem is that our labor-intensive manufacturing has sailed into choppy waters. More than 30 years ago, the same problem was faced by South Korea, Hong Kong, and Taiwan of China. Labor-intensive manufacturing was once very prosperous in these economies and even developed from a low-income into a middle-income sector. Then came the turning point of the labor force—around 1980 in South Korea. Consequently, many Korean enterprises lost their competitive edge at home and had to move to mainland China, thanks in large part to its policy of reform and opening-up. At that time, people in Taiwan and Korea had almost completely lost their confidence in the economy. That same problem is now in front of us. Yet when we look at how these economies previously coped with it in different ways, we might just be a bit more optimistic. They were very similar in economic structure three decades ago, but today is a different story with different circumstances. Yet there is one thing in common between them: they have all developed into high-income economies. In mainland China, we can also find successful examples, such as the city of Shenzhen. Judging by the World Bank's thresholds, many of China's coastal cities are already considered high-income regional economies. They are proof that there is innovation in China. So the key is to encourage innovation and guide it with good policy.

The other big problem is the allocation of resources, in particular our financial resources, in order to provide stronger support for innovation and economic restructuring. If our financial system fails to work, economic growth will be extremely difficult.

What is China's financial system like now? Over more than 30 years of financial reforms, China has made a world of difference in its financial system, which is characterized by a complete setup and large size but ineffective market mechanisms and problematic governance structures. It is true that China's financial system is growing ever-more-complete than before. In the past, there was only one financial institution in China. Today, there are the regulatory institutions known as One Bank and Three Commissions (i.e., the People's Bank of China—the Central Bank, China Securities Regulatory Commission, China Insurance Regulatory Commission, and China Banking Regulatory Commission), three policy banks, four state-owned commercial banks, over a dozen joint-stock commercial banks, and numerous securities companies, insurance companies, and asset management companies. Such institutions constitute a complete financial structure of enormous size. By contrast, the bond market is still underdeveloped in China. It was once the world's largest country in terms of bond financing, but is still incomplete as far as market mechanisms. China is a very big market, yet government intervention is quite serious across many fields and takes various forms, such as interest rate regulation, exchange rate regulation, cross-border capital flow control, etc.

The International Monetary Fund has released the IMF Financial Stress Indices of 91 countries, covering seven aspects. China ranked 87th overall on the index. Compared with other countries, China has a considerably higher degree of financial intervention. A commonsense reaction to this state of affairs is that, serious as it is, financial repression and intervention has not impeded our high-speed growth over the past decades. According to statistical analysis, the effect of financial repression on China's economic growth was positive in the 1980s and 1990s, but has been negative since the turn of the century. This finding was surprising when it was released. Later on, the Stiglitz Effect was discovered to back up this view. Joseph E. Stiglitz is a Nobel Prize winner at Columbia University. In the 1990s, when he was studying financial opening and emerging market economies, he noticed a strange phenomenon, which was that financial crises have become more and more frequent in emerging markets since the 1980s. He found that this issue is related to globalization—in particular financial globalization—so he concluded that if an economically-underdeveloped country opens its financial market ahead of time, it is likely to suffer adverse consequences. To Stiglitz, moderate financial repression is likely to favor economic growth, because it helps overcome fundamental problems, like information asymmetry, in a country's financial sector.

As a matter of fact, financial repression can actually have diametrically opposite effects on growth. The negative is what I call the Mckinnon Effect, and the positive is the Stiglitz Effect. In the late 20th century, financial repression had a positive effect on China's economic growth and was conducive to economic growth. As we all know, during the 1997 Asian Financial Crisis, bad debts soared up to 30% and even 40% at many Asian banks, but China maintained the stability of its financial system and was able to avert any serious setbacks. Why? Exactly because our government took responsibility for the country's financial stability. In the 21st century, however, financial repression has played a negative part in our economic growth. This turn of events has significant policy implications. In the past, we might as well get by without reform. But now, without reform, our economic growth will suffer. The current deceleration has proven that financial repression leads to lower allocation efficiency and thus affects economic growth. More importantly, many of our financial interventions no longer work anymore, and this is a direct reason why we must push forward with our reforms.

Take, for example, China's shadow banking. The definition of shadow banking varies from person to person. To many people, shadow banking means trust products, financial products, or entrusted loans. Why is it so prosperous recently? We all see the direct result: a strengthened control of interest rates and capital allocation. This is exactly because traditional financial repression is no longer sustainable. In the past, when people kept money in banks, they received an annual deposit rate of 3%. At times of high inflation, however, what they received was still that same 3%, which was practically equivalent to nothing when inflation is taken into account. Under such circumstances, shadow banking has come to the rescue as a covert form of disintermediation of banks by new instruments, such as trust products, financial products, etc. Much of the money is still in the banks, but put to different uses. Some people view shadow banking as a disguised or spontaneous—rather than government-driven—form of interest rate liberalization.

Anyone with a grasp of economics knows that there is always a shortage of resources. So the lack of money is universal, and everyone is lacking in money. Yet, strangely enough, this is all the more prominent in China—and particularly acute as of recent. As Vice President Li Yang puts it, with so much money and such high liquidity in our country, why is financing so difficult and so costly? We may see the issue from two perspectives, which are related.

On the one hand, financing difficulties have something to do with the aforementioned financial repression, a big part of which is interest rate regulation. On the formal financial market, banks (usually the central banks) control interest rates, keeping them "artificially low." A direct result of artificially low interest rates is that the allocation of funds is decided by the quantitative policy. When interest rates are set low, demand for loans outstrips the money supply, and the government must serve as an allocator of funds. Thus, quantitative restriction becomes a necessity for interest rate regulation. As a result, many small- and medium-sized enterprises are unable to raise funds. Financing may not be a problem for large, profitable, or state-owned enterprises, but under such circumstances, it is utterly impossible for poor and average enterprises to raise money on the open market, and consequently they are elbowed out. In a dual-market system with both formal and non-formal prices, when formal interest rates are set low, the non-formal rates are bound to be driven up. Therefore, we must recognize that financing difficulty and high financing costs are endogenous to interest rate regulation within this system.

Even with such an abundant money supply, financing remains difficult. It also has something to do with our overcapacity. In many eyes, China's leverage and debt ratios are both too high. Currently, the overall corporate debt-to-GDP ratio is 130% and state-owned enterprises account for 70–80% of China's corporate debts. Many enterprises are busy raising funds, but allocation is neither evenly-distributed nor determined by the market.

On the other hand, if shadow banking represents the spontaneous liberalization of interest rates, theoretically it must have improved the financing environment and facilitated corporate financing. This has turned out to not be the case. Instead, I deem it a poor form of interest rate liberalization. As soon as the new mechanism comes into play, countless state-owned enterprises and governmental institutions swarm into the market to issue bonds and other financial products. Bailed out by the government, they are jostling with private enterprises for funds on both the formal and non-formal markets, sometimes regardless of budget constraints or costs. Eventually, their financing cost becomes a new interest rate, which is anything but risk-free. As a result, other enterprises have to accept a higher interest rate to raise funds.

Over the past few years, the Chinese government has made many decisions designed to cope with financing difficulties and high financing costs. For example, prior to the rate hike in mid-November 2014, it had already introduced a policy to alleviate the high costs of financing. It is fine to develop a multi-tiered capital market and establish more small- and medium-sized financial institutions, including private ones, but these measures will hardly make any difference in the short run. Accordingly, we propose the regulation of interest rates and liquidity using total-control means and giving separate considerations to macro-prudential and macro-control policies, which have long been mixed up. Besides, we must solve the problem of the dual-track interest rates, which is the root of both the difficulty with and high costs of enterprise financing. To this end, we have to first cut our overcapacity.

To promote interest rate liberalization and give the final say to the market, we must carry out a series of reforms, such as the establishment of a deposit insurance system, budget constraints on fundraising institutions, the rationalization of risk-free yields of China Government Bond, and more.

Chapter 10
Productivity Under the New Normal: Latest Estimates and Interpretations of China's Total Factor Productivity

Harry X. Wu

1 Introduction: Economic Deceleration and Productivity Under Structural Adjustment

I shall begin this discussion on the productivity of the Chinese economy with what is called the "new normal." Almost overnight, everyone is talking about the new normal, and some economists have even jokingly suggested that it be taken as an economics course in universities. There is no denying that this term has rapidly enriched our political and economic context. Yet its point of origin is nothing new: it is about the growth rate, about how to accept the fact that the Chinese economy has slowed down and is very likely to bid farewell forever to double-digit growth. Meanwhile, as we have seen, almost all studies on macroeconomic policy are now oriented towards the struggle to find the new potential growth rate of the Chinese economy, which may as well be referred to as "the new normal growth rate." In stark contrast, as has been repeatedly highlighted by the current administration's initial policy objectives, the structural problems of this type of of growth seem to have faded out of this new

This chapter is based on a report given at the international symposium, "China's New Normal: Growth, Structure, and Momentum," organized by Chinese Academy of Social Sciences. In 2014, the English version of this report was presented at the Third World KLEMS Conference and the Asia-Pacific Productivity Conference (APPC), as well as symposiums hosted by Peking University, Nankai University, the CASS Institute of World Economy and Politics, the China Comparative Economics Association, the Organization for Economic Cooperation and Development (OECD), the Centre d'Etudes Prospectives et d'Informations Internationales (CEPII), and the Asian Development Bank (ADB). The author truly appreciates the constructive criticism and comments received at these meetings. Part of the report was published in *Comparative Studies* (Volume 69, 2013) as "Measuring and Interpreting Total Factor Productivity in Chinese Industry." The current version has omitted the mathematical derivation of the empirical studies, and for data cited herein, it only provides the source of relevant publications. The author takes full responsibility for the content.

H. X. Wu (✉)
Institute of Economic Research, Hitotsubashi University, Kunitachi, Japan
e-mail: harry.wu@ier.hit-u.ac.jp

F. Cai (ed.), *China's Economic New Normal*, Research Series on the Chinese Dream and China's Development Path, https://doi.org/10.1007/978-981-15-3227-6_10

political and economic context and have, in fact, been cast aside in China's actual policy practices.

For all the hopes pinned on the new normal to make people accept the fact of deceleration, over the past year, almost all macro-control policy instruments have been targeted at the declining growth rate instead of at the structural problem. Of course, I hope that I have guessed incorrectly, and that our macroeconomic policy has not been avoiding the important in order to dwell on the trivial. Yet I would hereby reiterate my view that the real problem with the Chinese economy is its distorted resource allocation, which is closely related to its structure and growth rate. In this chapter, I hope to gain a foothold in discussing the new normal in terms of productivity, a theme that is closely related to its structural issues.

China's misallocation of resources is deeply rooted in the government's direct involvement and indirect intervention in resource allocation (see Wu 2008) to serve its high growth goal and the high income of related interest groups. Of course, we all know the result—an abnormally high rate of development and a twisted economic structure. Therefore, if we are to reform, we must give play to the decisive role of the market in resource allocation. In this light, the so-called new normal is more precisely a regression of the Chinese economy from an abnormal state to a normal, free-market-based state. This will definitely involve the growth rate. Regardless of external factors, the growth rate of an economy based on its market fundamentals is what we call a normal rate, which fluctuates along a potential growth rate determined by the long-term supply curve. Such a potential growth rate is usually related to the stage of development of a given economy, which reflects the gap between it and economies at the bleeding edge of financial and technological development. Not surprisingly, through the emulation of more mature technology, a backward economy will certainly grow faster than those developed economies that count on technological innovation for growth. This has been borne out, time and again, by the economic rise in East Asia after World War II, in China since the start of its reform and opening up, and in emerging market economies since the late 1990s.

Nonetheless, no matter what stage it is in, a government-dominated economy always has the ability to grow at an exceptional rate. In addition to the state's strong capacity for resource mobilization, it is also possible to hold down the costs of certain factors through institutional arrangements that boost growth by overdrafts. Yet such a growth rate is unsustainable. Once the market resumes its decisive role in resource allocation, growth is bound to slow down. Based on what has happened in China over the past two decades, I am convinced that its growth will slow down regardless of whether it implements substantial structural reforms or not. Since the 1990s, especially after China's entry into the WTO, competition for economic growth has been intensifying among its local governments, which has resulted in a fierce race to promote investment and a variety of ways to hold down the prices of factors.[1] The

[1] On the motivations of local government officials for growth, see Li and Zhou 2005.

serious negative externalities of such practices are no different from encouraging overinvestment and overproduction.[2]

Thus, growth stimulates investment, and further investment accelerates growth, and such a chain reaction has driven the rapid expansion of the downstream manufacturing sectors oriented to the global market. In turn, such expansion has greatly increased the demand for infrastructure facilities, materials, and energy resources within the upper stream. When it is aware of the importance of resources for manufacturers' expansion in the global market, the government has chosen direct involvement and intervention in resource allocation in response to such demand. By restructuring and subsidizing large-sized state-owned enterprises and providing other enterprises with various means of support, it has driven the rapid development of the upstream industries, which are long in terms of investment cycles, low in returns, and without comparative advantages. As a matter of fact, supported by the upper-stream industries, China's downstream manufacturing had expanded until 2008, when the global financial crisis put an end to it. Thereafter, what we saw was an unprecedented capital injection by both central and local governments. Yet given its short-term effect, the measure was unable to stop the slowdown trend. Meanwhile, investment efficiency deteriorated, and overcapacity spread across the real economic sectors.

The aforesaid problems are already widely known. For macroeconomists, the challenge is how to logically imbed such problems into an analytical framework. As we know, both government behavior and resource misallocation are so complex that it is impossible to make direct statistical observations and measurements of them. Fortunately, while these issues are seemingly inexplicable through standard market-behavior modeling, there is an analytical instrument that will best serve our purpose, which is the production function analysis based on the producer theory of microeconomics and within the framework of national accounting in macroeconomics. Its decomposition of an economy's input factors—in particular its total factor productivity (TFP)—is more than capable of providing us with a valid reference frame for efficiency analysis. Thanks to the establishment of the China Industry Productivity Database (CIP) through long-term efforts, we are now better positioned to make more in-depth estimates at the industry/sector level and explore the efficiency and/or productivity of those industries/sectors under varying degrees of government involvement and intervention, as well as their effects on the overall efficiency and/or productivity of the economy.[3] In this way, we have successfully introduced an economic framework into our studies on productivity. A good many empirical studies in economics have proven that government may be able to solve the problem of growth, but it is unable, or at least difficult, to solve that of efficiency. The above-mentioned approach represents significant progress in my recent research of total factor productivity at the industry/sector level. It serves to verify this argument and

[2]A negative externality is a production cost suffered by a third party, which can be an individual, the public, or even society as a whole (see Fig. 1).

[3]Under this analytical framework of growth measurement, we are unable to further decompose efficiency and technical changes, and therefore our estimates of TFP changes are the net effect of efficiency and technical changes.

is particularly conducive to the current policy debate on the modal transformation of China's economic growth.

In my paper published in *Comparative Studies* (Volume 69, 2013), I introduced my estimates and interpretations of China's total factor productivity in more detail using the CIP Database. As an extension of that paper, this chapter covers all 37 sectors of the Chinese economy,[4] adding the country's 13 non-industrial sectors to its 24 industrial sectors. Such an extension has revealed the country's input-output relations and resource mobility among China's industrial and non-industrial sectors, and thus enabled us to make a full observation of the productivity of the Chinese economy.

In the following, I will first discuss why total factor productivity is an institutional issue. Next, under an exploratory conceptual framework and using the example of government intervention in the industrial economy, I will explain my hypothesis of "cross-subsidization" among the upstream and downstream sectors. After that, I will briefly introduce the methods and statistics used in this chapter, highlighting their importance for settling the research problems herein. Finally, I will share my overview and interpretations of the estimated total factor productivity of the Chinese economy from 1980 to 2010. It should be noted that, to highlight the effect of the significant improvement in methodology and data application on our estimates of the overall TFP growth, we will divide the results into three parts according to different approaches of estimation, namely, the production function for gross sectoral output value, the production function for the aggregate production possibility frontier (APPF), and the aggregation and decomposition of industrial/sectoral factors using Domar weights under the APPF framework.[5]

2 Total Factor Productivity as an Institutional Issue

A production function gives the relation between the input and output of an economy (under given institutional conditions), or, otherwise put, how the output changes with increases and decreases in the factor input in production. Through production function analysis, we can decompose major determining factors and probe into the momentum of economic growth. The primary concern of economists, however, is more than each factor's contribution to growth, which can be directly observed in production function analysis. More importantly, they will discover an output "residual" generated from such analysis, which is inexplicable using any of the factor

[4]This classification is based on China National Bureau of Statistics' (NBS) industrial classification. The two classifications are mutually convertible, but do not completely overlap with each other.

[5]For a better understanding of the "cross-subsidization hypothesis," I also estimated the unit labor cost (ULC) and the marginal product of capital (MPK) of Chinese industries and sectors under varying degrees of government intervention in my paper in Volume 69 of *Comparative Studies*, which focused on the total factor productivity of Chinese industry. Although the MPK estimation was largely based on hypotheses, it is still a useful reference.

changes directly observed. This is what Robert M. Solow referred to as total factor productivity or TFP, drawing our attention to the significant role of institutional factors.

I have implicitly mentioned the institutional problem earlier in this chapter. The Solow Model is largely grounded in an institutional hypothesis and behavioral hypothesis, that is, it is set against the context of a perfect, barrier-free market for factor mobility (e.g., with complete information, zero transaction cost, etc.), where profit maximization is the only motivation for the market competition of producers. Under such circumstances, returns to scale are constant (and there are always demands). If these hypotheses were true, it is not difficult to see that there would be no problem with a given economy's efficiency or resource misallocation. In other words, an economy's production possibility frontier would overlap with its efficiency frontier and its TFP would never turn negative (unless caused by technical regression, which is impossible under normal circumstances). A positive TFP growth indicates an outward shift of the production possibility frontier, which reflects the contribution of Hicks neutral technological progress to economic growth (Solow 1957). Only such technological progress or innovation can increase the output of resources that are already being fully and efficiently utilized or improve the productivity of available resources.

In reality, loss of resource efficiency can occur due to various institutional deficiencies (e.g., government intervention, price control, and information monopolies), factor mobility barriers, resource misallocation, motivations of economic participants other than profit maximization, etc. Therefore, the Solow residual must have taken into account such factors as efficiency, institutions, and even data errors (Hulten 2001). When loss of efficiency offsets technological progress, the Solow residual would be zero; when it exceeds the contribution of technological progress, the Solow residual would be less than zero. As economic development and reform usually go hand-in-hand with the improvement of market institutions, economic growth as we observe it is theoretically attributable to any one of the following or any combination thereof: resource input (e.g., labor, equipment, energy, and materials), efficiency improvement, and/or technological progress. Any room for efficiency improvement may disappear sooner or later, because our market institutions are heading toward perfection. Yet, no matter how these factors change, limited resources have endowed TFP growth with a special institutional sense. Technological progress can also transform unused or unknown resources into economic resources that create wealth. This requires a complete system that not only protects private property (including intellectual property) but also rewards the innovation-driven appreciation of property values. Economic history has proven, however, that such a system must be directly derived from private entrepreneurs' persistent, profit-driven activities towards technological innovation and efficiency improvement. For economies that lag behind the world's technology frontier, such a system is the only guarantee for the efficient acquisition and emulation of existing knowledge and technology.

What should also be noted is the commonly-used approach to TFP estimation, which is an indexical method based on Solow's theory and designed to account for growth factors. In this method, it is impossible to decompose the Solow residual into efficiency and technology factors. Despite the significance of such decomposition (see Milana and Wu 2013), we have followed this method for the sake of convenience in comparison, without breaking down TFP into efficiency and technology factors. Thus, changes in efficiency and technology will be included in the TFP estimates, reflected as the "net effect" of efficiency and technology. Based on China's economic reality, it is unwise to replace the concept of efficiency improvement (or deterioration), which is implied in real TFP estimates, with Solow's technological changes, a concept of standard neoclassical economics.

3 Cross-Subsidization in the Chinese Economy: An Exploratory Conceptual Framework

In this section, we will discuss the government's role in the Chinese economy using the "cross-subsidization" hypothesis. Directly or indirectly, the government intervenes in the economy by means of administrative control and subsidies. Such intervention is industrially selective, based on either a given industry's distance from the final demand or its position on the industrial chain.

Arguably the biggest lesson the Chinese government has drawn from its past industrial policy is that product manufacturing industries—in particular export-oriented ones—must be competitive. Therefore, those nearest to the final market must be subject to the least direct intervention, and when they need support, indirect subsidies must be the major means through which they receive it. On the other hand, upstream industries are supposed to be "of strategic significance" and therefore must be subject to administrative control and direct subsidies. Direct subsidies come from government revenue; indirect subsidies usually take the form of lower costs (of land, labor, energy, environment, and capital), which are ultimately borne by the public as well. Different types of interventions and subsidies can have different influences on industrial efficiency and productivity. For instance, based on its monopoly position, the state-owned energy industry in the upper stream is highly profitable and thus able to pay high salaries, and, meanwhile, provides relatively cheap energy products to benefit all the downstream industries.

Our working hypothesis is that different methods of intervention have different effects on behavior, and given that downstream industries are higher than upstream ones in terms of productivity, the Chinese government's intervention is a type of cross-subsidization. The goal of such cross-subsidization is a "positive net income," that is, the total (net) income should always be greater than the total subsidy. The key to such cross-subsidization is the capacity of the downstream industries for higher output and productivity growth. In this case, they have increased their "competitiveness" and thus gained greater income due to cheaper energy products and basic materials provided by the upstream industries. In turn, the government is able to collect more tax revenue from these "more competitive" downstream industries and is better positioned to

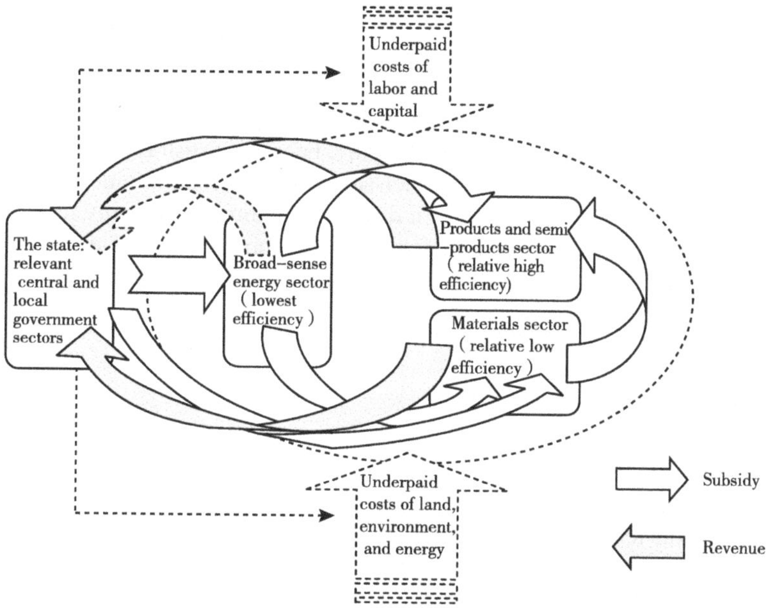

Fig. 1 The government's role, cross-subsidization, and cost overdraft in the Chinese economy

justify, maintain, or increase subsidies for the upstream industries. Figure 1 shows how such cross-subsidization works.

To simplify the process, we postulate an economy without non-industrial sectors in Fig. 1, because the inclusion of non-industrial sectors will not change the nature of the problem, but *will* make it more complex. Departing from the government, which is the initial point of this cross-subsidization, the white arrow represents government support for the energy sector in the form of subsidies. As the arrow splits and extends, the energy sector provides subsidy-inclusive energy resources for both the materials sector and the products and semi-products manufacturing sector. Likewise, the materials sector also provides the manufacturing sector with subsidy-inclusive intermediate materials. Consequently, as the largest gray arrow shows, the products and semi-products manufacturing sector increases its "competitiveness" and generates higher revenue as a public resource, and has thus become a major source of the government's funds for maintaining and increasing further subsidies. In Fig. 1, different sizes of arrows are used to indicate the contributions of different sectors. Obviously, the primary source of revenue is the downstream sectors. As can also be seen in Fig. 1, due to government intervention, all sectors have benefitted from the underpaid costs of factors such as labor, capital, land, and environment (see Huang and Tao 2010). Such costs are an overdraft on the future.

It is easy to see that the key to sustaining such a cycle of cross-subsidization is to promote the capacity of the products and semi-products sector for generating profits, which has to sustain strong growth and continually improve its efficiency. When its

TFP growth slows down, it will have to speed up and expand its output to offset the income decline due to decreases in efficiency. Nevertheless, this will require higher subsidies for costs to maintain the "market competitiveness" of the downstream producers, which is obviously unsustainable. In this sense, cross-subsidization is to spin a cocoon around the Chinese economy, because it distorts the motives and behaviors of all producers. No matter which sector they are in, how much of a subsidy they receive, and whether they receive it directly or indirectly, the only result is that they will invariably lose motivation for both the improvement of efficiency and technological innovation, and eventually turn into misbehaving "bad kids."

4 Research Objectives

The cross-subsidization hypothesis has raised an important argument: under varying degrees of government involvement or intervention, the growth and productivity of industries/sectors tend to influence, more or less, the overall production function and the overall TFP growth through some mechanism. If so, the estimation and interpretation of such an influence will be highly significant to the formulation, evaluation, and revision of economic policies. What's more, the hypothesis also suggests that, when statistical conditions permit, we might as well reveal the governmental influence on resource allocation by means of predesigned industrial grouping, as well as how it flows through inter-sectoral economic activity to the overall economy and affects the overall economic efficiency or productivity.

The above research objectives place strict demands on both our methods and statistics. Methodologically, we must build a quantitative model that will enable us to not only estimate the sectoral productivity and the effect of cross-sectoral factor reallocation in order to match different levels of productivity, but also establish a logical relation between the total and sectoral outputs. When constructing such an analytical framework, we must minimize the effect of overly strong restrictive assumptions, but take into full consideration that, due to market defects, different industries/sectors or different links of the industrial chain are very likely to be faced with different factor prices, and are therefore different in their production functions for gross output value.[6] Statistically, in contrast to most studies on China's overall TFP, this study requires quality sectoral statistics that will not only meet the demands of the production function analysis of gross sectoral output value, but also conform to the logical relation between sectoral inputs and the total input and output in national accounting.

[6]Note that "gross output value" differs from "gross output" in that the former includes intermediate inputs, while the latter equals "value added."

5 Basic Statistics, Groupings, and Staging

The first step is to decide upon the basic statistics. Even in traditional production functions for the overall economy, TFP estimates are usually very sensitive to the quality of input-output statistics, in particular to a factor's growth rate and its share of national income. Hence, a discussion of statistics is a must for our analysis of TFP growth. As I once pointed out (Wu 2014b), the key to settling the current dispute over TFP lies in the transparency of data processing as well as data accessibility (for result rechecks). Undoubtedly, the statistics of industrial/sectoral production functions involved herein are far more complex than those in traditional production functions for the overall economy. It is through long-term efforts that we have preliminarily settled the issue of sectoral input-output statistics and, in particular, determined the relations between the sectoral and overall variables, and eventually established the China Industry Productivity Database (CIP). The significance of CIP lies in the fact that it has—for the first time ever—straightened out the logical links between the gross output value, value added, investment, and employment of all sectors of the Chinese economy ranging from 1980 to 2010, based on consistent economic concepts, statistical classifications, and survey coverage, and is in line with the logical relations between the aggregate and sectoral outputs. Based on the national accounting and through the logical processing of inconsistencies, fractures, and gaps in historical official statistics—as far as possible, it has preliminarily integrated the statistics of industrial enterprises of different sizes, various categories of labor and employment statistics, and sectoral investment statistics. Although some discrepancies still remain between the concept and the reality when it comes to certain indicators, the basic statistics roughly satisfy the demands of our research.[7]

My paper on the estimation and interpretation of China's total factor productivity, which was published in *Comparative Studies* (Volume 69, 2013), more or less introduced the handling of the main input-output variables. For the details of our data processing, please refer to the latest series of papers by me and my coauthors,[8] which also include our earlier discussions on China's economic statistics.

The second step is industrial grouping. To study the influence of government industrial policy on resource allocation and its effect on productivity, we have

[7] Many scholars have cast doubts on China's economic statistics in their research literature, including myself (Maddison and Wu 2008). See Wu (2014b) for a summary of this issue. Nonetheless, the basic principle of the CIP Database is to accept the official output estimates, primarily because there is simply no substitute for them at the sector level.

[8] Basically, the CIP Database was established in accordance with the principles of the KLEMS approach. KLEMS stands for K(C)apital, Labor, Energy, Materials, and Service, the basic factors and intermediate outputs and inputs in the production function for gross output (O'Mahony and Timmer 2009). For the CIP output statistics, including input-output tables, national accounting, and producers' prices, please refer to Ito and Wu; for details of the establishment of the CIP employment and payoff matrices and the CIP labor hour estimates, please refer to Wu and Yue (2012; Wu, et al. 2015); for the establishment of the CIP capital stock and the CIP capital input estimates, please refer to Wu (2015).

classified the 37 sectors of the Chinese economy in the CIP Database into eight groups/industries.[9]

To begin with, agriculture and construction are regarded as two separate groups. Next, the 24 industrial sectors are divided into three groups according to their positions on the industrial chain, similar to the divisions in Fig. 1. These are, specifically, the "energy industry (broad-sense)," which includes four sectors: coal mining; oil and natural gas; refining, coking, and nuclear power; and coal gas. "Materials industry" includes seven sectors: metal mining; non-metal mining; textiles; paper and printing; chemical raw materials; building materials; and metal smelting and pressing. "Products and semi-products" includes 13 sectors: food; tobacco; clothing; leather; wood and furniture; rubber and plastics; metal products; general- and special-purpose equipment; electrical equipment; electronic and communications equipment; instruments and apparatuses; transportation equipment manufacturing; and other manufacturing. Finally, the eleven service sectors are also divided into three groups, according to their statuses in the market. Specifically, "monopoly services" includes three sectors monopolized or dominated by state-owned enterprises: transportation and storage; telecommunications and postal services; and finance and insurance. "Non-market-oriented services" includes three sectors: government and public administration; education; and healthcare. "Market-oriented services" includes five sectors: wholesale and retail sale; hoteling and catering; real estate; research, technology, and consultation; and other services.

The last step of our data processing is staging. To study the influence of changes in policy and market conditions, we divide the 30 years from 1980 to 2010 into four periods in order to best estimate the average annual growth rates of the aforementioned variables. The years from 1980 to 1991 were the early period of China's reform, beginning with agricultural reform, going through the opening-up and the industrial reform marked by a dual-track price system, and ending with political unrest in 1989 over the deepening of the previous economic reform. From 1992 to 2001 was a further period marked by the comprehensive deepening of China's reform, which started with the official acceptance of "the socialist market economy" largely attributable to Deng Xiaoping's Southern Tour, went through the state-owned enterprise reform, the establishment of a factor market, a large-scale infrastructure expansion, and China's overall opening-up, and ended up with the Asian Financial Crisis and the three or four years of deflation that subsequently followed. The period from 2002 to 2007 was one characterized by the rapid rise of China as "the world's factory" upon its entry into the WTO, a period that also witnessed the reorganization of the country's state-owned enterprises in order to restore dominance in many fields alongside the deepening of the local government's involvement or intervention in the local economy by means of intensified "land financing". The last period was from 2008 to 2010, which is quite short due to statistical limits, but nonetheless

[9] It must be pointed out that our grouping utilizing the currently-available industry classification may not be very accurate. In some cases, it is very hard to define the nature of a sector, inevitably resulting in an obscure boundary between neighboring groups. For instance, both "wood and furniture" and "paper and printing" include "materials (pulp and board)" and "products and semi-products (furniture and paper products)."

necessitating being discussed separately. This period saw the biggest global financial crisis since WWII, during which both the central and local governments injected unprecedented amounts of funds into the economy to support growth. Therefore, it is necessary to make a close observation of this period.

6 Growth Accounting Methods

To achieve our research objectives, the most appropriate empirical method is the Domar aggregation of the production function for gross sectoral output value within the analytical framework of the production function for aggregate production possibility frontier (APPF) and by use of Domar weights (see Domar 1961; for further interpretations see Hulten 1978).

The APPF method was developed by Jorgenson (1966) and later applied in a series of studies on US productivity (Jorgenson, 2001; Jorgenson, et al. 2005), the productivity of EU countries, and a comparison of productivity between the US and EU economies (van Ark, et al. 2008). In their monograph on US productivity, Jorgenson, et al. proposed aggregating sectoral input factors using Domar weights under the APPF framework. This analytical framework has established a strict logical system amongst both total and sectoral outputs, and thus linked overall productivity with sectoral productivity and the inter-sectoral influence of productivity differences. It basically meets the requirements of our studies on the Chinese economy, because it has taken into account the fact that, due to market defects, different industries/sectors on different links of the industrial chain are very likely to be faced with different factor prices and are different in their production functions (for gross output value).

With its consistency in sectoral and total productivity, the APPF analytical framework is diametrically opposed to the aggregate production function (APF), which has been widely used for a long time in literatures on economic growth. The APF model contains an implicit assumption that all industries/sectors are homogenous, and practically aggregates the outputs of different industries/sectors at the same constant price using the same fixed weight. In other words, it assumes a fixed price for various types of assets and human capital across all industries/sectors and, on that basis, comes up with the same production function. Moreover, such overly strong restrictive assumptions have ignored the tremendous differences likely to arise among different industries/sectors in terms of growth and productivity during economic expansion and contraction, especially under external impacts. Yet the effects of such differences, which have no way to offset each other, are of great importance for the observation of changes in the aggregate production function.

In the following paragraphs, in order to highlight the influence of sectoral factors on overall TFP, we will briefly explain the production function for sectoral and aggregate production possibility frontiers (i.e., the APPF model) and the Domar-weighted production function for gross sectoral output value in comparison with the APF estimation of the overall TFP. To make our estimation more explicit, we express the growth rate as the first-order differential of a logarithm, omitting the symbol of time. First, we define the normal-form representation of the overall TFP growth rate in the APF model ($v^{T(APF)}$) as

$$v^{T(APF)} = \Delta \ln V^{(APF)} - \bar{v}^k \Delta \ln K - \bar{v}^L \Delta \ln - \bar{v}^L \Delta \ln L \quad (1)$$

where $V^{(APF)}$ stands for the gross value added or GDP in the APF model; K and L, respectively, for the total capital and labor inputs, including the values of service; v^k and v^L, respectively, for the nominal capital and labor shares of income in the national income, namely, the ratios of capital and labor gains to GDP at current price; $\bar{v}^k$ and $\bar{v}^L$ for averages of such ratios in two adjacent periods. Remember that all industries/sectors are implicitly assumed to be homogenous in this widely used model.

Now we plug an industry or a sector (j) into the APPF framework. Let's just leave aside the APF (implicit) assumption of a fixed price for the value added of all industries/sectors, and define the growth rate of the gross value added as that of the weighted ($w_j = \frac{V_j}{\sum_j V_j}$) aggregate of the nominal value added of all industries/sectors, and meanwhile follow the definitions of total capital and labor inputs in Eq. 1. Then, the overall TFP growth rate in the APPF model ($v^{T(APPF)}$) is

$$v^{T(APPF)} = \sum_j \overline{w}_j \Delta \ln V_j - \bar{v}^K \Delta \ln K - \bar{v}^L \Delta \ln L \quad (2)$$

Moreover, we have to take into account the differences among the industries/sectors (j) in their costs of factor and intermediate inputs. We must modify the production function for gross sectoral output value to ensure that the estimation of every industry/sector has included the intermediate input marked as M. After the homogenization of different types of productive assets and human capital using the user cost,[10] the production function for the gross output value of industry/sector j is now expressed as

$$\Delta \ln Y_j = \bar{v}_j^K \Delta \ln K_j + \bar{v}_{jt}^L \Delta \ln L_j + \bar{v}_j^M \Delta \ln M_j + v_j^T, \quad (3)$$

or

$$v_j^T = \Delta \ln Y_j - \bar{v}_j^K \Delta \ln K_j + \bar{v}_{jt}^L \Delta \ln L_j + \bar{v}_j^M \Delta \ln M_j, \quad (3')$$

or

$$\Delta \ln Y_j = \bar{v}_j^V \Delta \ln V_j + \bar{v}_j^M \Delta \ln M_j \quad (4)$$

[10]Reference to a series of important literatures is omitted here. See the author's paper in English (Wu 2014a) and the early works by Griliches (1960), Denison (1962), and Jorgenson and Griliches (1967).

We can even derive the following equation from Eqs. 3 and 4:

$$\Delta \ln V_j = \frac{\bar{v}_j^K}{\bar{v}_j^V}\Delta \ln K_j + \frac{\bar{v}_j^L}{\bar{v}_j^V}\Delta \ln L_j + \frac{1}{\bar{v}_j^V}v_j^T \tag{5}$$

The next step is the Domar aggregation, which is used to illustrate the relation (ratio) between the industrial/sectoral weight in the gross value added ($\bar{w}_j$) and the industrial/sectoral ratio in the gross value added($\bar{v}_j^V$). Based on Eqs.2 and 2 and using Domar weights, we express the growth rate of the gross value added as

$$\Delta \ln V \equiv \sum_j \bar{w}_j \Delta \ln V_j = \sum_j \bar{w}_j \frac{\bar{v}_j^K}{\bar{v}_j^V}\Delta \ln K_j + \bar{w}_j \frac{\bar{v}_j^L}{\bar{v}_j^V}\Delta \ln L_j + \bar{w}_j \frac{1}{\bar{v}_j^V}v_j^T \tag{6}$$

By now, through this Domar-weighted aggregation under the APPF framework, we are finally able to express the growth rate of the overall TFP as the sum of the three major factors in Eq. 7: (1) the industrial/sectoral effect of the Domar aggregation, (2) the effect of TFP growth from capital reallocation (ρ^K), and (3) the effect of TFP growth from labor reallocation (ρ^L). What's more, we are also able to calculate the Domar-weighted growth rates of industrial/sectoral capital and labor inputs under the effect of factor reallocation.

$$\begin{aligned} v^{T(APPF)} &= \left(\sum_j \frac{\bar{w}_j}{\bar{v}_j^V}v_j^T\right) + \left(\sum_j \bar{w}_j \frac{\bar{v}_j^K}{\bar{v}_j^V}\Delta \ln K_j - \bar{v}_K \Delta \ln K\right) \\ &+ \left(\sum_j \bar{w}_j \frac{\bar{v}_j^L}{\bar{v}_j^V}\Delta \ln L_j - \bar{v}_L \Delta \ln L\right) = \sum_j \frac{\bar{w}_j}{\bar{v}_j^V}v_j^T + \rho^K + \rho^L \end{aligned} \tag{7}$$

7 The Principle of Theoretical, Methodological, and Statistical Consistency

In growth accounting using the production function, we must strictly follow the principle of theoretical, methodological, and statistical consistency emphasized by Jorgenson and Griliches (1967). This principle was first applied by Jorgenson et al. in their studies on US economic growth.[11] Under a given supply and market conditions, factor prices are determined by producers for the maximum profit or the minimum cost of factors. Factor cost equals the marginal product of the factors, and the total factor cost equals the gross product in national accounting, identical to the gross revenue (known as the principle of equality between production, income, and

[11] See (Jorgenson 1990) for a summary of this method and a comparison with other methods.

consumption or expenditure in macroeconomics). Following this theory, if we start with the smallest producer and add up all the production accounts, the sum of such production accounting must be completely consistent with the national accounts. On the other hand, we must treat the gross product, value added, and gross factor income in the national accounts as "controlled variables" in "microscopic" statistical processing, so as to define—in the economic sense—the relations between the gross and industrial/sectoral statistics in light of cost and income. Any deviation from this principle (a common problem with current studies) will result in the loss of economic significance for our statistical work.

Of course, based on China's economic reality, we have every reason to doubt the theoretical basis of this principle—the neoclassical producer theory—but it is very difficult to subvert or challenge this fundamental principle. We may add the institutional factor to the constraints and, meanwhile, modify the profit maximization into profit optimization. Yet we are unable to change the equality between the total cost of factors and the gross revenue in the national accounts, the relation between the gross and industrial/sectoral statistics, the cost-income relations among the industries/sectors, or the significance of the aforementioned "controlled variables" to the industry-based statistical calculation and estimation.

8 Estimates of Industrial/Sectoral Total Factor Productivity

Our discussion of TFP growth estimates will begin with the production function for the gross industrial/sectoral output value, expressed as Eq. 3 in Sect. 6. Writing on the US economy, Jorgenson, et al. (2005) identify such an aggregate production function as the "building block" of the APPF model, because it is the basis of the total productivity of all industries/sectors. In this section, we will make a simple, isolated analysis of the industrial/sectoral production function using Eq. 3, instead of the complex, weighted aggregation of the industrial/sectoral growth and productivity into the gross product or the total growth rate and productivity, as in Eqs. 6 and 7. This is because we hope to base our estimates on industrial/sectoral statistics. Using the aggregate production function, we calculate the gross output values of eight chosen sectors, the average annual growth rates of their gross output values, and the contribution of various inputs to the annual growth rates (in percentages of gross output value). Moreover, to directly observe these sectors' changes in total factor productivity from 1980 to 2010, we have drawn the TFP index of each sector in Fig. 2, with 1980 as the base year. While the results of our calculation are divided into four periods, we may summarize the overall performance of these sectors from 1980 to 2010 by reference to the TFP indexes in Fig. 2. In terms of the annual growth rate of gross output value, the category of products and semi-product manufacturing (15.4%) is the highest of all; construction, materials, monopoly services, and market services are all approximately at the same level, ranging between 10 and 11%, with construction higher than the others; the energy industry is the lowest of all, up by only 5.9% annually. In terms of the growth of labor input, the non-market services category

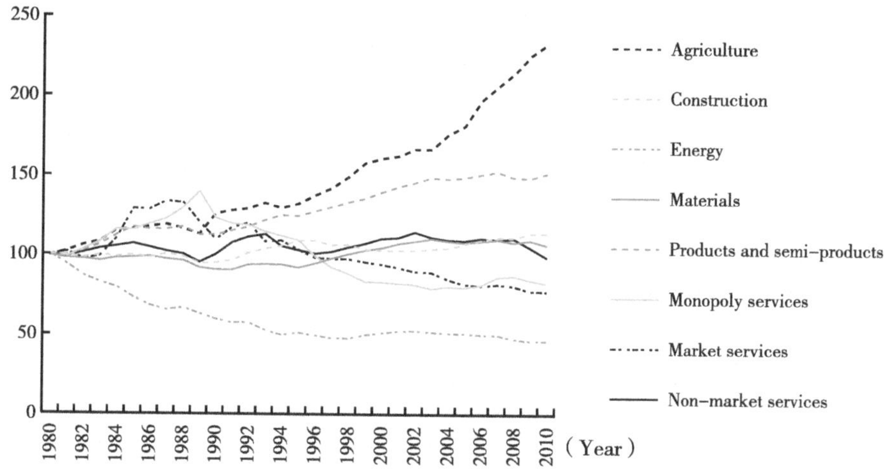

Fig. 2 Gross-output-based sectoral TFP indexes of the Chinese economy (1980 = 100). *Source* The author's estimation using Eq. 3

(government, healthcare, and education) is the fastest of all, with a 3-percentage-point contribution of labor input to the 8.3% annual growth of the sectoral gross output value. In terms of the growth of capital input, monopoly services (transportation, telecommunications, and finance) is the fastest of all, with a 5.6-percentage-point contribution of capital input to the 10.2% annual growth of the sectoral gross output value. By contrast, agriculture is the slowest in the growth of factor input, with only a 0.8-percent-point contribution of capital input to the 6.1% annual growth of the sectoral gross output value and a 0.2-percent-point annual decline in labor input. In terms of the growth of intermediate input, products and semi-product manufacturing is the fastest of all, with an 11.7-percentage-point contribution of intermediate input to the 15.4% annual growth of the sectoral gross output value.

The most eye-catching among our findings is probably the TFP growth of China's agricultural sector. In each of the four periods we examine, agriculture has been higher than the other sectors in terms of TFP growth (see Fig. 2). In fact, TFP has been the only source of China's agricultural growth since 2000, when its labor input started to decline sharply. Besides, agriculture is the only one of the eight sectors that has achieved sustained TFP growth even in the context of the global financial crisis. On the one hand, it reflects a fairly common phenomenon of this stage of economic development, that is, agricultural productivity increases greatly with the shift of agricultural resources to non-agricultural activity. Meanwhile, compared with the other sectors, agriculture is subject to probably the least amount of government intervention. On the other hand, we have to admit that the agricultural TFP may have been exaggerated due to some defects with the statistics. Principally, we have so far been unable to give due weight to the contribution of land to agricultural output, and as a result, we must have underrated the return on capital and overrated labor remuneration in China's agricultural sector.

In each of the four periods examined, the category of products and semi-products has been the fastest in terms of the growth of its gross output value, and, following closely, materials also demonstrated potent growth in gross output value from the 1990s up through the eve of the global financial crisis. They are therefore the cornerstones of "the world's factory" in China. In terms of TFP growth, though, the best time period for these two sectors was the decade following Deng Xiaoping's Southern Tour Talks. Both have, however, experienced diminished TFP growth since China's entry into the WTO. Likewise, the TFP growth rate of products and semi-products declined from 2.2% between 1991 and 2001 to 1.0% between 2001 and 2007, and that of materials was down more sharply—from 1.6 to 0.4%—over the same period. In fact, these categories have demonstrated the fastest intermediate input growth, despite a slowdown resulting from the global financial crisis. On the other hand, we can assert that, with their increasing dependence on intermediate input, their productivity will be increasingly affected by the other sectors. Of all the industrial sectors, products and semi-products has been the best performing in terms of productivity over these past three decades, largely because it is the nearest to the final demand, directly engaged in the international competition, and subject to the least government intervention. This conclusion is basically in line with our expectation (see Fig. 1). That being said, it is also consistent with the expectation that its TFP growth will have slowed down in the post-WTO period with the enhancement of the government role and practically stagnated during the large-scale government capital injection after the global financial crisis. Figure 2 shows the overall TFP of products and semi-products, with 1980 as the base year. According to the index therein, the annual growth rate of its TFP averaged 1.4% over the 30 years. While only half that of agriculture (2.8%), it is still the highest of all the non-agricultural sectors nonetheless.

Sharply contrasting products and semi-products is the broad-sense energy sector. In China's early period of reform, this state monopoly sector suffered the most serious negative growth of its TFP (down by 5.0% annually from 1980 to 1991). In the years that followed, its efficiency improved somewhat, but its TFP remained negative even before the global financial crisis (down by 1.0% from 1991 to 2001 and 0.5% from 2001 to 2007 annually). With the outbreak of the global financial crisis, however, alongside the government's enhanced role, its TFP began to deteriorate rapidly (down by 2.1% annually from 2007 to 2010). As shown in Fig. 2, the energy sector has never been able to restore its TFP to the level it boasted in 1980. As a matter of fact, its 2010 TFP was only about half that of 1980. Nothing can be more shocking than such a huge efficiency loss in this large interest group over the past years, which has been nourished by a state monopoly and high-level government involvement. Nonetheless, based on the hypothesis depicted in Fig. 1, this result is exactly in accordance with our expectations.

Besides agriculture, construction is the only sector that has experienced TFP improvement since China's entry into the WTO and achieved slight TFP growth in the years after the global financial crisis. Presumably, this is closely related to the government's increasing reliance on infrastructural investment to sustain growth and the long-term property bubble in the country, yet the necessity for further research remains. Finally, the service sectors are generally slow in productivity growth because they are labor-intensive technically speaking. In the early period of China's reform, almost all service sectors performed extremely well in terms of TFP, and their TFP contributions to gross output value invariably exceeded that of products and semi-products, which seemed to be rebounding after the long-term inhibition of their development,. In the 1990s, however, the TFP growth of non-market services fell by more than half (from 0.7% between 1980 and 1991 to 0.3% between 1991 and 2001). Meanwhile, TFP growth declined sharply in both monopoly services and market services, from 1.6% and 1.4% to −3.7% and −2.3%, respectively. As reflected in Fig. 2, the cumulative effect of such TFP changes resulted in the constant decline of the TFP indexes of monopoly services and market services since the late 1980s, dropping from 130 to 80 (1980 = 100).

9 APPF Estimates of Total Factor Productivity

Based on the production function for industrial/sectoral gross output value, we are now able to analyze the APPF estimates of TFP growth. The APPF model has abandoned the (implicit) assumption of a fixed price for the value added of all industries/sectors and instead estimates the weighted aggregate of their value added. Thus, we can test the APF hypothesis of the fixed price for industrial/sectoral outputs by comparing the growth rates of the value added in the APPF and APF models, respectively. If the APPF estimate minus the APF estimate is positive, an industry/sector with a bigger proportion in the gross value added will be identified as growing at a faster rate. This usually occurs in the context of the market-based adjustment of resource allocation as a result of declining prices. Conceptually, the APPF model is closer to China's economic reality in view of the government's intervention in resource allocation as well as the institutional defects of the country. Moreover, through the APPF-APF comparison, we can also observe whether China's reallocation of its gross value added among its industries/sectors accords with the logic of the market economy.

In Part 1 of Table 1, we compare the APPF and APF growth rates of gross value added over the three decades and in the four periods, respectively. As we can see, the annual growth rate of the Chinese economy (value added or GDP) averaged 9.16% from 1980 to 2010, but the reallocation of its gross output (or value added) among its industries/sectors had a negative effect (−0.26) on the economy, which is calculated by subtracting the 9.42 in APF from the 9.16 in APPF. Separately speaking, the reallocation effect was positive in the early period of China's reform, but was negative throughout the other three periods with its absolute value constantly increasing, which reflects a serious problem in resource misallocation from an output perspective. That is, in the production structure calculated at the constant price, the most heavily weighted industries/sectors are not necessarily the ones with the most potential. Moreover, resource allocation among the industries/sectors has not necessarily kept up with the changes in the output prices, and, as a result, timely

Table 1 Contributions of sectoral growth and factor-input and productivity growth to China's economic growth (annual growth of value added in percentage; weighted contributions in percentage points)

	1980–1991	1991–2001	2001–2007	2007–2010	1980–2010
Effects of the reallocation of the gross value added					
APF gross value added (%)	7.28	9.69	11.99	11.23	9.42
APPF gross value added (%)	7.72	9.15	11.23	10.30	9.16
Reallocation effects	0.44	−0.54	−0.75	−0.93	−0.26
Contribution of sectoral growth to the overall growth of gross value added					
APPF gross value added (%)	7.72	9.15	11.23	10.30	9.16
Agriculture	1.75	1.18	0.50	0.48	1.18
Construction	0.38	0.64	0.68	0.89	0.58
Energy (broad-sense)	−0.06	0.33	0.74	0.37	0.27
Materials	0.90	1.49	1.57	1.21	1.26
Products and semi-products	1.91	2.69	2.83	2.54	2.42
Monopoly services	0.93	0.66	1.61	1.36	1.02
Market services	1.50	1.78	2.37	2.66	1.89
Non-market services	0.39	0.37	0.94	0.80	0.53
Contribution of factor-input and TFP growth to the overall growth of gross value added					
APPF gross value added (%)	7.72	9.15	11.23	10.30	9.16
Capital input:	4.95	6.11	8.49	10.57	6.61
- Net stock	4.94	6.18	8.56	10.55	6.64
- Asset portfolios ("quality")	0.01	−0.06	−0.07	0.02	−0.03
Labor input:	1.39	1.26	1.19	1.53	1.32
- Labor hours	1.34	0.88	0.71	0.36	0.96
- Human capital ("quality")	0.05	0.38	0.48	1.17	0.35
Overall TFP	1.39	1.79	1.57	−1.80	1.24

Source APF estimation using Eq. 1; APPF estimation using Eq. 2

adjustments might not have been made to improve allocation efficiency. In other words, the principle of the market economy was probably violated in such resource allocation. What's worse, there was a tendency towards the deterioration of such resource misallocation, as the reallocation effect dropped further from −0.54 in the 1990s to −0.93 in the post-crisis period.

In Part 2 of Table 1, we estimate the contributions of the eight major sectors of the Chinese economy to the growth of the APPF gross value added over the three decades and in the four periods, respectively. In the span of 30 years and in every period before the global financial crisis, the category of products and semi-products was the most important sector of the Chinese economy. Market services follow. This category has been on the rise over the last three decades and has surpassed products and semi-products in the post-crisis period from 2007 to 2010. These two sectors now account for more than half of the overall growth of the Chinese economy, judging by their contributions that add up to 5.2% points (2.66 plus 2.54) in the average overall growth of 10.3% from 2007 to 2010. By contrast, the contribution of agriculture to the overall growth of value added has been on the decline. In terms of its contribution to growth, agriculture is the second smallest of all sectors either at present or after the financial crisis, second only to energy. The energy sector is relatively small and fairly unstable in terms of its growth contribution, but it plays a very important role in the Chinese economy (see Fig. 1). According to our groupings, energy, materials, and products and semi-products constitute the whole Chinese industry and account for 40% of the overall economic growth, which is 4.2% points in the average overall growth of 10.3% from 2007 to 2010.

In Part 3 of Table 1, we conduct a growth accounting of the Chinese economy using the APPF model. In this procedure, we decompose the growth rate of the APPF gross output value into the contribution of factor inputs and TFP growth. We not only calculate the contributions of capital and labor inputs, but also break these contributions down into the effects of the net capital stock, the changes in capital "quality" measured by the asset structure, labor hours, and the changes in labor "quality" as measured by the labor structure.

Over these past three decades, the Chinese economy has been growing at an annual average rate of 6.16%, of which capital input accounts for 6.61% points, labor input for 1.32% points, and total factor productivity for 1.24% points. That is to say, for more than 30 years—since 1980—the contribution of capital to China's economic growth has been 72.5%, while that of labor and that of total factor productivity are 14.0% and 13.5%, respectively. It is true that capital input has been the engine for China's economic growth. If we look back upon the four periods identified in this study, the contribution of capital input has increased from 64% in the 1980s to 76% in the periods after China's entry into the WTO. The contribution of capital "quality" has been quite close over these periods, but in our view this is simply because the currently available data cannot fully reflect the effect of changes in asset structure. On the other hand, the contribution of labor input has stabilized between 1.2 and 1.5% points. Specifically, the contribution of labor hours has experienced a rapid slowdown, dropping from 1.34 in the 1980s to 0.36 after the global financial crisis; fortunately, however, such negative impact of labor hours on labor input seems to have been offset by the growth of human capital, increasing from 0.05 to 1.17 over the same period. Nonetheless, the close-to-zero growth rate of labor hours does prove that the country's demographic dividend has indeed been disappearing, while the rapid rise in human capital has borne out the generally-observed increase in labor cost.[12]

[12]For discussions on the demographic dividend and the Lewis turning point, see (Cai 2010).

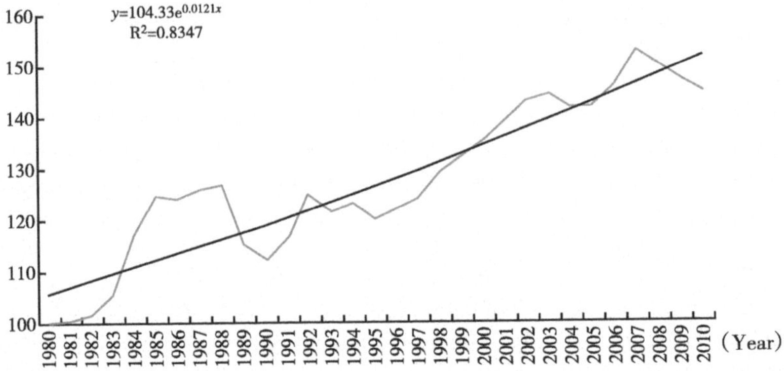

Fig. 3 (APPF) TFP index of the Chinese economy (1980 = 100)

Notably, due to the enormous government injection, the contribution of capital input has even exceeded the growth rate of the gross value added after the global financial crisis. This makes it clear that capital-input-based growth is bound to cause increasingly large losses in efficiency, which is also reflected by the TFP values in Table 1. At the end of Table 1, we estimate the TFP growth rate of every period as "the Solow residual." Meanwhile, we also draw a TFP Index of the Chinese Economy in Fig. 3. As the start of the country's all-round reform, the 1990s witnessed the fastest growth of China's TFP, during which the annual growth rate increased from 1.39% between 1980 and 1991 to 1.79% between 1991 and 2001. From 2007 to 2010, however, the contribution of TFP was negative, down by 1.8% points annually, whereas capital and labor inputs accounted for 10.6% and 1.5% points, respectively, in the 10.3% growth of the gross value added.

Given the above, our estimate of TFP decline after the financial crisis is merely based on the statistics of three years (i.e., the average growth rate from 2007 to 2010, with 2007 as the base year), which are not enough for a full observation of the changes in the basic conditions affecting the potential growth rate of the Chinese economy. According to the latest official estimates, China's GDP growth has been decelerating rapidly since 2010, down from over 10% to 7.5% and even lower. If this trend turns out to be irreversible, it would pose a significant challenge to pull China's TFP back to the 30-year "trend rate of growth" (see the regression line and the growth rate of the regression equation in Fig. 3). As we see it, if China's TFP growth remains negative from 2010 onwards—as it was in the first three years after the financial crisis—it is probably not a short-term or periodic phenomenon, but the effect of more fundamental factors. If this proves to be true and in line with what Fig. 3 implies, there is perhaps only one way to get it back on the growth track—that is, to implement fundamental reforms as the country did in the first half of the 1990s.

10 Domar-Weighted Decomposition of China's TFP into Sectoral and Factor-Reallocation Effects

According to the method introduced in Sect. 6, we can decompose TFP growth into industrial/sectoral and factor-reallocation effects using Domar weights under the APPF framework. This significant progress in growth accounting has loosened the APF model's strong assumption of a fixed factor cost for all industries/sectors. Thus, we are not only able to systematically observe the productivity of various industries/sectors under the influence of different factor costs, we can also examine to what extent industrial/sectoral productivity has influenced overall TFP through Domar-weighted aggregation. Containing the least restrictive assumptions, the Domar-weighted APPF model enables us to estimate industrial/sectoral effects on the overall economy from both the input and output perspectives. Compared with the single APPF model, it is able to establish more comprehensive logical relations between the aggregate and sectoral growth and productivity (Jorgenson, et al. 2005). In Table 2 we estimate the Domar-weighted sectoral and factor-reallocation effects on TFP, and in Fig. 4 we draw the indexes of capital and labor reallocation effects from 1980 to 2010.

Overall, the 1.24% average annual growth of China's TFP from 1980 to 2010 is decomposed into a sectoral effect (or Domar-weighted sectoral contribution to the overall TFP) of 0.84% points and a factor-reallocation effect of 0.40% points, as the sum of a labor reallocation effect of 0.56% points and a capital reallocation effect of −0.16% points. In the sectoral contribution to TFP of 0.84% points, agriculture

Table 2 Decomposition of China's TFP: Domar-weighted sectoral and factor-reallocation effects (TFP growth in percentage; sectoral and factor-reallocation effects in percentage points)

	1980–1991	1991–2001	2001–2007	2007–2010	1980–2010
Overall TFP growth (%)	1.39	1.79	1.57	−1.80	1.24
1. Domar-weighted sectoral effect on TFP	0.74	1.81	0.98	−2.31	0.84
Agriculture	0.99	0.75	0.82	0.76	0.85
Construction	−0.05	0.12	0.29	0.22	0.10
Energy (broad-sense)	−0.76	−0.24	−0.33	−0.57	−0.48
Materials	−0.50	0.77	0.21	−0.61	0.05
Products and semi-products	0.35	1.39	0.59	−0.27	0.68
Monopoly services	0.30	−0.58	0.55	−0.03	0.02
Market services	0.36	−0.37	−0.76	−1.10	−0.25
Non-market services	0.06	−0.03	−0.40	−0.71	−0.14
2. Capital reallocation effect on TFP (ρ^K)	0.30	−0.03	−1.15	−0.30	−0.16
3. Labor reallocation effect on TFP (ρ^L)	0.35	0.01	1.73	0.81	0.56

Source Estimation of Domar-weighted sectoral and factor-reallocation effects using Eq. 7

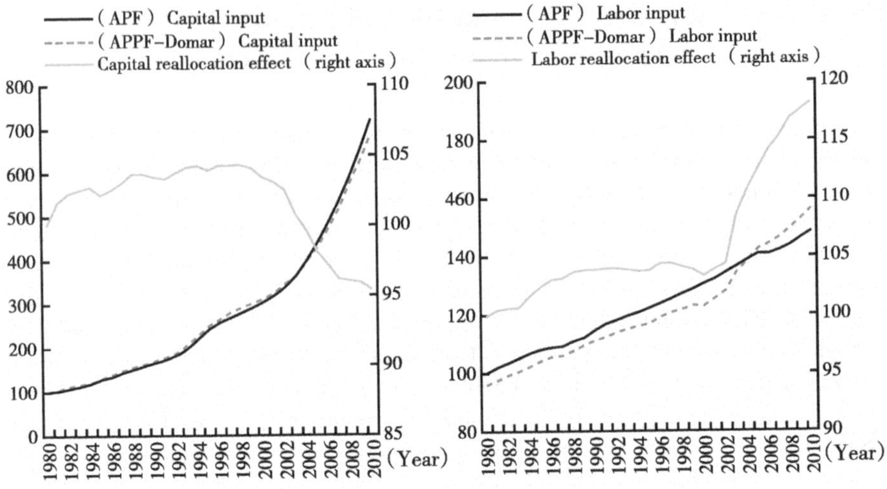

Fig. 4 Reallocation of capital and labor in the Chinese economy and the effects on TFP (1980 = 100). *Source* See Table 2

and products and semi-products are the biggest contributors, accounting for 0.85 and 0.68, respectively. In contrast, energy, market services, and non-market services have invariably played a negative role, which adds up to −0.87 and more than offsets the agricultural contribution to TFP.

A positive effect of factor reallocation on TFP reflects more efficient allocation of resources in line with the principle of the market economy. Such reallocation improves the efficiency element contained within TFP growth, and thus increases the overall TFP growth rate. Over the three decades included in this study, a positive effect of capital reallocation on TFP was achieved only in the early period of China's reform, which was 0.30 in the 1980s and very close to the effect of labor reallocation on TFP (0.35) over the same period. When China witnessed the most rapid TFP growth (1.79%) amidst its deepening of reform and opening-up in the 1990s, however, the effect of capital and labor reallocation was fairly insignificant on TFP growth (capital reallocation accounting for −0.03 and labor reallocation for 0.01).

It is worth noting that, in the post-WTO period (2001-2007), capital reallocation had a significant negative effect (−1.15) on TFP growth whereas labor reallocation had a very significant positive effect (1.73). It follows that the cross-sectoral mobility of labor resource was consistent with sectoral TFP growth and thus improved the overall TFP of the Chinese economy, which is also demonstrated by improvements in human capital in this period (see Table 1). On the other hand, the cross-sectoral mobility of capital resource worked against sectoral TFP growth. In other words, a timely adjustment of capital allocation conducive to productivity growth was not made to adapt to the relative changes in sectoral productivity in this period. Such a discrepancy persisted even after the global financial crisis, though the extent of deviation declined—a normal response under the pressure of income decline during the crisis, which is further demonstrated in Fig. 4. In view of the sustained TFP worsening in the energy industry and some service sectors since 2000, we are firmly convinced that increasing government intervention in resource allocation has affected the market-based mobility of capital and thus reduced the efficiency of overall capital allocation of the economy.

11 Conclusions

In this chapter, we have estimated the total factor productivity of the Chinese economy from 1980 to 2010 using a growth accounting method within the neoclassical economics framework to get as close as possible to the real economy, in particular the reality of the Chinese economy. This is the first time that the Domar-weighted APPF analytical framework—based as it is on industrial/sectoral statistics—has been systematically applied to the China Industry Productivity Database, which was built using the same analytical method. In addressing this data, we have not challenged the official statistics, but instead sorted them for consistency in terms of concept, classification, and coverage. At the same time, we have strictly homogenized the input factors and established strict logical relations between sectoral costs and the national input-output accounts. According to our estimates, the average annual growth rate of China's GDP was 9.16% over the three decades, much lower than the 10% or even higher officially estimated and widely accepted. Meanwhile, according to our estimates, the average annual growth rate of China's TFP was only 1.24% over the same period, also much lower than the cheerful 3–4% in some literatures but closer to the more conservative 1–2% found in others. Moreover, our estimates also reveal an increasingly dire misallocation of resources from the perspectives of both output and capital input, which have caused losses in efficiency. Our analysis at the industrial/sectoral level practically supports the hypothesis of "cross-subsidization" as a form of government involvement or intervention. That is, a higher efficiency of product and semi-product manufacturing, a sector oriented toward market competition, exists side by side with the long-term low efficiency of the state-monopolized energy industry and certain service sectors. What's more, this is the first time that China's TFP and the effects of factor reallocation on it after the global financial crisis have been measured using the industrial and sectoral statistics. The results clearly show that the huge injection of government capital has not only aggravated resource misallocation, but also generated an overall decline in sectoral efficiency.

Our estimates of China's TFP have also made it clear that under the current model of development, the Chinese economy is close to hitting the ceiling on growth. Therefore, our understanding of China's growth potential should not be based on the premise of maintaining existing institutions and structures, our conclusions should not be drawn merely on the basis of the gap in GDP per capita between China and developed economies, and, furthermore, our suggestions for possible solutions should not be made simply by referring to the so-called "middle income trap" that has been discovered through empirical observation yet remains unsupported by systematic economic theory. Rather, a more scientific and persuasive judgment of the country's growth potential has to be based on an analysis of total factor productivity and factor costs using the production function at the sectoral level.

A government-dominated economy has the capacity to grow at an exceptional rate. Once the market resumes its decisive role in resource allocation, however, growth is bound to slow down. Yet unfortunately we cannot expect either a quick or big "dividend" from the rectification of such resource misallocation, because the Chinese economy has gone too far and sunk too deep in a distorted structure. This problem of China has already transcended national boundaries and become a global problem. Likewise, the overcapacity of the Chinese economy means the overcapacity of the world economy. Over a long period of time, China will likely suffer from a reduction in its production capacity, not only because it does not have and is unlikely to have all at once a consumption capacity that matches its current production capacity, but also because its rapid rise and expansion as "the world's factory" has already put an end to the "technology-economy paradigm" that has endowed it with all types of mature technology.

In order to solve the existing deep-seated problems in the Chinese economy and transform its model of growth as quickly as possible, the role of the government must be transformed while pulling it out from competitive economic activities. What we need to do is keep the government neutral on economic interests or "economically disinterested," committed only to maintaining and improving the market economy system, rather than intervening in the country's economic operations for any variety of reasons. Any government intervention on the basis of the national interest must be clearly defined and confirmed through public hearings, and the resulting economic activities must be plainly restricted to the production of public products or services. It is supported by numerous facts that supporting the development of state-owned enterprises in the so-called "strategic industries"—whether by means of subsidies, encouragement policies, or cheap credit—may increase our growth rates but will also cause us to suffer losses to our efficiency. This also applies to the race among local governments for investment in and strategic development of infrastructure facilities. Such an extensive mode of development cannot do without skewed incentives and therefore has inevitably led to low efficiency. Accordingly, we must be on guard against such propositions that involve the government undertaking structural adjustments. Any attempt to solve the problem rooted in the government's over-intervention through further government intervention is bound to make a bad situation worse.

References

Cai, F. (2010). Demographic transition, demographic Dividend, and Lewis turning point in China. *China Economic Journal, 3*(2), 107–119.

Denison, E. F. (1962). *The sources of economic growth in the United States and the alternative before US*. New York: Committee on Economic Development.

Domar, E. D. (1961). On the measurement of technological change. *The Economic Journal, 71*(284), 709–729.

Griliches, Z. (1960). Measuring inputs in agriculture: A critical survey. *Journal of Farm Economics, 40*(5), 1398–1427.

Huang, Y., & Tao, K. (2010). Factor market distortion and the current account surplus in China. *Asian Economic Papers, 9*(3), 1–36.

Hulten, C. R. (1978). Growth accounting with intermediate inputs. *Review of Economic Studies, 45*(3), 511–518.

Jorgenson, D. W. (1966). The embodiment hypothesis. *Journal of Political Economy, 74*(1), 1–17.

Jorgenson, D. W. (1990). Productivity and economic growth. In E. R. Berndt & J. E. Triplett (Eds.), *Fifty Years of Economic Measurement: The Jubilee of the Conference on Research in Income and Wealth* (Vol. 54). National Bureau of Economic Research.

Jorgenson, D. W. (2001). Information technology and the US economy. *American Economic Review, 91*(1), 1–32.

Jorgenson, D. W., & Griliches, Z. (1967). The explanation of productivity change. *Review of Economic Studies, 34*(3), 249–283.

Jorgenson, D. W., Ho, M. S., & Stiroh, K. J. (2005). Information technology and the American growth resurgence. In *Productivity* (Vol. 3). Cambridge, MA: MIT Press.

Li, H., & Zhou, L. (2005). Political turnover and economic performance: The incentive role of personnel control in China. *Journal of Public Economics, 89*(9–10), 1743–1762.

Maddison, A., & Wu, H. X. (2008). Measuring China's economic performance. *World Economics, 9*(2), 13–44.

Milana, C., & Wu, H. X. (2013). China's *Productivity performance in the government-engineered growth: A 'true' index number approach.* Presented at the IARIW-UNSW Conference on Productivity: Measurement, Drivers, and Trends. Sydney, Australia, November 26–27.

O'Mahony, M., & Marcel, P. T. (2009). Output, input, and productivity measures at the industry level: The EU KLEMS database. *The Economic Journal, 119*(June), 374–403.

Solow, R. M. (1957). Technical change and the aggregate production function. *Review of Economics and Statistics, 39*(3), 312–320.

van Ark, B., O'Mahony, M., & Timmer, M. P. (2008). The productivity gap between Europe and the US: Trends and causes. *Journal of Economic Perspectives, 22*(1), 25–44.

Wu, H. X. (2014a). *On China's strategic move for the new stage of development: A productivity perspective*. Presented at the Third World KLEMS Conference. Tokyo, Japan, May 19–20.

Wu, H. X. (2014b). China's Growth and Productivity Performance Debate Revisited: Accounting for China's Sources of Growth in 1949–2012. In *The Conference Board Economics Working Papers*, EPWP1401.

Wu, H. X. (2015). Constructing China's Net Capital Stock and Measuring Capital Service in China, 1980–2010. *RIETI Discussion Papers*, 15-E-006. (http://www.rieti.go.jp/en/publications/summary/15010007.html).

Wu, H. X., & Yue, X. (2012). Accounting for Labor Input in Chinese Industry, 1949–2009. *RIETI Discussion Papers*, 12-E-065. (http://www.rieti.go.jp/jp/publications/nts/12e065.html).

Wu, H. X., Yue, X., & Zhang, G. (2015). Constructing Annual Employment and Compensation Matrices and Measuring Labor Input in China. *RIETI Discussion Papers*, 15-E-005. (http://www.rieti.go.jp/en/publications/summary/15010006.html).

Wu, J. L. (2008). *The choice of China's growth model*. Shanghai: Shanghai Far East Publishers.

Harry X. Wu is a professor at the Institute of Economic Research, Hitotsubashi University, Japan. He is also Senior Advisor and Research Director at The Conference Board China Center for Economics and Business. E-mail: harry.wu@ier.hit-u.ac.jp or Harry.Wu@conference-board.org. For details and sponsorship of this research program, please refer to Wu, Harry X., "On China's Strategic Move for the New Stage of Development: A Productivity Perspective," presented at the Third World KLEMS Conference, Tokyo, May 19–20, 2014.

Chapter 11
New Trends and Determinants of China's Income Gap

Juzhong Zhuang

China's income gap is an important issue under the conditions of the new normal.

In recent years, China's widening income gap has received a great deal of attention. According to statistics presented by the Chinese National Bureau of Statistics (NBS), China's Gini coefficient for per capita household income has dropped from its peak of 0.491 in 2008 to 0.473 in 2013. People's views are divided as to the veracity of these figures. Some cast doubts on them. Others believe that such figures validate the Kuznets hypothesis and that China's income gap has passed its peak, so its Gini index will only decline further.

In this chapter, I would like to review the changes and determining factors of China's Gini coefficient over the past three decades, and on that basis, I will explore the reasons for its decline in recent years and forecast its direction for the future.

This chapter is based on my working paper co-authored with my colleague at the Asian Development Bank (ADB), and as such is still crude to some extent but provides a good frame of reference. Our basic conclusion is that the recent decline in China's Gini coefficient is well-grounded in both theoretical and empirical evidence, but it is still too early to tell whether it has peaked already.

To begin with, let's look at the changes to China's Gini coefficient over the past three decades (see Fig. 1). Historically, the Gini coefficient declined in the early 1980s mainly because the country's earlier rural reforms had both raised farmers' income and narrowed the urban-rural income gap. With the focus of reform shifted to the cities, however, it began rising in the mid-1980s. It was not until the mid-1990s that China's Gini coefficient started to decline again, this time when the second round of rural reforms—including that of the grain price system—and the development of township enterprises increased farmers' incomes. With China's entry into the WTO, the Gini coefficient started rising again in the late 1990s and reached 0.491 in 2008, whereupon it began to decline again, dropping to 0.473 in 2013.

J. Zhuang (✉)
Asian Development Bank, Manila, Philippines
e-mail: jzhuang@adb.org

F. Cai (ed.), *China's Economic New Normal*, Research Series on the Chinese Dream and China's Development Path, https://doi.org/10.1007/978-981-15-3227-6_11

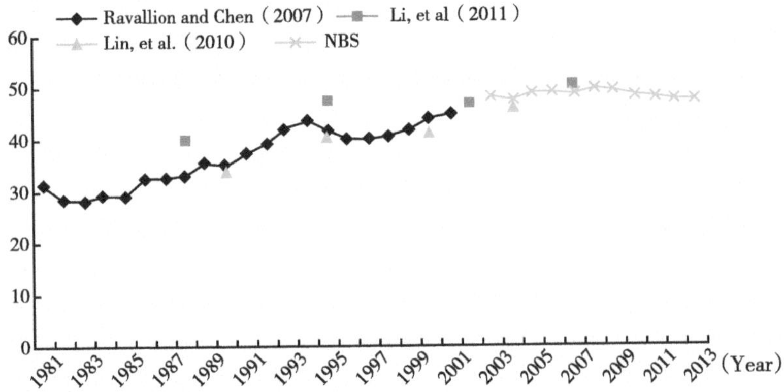

Fig. 1 China's Gini coefficient, 1981–2013

To analyze why China's Gini coefficient has declined in recent years, we have created a simple model (see Eq. 1). In this model, per capita household income is the sum of per capita capital income and per capita wage income. The former is household capital (or wealth) multiplied by the return on capital and divided by the number of household members, and the latter is the number of household laborers multiplied by the wage rate and divided by the number of household members. It should be noted that human capital is included not in wealth, but in the labor force category. Hence, the income gap is determined by the distribution of wealth, labor force, and human capital among households, the return on capital, the relative wages of the different types of labor forces, and the relative share of wages and the return of capital in the national income.

$$\frac{Income}{H} = \frac{WL}{H} + \frac{RK}{H} \tag{1}$$

In Eq. 1, *Income* refers to household income; *K* stands for capital or wealth, *R* for return on capital, *L* for labor force (including human capital), *W* for wage, and *H* for household size or the number of household members. What, then, are the determining factors of such variables in our model?

The distribution of wealth, the labor force, and human capital amongst households is determined by their initial distribution, household savings and investment decisions, individual efforts, governmental behavior (including land reallocation, taxation, and public investment in human capital), the quality of public governance, household fertility decisions, and more.

The wage rate and the return on capital are determined by market demand and supply, factor market efficiency, government behavior (including labor market regulation and taxation on capital and labor income), etc.

The relative shares of capital and labor income within the national income is determined by the relative return on capital, labor, and human capital, the capital-labor ratio, etc., all of which are subject to technological progress, the relative bargaining power between labor and capital, and governmental behavior.

Within this framework, the income gap widens when such variables—the wage rate, the return on capital, the distribution of both the capital and labor force (including human capital), and the shares of capital and labor income in the national income—change in a direction that favors the relatively wealthy.

Such changes include: (1) a rise in the wages of skilled workers relative to unskilled workers, known as the skill premium, which widens the gaps in wage income; (2) a rise in returns to factors (including capital and labor) in urban and coastal regions relative to rural and inland regions, which enlarges interregional income disparities; (3) a decline in the wage share of per capita income, which also widens the gaps in per capita income because wage gaps are usually smaller than capital income gaps; (4) widening wealth gaps; and (5) widening human capital gaps. The following are our empirical analyses of these aspects.

Figure 2a shows the proportions of national income gaps resulting from differences in education. In China, education gaps accounted for less than 10% of the

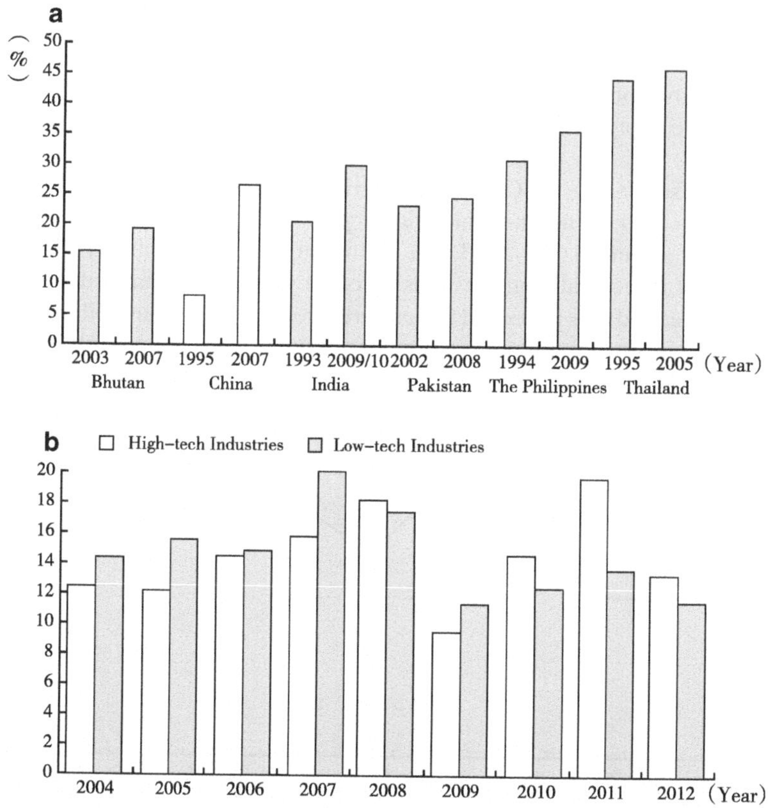

Fig. 2 **a** Proportions of income gaps accountable by education gaps (%). *Source* ADB (2012). **b** Wage growth in China's high-tech and low-tech industries (%). *Source* china statistical yearbooks

income gap in 1995, but rose to over 25% in 2007, which indicates the growing importance of education as a determinant of income. The widening of the income gap due to differences in education implies a rise in skill premium over this period.

According to statistics, however, China's skill premium has declined in recent years. In Fig. 2b, we compare the average annual wage growth rates in China's high-tech and low-tech industries and find faster growth in the low-tech industries in recent years (2008, 2010, 2011, and 2012). Part of the reason is probably the significantly increased input to China's higher education over the past few years. For example, the number of college graduates has increased from fewer than one million in 1995 to over seven million today, and the supply of skilled workers has also increased quickly. To the contrary, wage growth has been slower in the country's high-tech industries relative to its low-tech industries.

A second reason for China's declining skill premium is the government's endeavors to raise the minimum wage in recent years, which has greatly lifted the wage floors in China, in particular along its coastal regions. Hence, the recent narrowing of China's income gap can also be attributed to the decline in the skill premium.

Let's look at China's interregional income gaps, including urban-rural and inter-provincial disparities. Research shows that the widening of urban-rural and inter-provincial income gaps is a major reason for the rise of China's Gini coefficient over the past three decades. According to an ADB study, interregional income gaps accounted for over 50% of China's overall income gap in 2007, that is, over 50% of China's income gap was caused by interregional (urban-rural and inter-provincial) income gaps.

As we can see in Fig. 3, China's urban-rural income gap has been narrowing in recent years, and its urban-rural ratio of per capita income has dropped from 3.4 in 2008 to around 3.0 in 2013. An important reason is probably the massive workforce shift from rural to urban areas in recent years, which has reduced surplus rural labor forces and thus improved agricultural productivity. Meanwhile, supportive government policies for agriculture have also contributed to an overall increase in farmers' income.

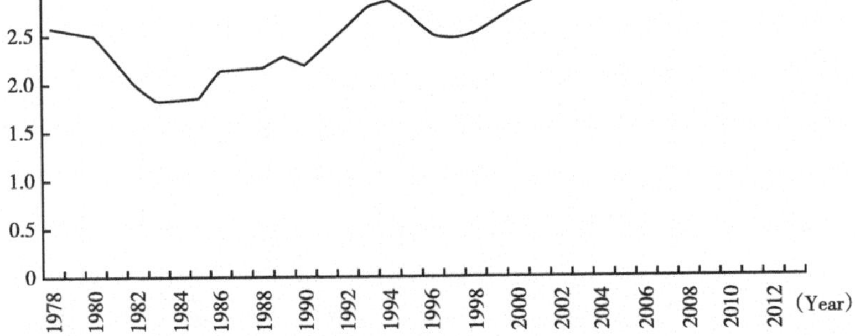

Fig. 3 China's urban-rural income gap. *Source* China statistical yearbooks

Figure 4 shows the Gini coefficients of provincial per capita income in three Asian countries: China, India, and the Philippines. Since 2003 or 2004, China's inter-provincial (region-to-region) income gap has been narrowing, which is related to the implementation of the country's Western Development Strategy over the past few years.

According to Figs. 3 and 4, the narrowing of both urban-rural and inter-provincial income gaps is part of the reason for the decline of China's Gini coefficient in recent years.

The third reason lies in changes to the shares of capital and labor income. According to many studies, the wage share of China's national income has declined over the past 20 years, which has widened the gaps in per capita income because wage gaps are usually smaller than capital income gaps. Nonetheless, as we can see in Fig. 5, the share of labor income in the value added of China's manufacturing has been increasing in recent years. This seems to coincide with the recent workforce shortage and rapid rise in wages in China's coastal provinces as well as the approaching

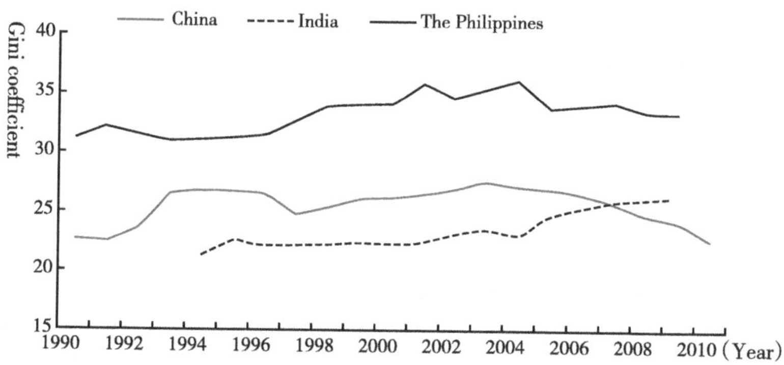

Fig. 4 Interregional income gaps in selected Asian countries. *Source* ADB (2012)

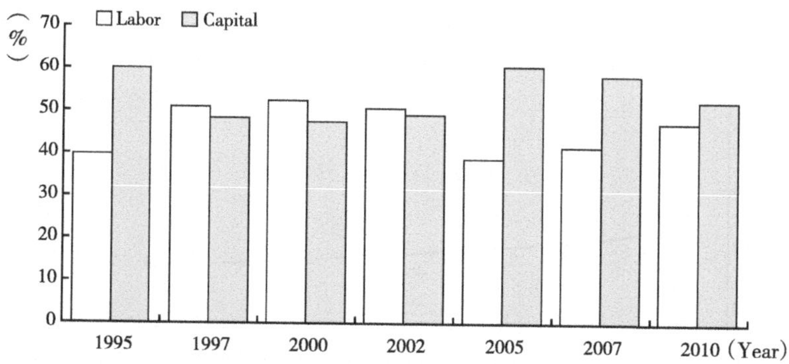

Fig. 5 Shares of capital and labor income in the value added of China's manufacturing. *Source* CEIC data (based on China input-output tables)

Lewis Turning Point espoused by some people. In a word, the rising wage share is probably another reason for the decline of China's Gini coefficient.

The fourth aspect of our empirical analyses is the wealth gap. Drawn from work published by Professor Li Shi and his colleagues, Fig. 6 shows that China's wealth gap has widened considerably over the past two or three decades. From 1988 to 2012, the Gini coefficient for China's wealth distribution doubled, from 0.35 to above 0.7. In other words, the widening wealth gap is also responsible for China's widening income gap over the past 20–30 years. Yet we still need further statistics to predict how this wealth gap will change in the future. Nevertheless, one thing is clear—unless we reform the tax system, it would be extremely difficult to find a driving force capable of narrowing the wealth gap.

The last aspect of our empirical analyses is the human capital gap among Chinese families. As we can see in Fig. 7, the overall human capital gap narrowed in China from 1989 to 2004, during which time the Gini coefficient for education dropped from 0.44 to 0.38. This is conducive to narrowing the income gap. On the other hand, some studies have discovered a widening human capital gap among those with

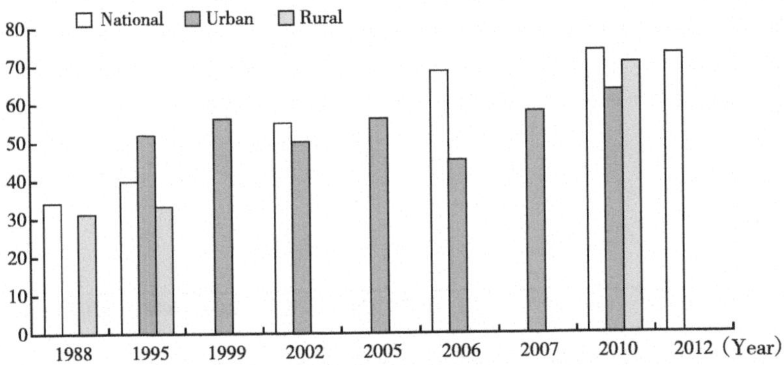

Fig. 6 China's wealth distribution gaps. *Source* Li, et al. (2014)

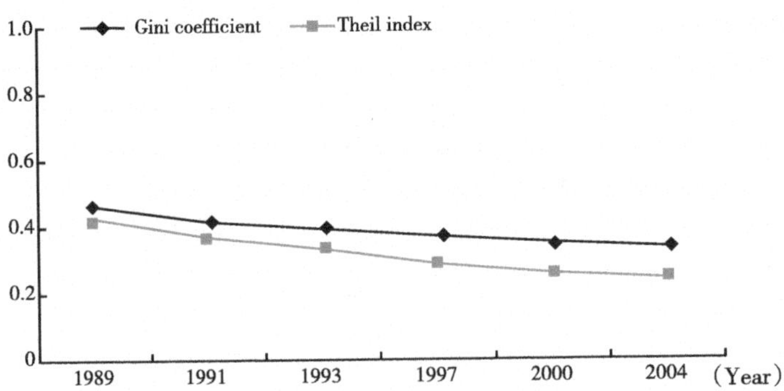

Fig. 7 China's human capital gap. *Source* Saccone (2008)

a junior high school education and above during the same period (1989–2004). But here we would once again reiterate that we need further statistics to predict the trend of China's human capital gap in the future.

Based on the above theoretical model and empirical analyses, we can conclude that the rise in the skill premium, the decline in the wage share of the national income, the widening interregional (urban-rural and inter-provincial) income gaps, and the growing wealth gap were the major reasons for the widening of China's income gap over the past 30 years. In recent years, however, the above factors have reversed—except for the wealth gap, which has been the major contributor to the decline of China's Gini coefficient.

Nonetheless, we should not conclude from the recent decline in the Gini coefficient that China's income gap has already peaked. There are many reasons for this, in fact. First of all, the reversal of the aforementioned factors is in part the result of government policies, not totally market-based behavior. Secondly, the wealth gap is likely to widen further and account for a bigger part of the income gap. Thirdly, it is still difficult to forecast the trend of the human capital gap without the latest statistics. Finally, an important precondition for the Kuznets hypothesis is the increase in income redistribution by the government through taxation with a country's economic and middle-class growth. In developed countries, individual income tax and transfer payment reduces one-third of the income gaps, but in China, the effect of individual income tax is still quite limited on the income gap.

In Fig. 8 and Table 1, we compare the pre-tax and after-tax Gini coefficients of OECD countries and China. Of the OECD countries, the pre-tax and after-tax Gini coefficients average 0.46 and 0.32, respectively. This translates into a more than 30% decline in the average Gini coefficient by way of tax adjustment. By contrast, there is not much difference in the pre-tax and after-tax urban Gini coefficients of China, a conclusion drawn by Professor Li Shi using the available 2009 statistics.

In conclusion, the decline in China's Gini coefficient over the past years is very inspirational, but it is still too early to tell whether it has peaked or not. China's income gap is likely to remain at a high level without the implementation of corresponding policies, such as the household registration system reform designed to meet the demands of migrant workers, the improvement of the social security system, increased public investment in education and healthcare aimed at narrowing the human capital gaps, tax system reform (including individual income tax reform), the promotion of urbanization and the development of services aimed at creating more jobs, the facilitation of equal opportunities, and sustained anti-corruption efforts for an honest and clean government.

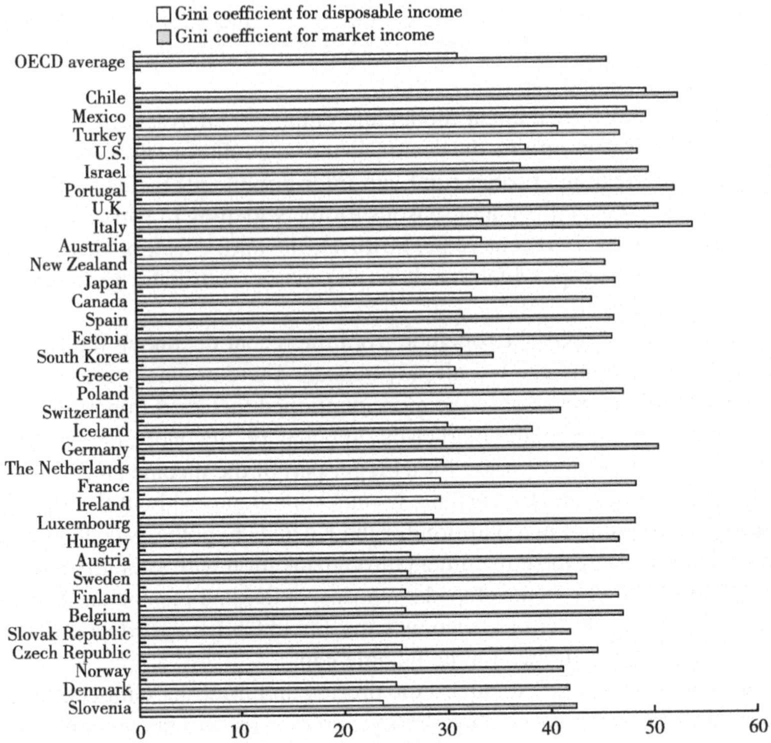

Fig. 8 Pre-tax and after-tax Gini coefficients of OECD countries

Table 1 Pre-tax and after-tax urban Gini coefficients of China

Year	Pre-tax Gini coefficient	After-tax Gini coefficient
1997	30.1	29.6
2002	32.5	31.8
2005	35.2	34.2
2008	36.3	35.1
2009	34.7	33.5

Source Li, et al. (2011)

References

ADB. (2012). *Asian development outlook 2012: Confronting rising inequality*. Manila: ADB.

Li, S., Luo, C., & Sicular, T. (2011). *Overview: Income inequality in China: The intergenerational dimension*. CIBC Centre for Human Capital and Productivity Working Paper No. 201113. Ontario: University of Western Ontario.

Li, S., Wan, H., & Xie, Y. (2014). *Widening trend of Chinese household wealth inequality*. China Institute for Income Distribution Working Paper No. 201424. Beijing: Beijing Normal University.

National Bureau of statistics. *China statistical yearbooks*; *China statistical annual reports*.

Saccone, D. (2008). *Educational inequality and educational poverty: The Chinese case in the period of 1975–2004*. Department of Economics Working Paper No. 08/2008. Torino: University of Torino.

Chapter 12
Changes in China's Labor Share: Estimation and Interpretation

Juwei Zhang

1 The Labor Share Dispute

There has been some dispute recently over China's labor wage. Over the past two years, this has been a particularly hot topic, with many big names weighing in. Yet, as far as I can tell, no consensus has been reached. An important reason for this is that the grounds of discussion are not the same. For example, some people argue that China's labor wage is too small and is rapidly shrinking, while others disagree after a comparison of various statistics. Only on the basis of an accurate calculation are we able to find out whether the labor wage has increased or decreased, which is significant for an appropriate understanding of China's economic development.

An important change to China's investment structure is in the ongoing relationship between capital and labor shares in the national income. In my view, it is necessary to begin anew when thinking about the structural relationship between investment and consumption. For example, how should we define investment and consumption in the first place? From an economic point of view, both investment and consumption are domestic demands, and the only difference lies in who is in need of them.

More often than not, consumption refers to the final consumption of domestic residents. In fact, however, investment is a form of intermediate consumption or corporate consumption. Given this, should we define government investment and consumption as investment, or as consumption? We generally regard it as investment now, but if we give it a second thought, we will find this definition far more complex than "investment" would indicate. In this sense, investment and consumption can mean quite different things when viewed from a new perspective. For a long time now, we have been constrained by conventional economic cognitions or classifications. Now, it is time we open up to new ideas and insights.

J. Zhang (✉)
CASS Institute of Population and Labor Economics, Beijing, China
e-mail: zhangjw@cass.org.cn

F. Cai (ed.), *China's Economic New Normal*, Research Series on the Chinese Dream and China's Development Path, https://doi.org/10.1007/978-981-15-3227-6_12

Some people say we must increase our consumption rate. This is true, but we have thus far failed to no matter how hard we try. Why? Because our remuneration is so low and so is people's income.

To some degree, the argument over whether China's labor wage has shrunk is due to a shortage of consistent statistics. Meanwhile, when we are to compare Chinese and international statistics, we find them hardly comparable, because they are different in their range of statistics. The Chinese wage statistics, drawn from three sources, have invariably included the income of the self-employed, without singling out the remuneration of employees.

2 Changes in China's Labor Share: Estimates and Interpretations

In the first place, we must straighten out, statistically, the real changes in the labor wage of China's national income. This is heavily dependent on data released by China's National Bureau of Statistics (NBS). The problem with the NBS wage statistics, however, is in the scope of labor income covered. As previously mentioned, this has included the income of the self-employed and thus caused confusion. That being the case, it is necessary to distinguish self-employment sectors from employment sectors so as to clear up misunderstandings. Theoretically, factor income distribution is exclusive to employment sectors. For self-employment sectors, distribution between factors is of a quite different nature, and is even unnecessary. It is unnecessary to distribute between capital and labor in self-employment sectors, such as individual economies and rural household businesses, because both factors are in the possession of the owner.

What, then, is the reality of the labor wage of China's employment sectors? How is it supposed to change theoretically? To estimate its theoretical changes, we must distinguish between the formal and mixed sectors of the Chinese economy, as well as estimate the theoretical changes in their respective labor wages. On that basis alone will we be able to pinpoint the reality and meaning of the labor wage by contrasting the theoretical changes and the real statistics.

As shown in Figs. 1 and 2, the labor wage is generally on the rise in developed countries if measured by the proportion of employee wages in GDP.

Economic development is a process of formalizing various types of economic activity. Figure 3 shows the changes in the proportion of self-employed sectors in the US GDP from 1900 to 2009. Currently, self-employed sectors account for around 10% of the US GDP.

Based on the NBS definition of economic accounting for the self-employed and formal sectors, we have cross-checked relevant statistics released by the NBS. Figure 4 shows the changes in both the output value and structure of China's self-employed sectors.

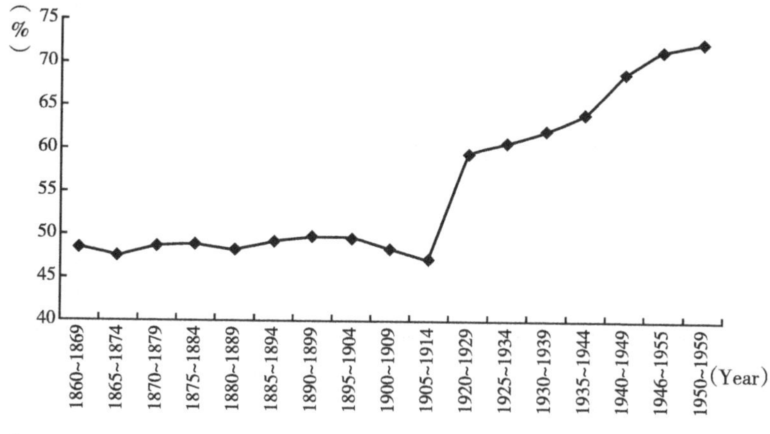

Fig. 1 Proportion of employee wages in UK GDP

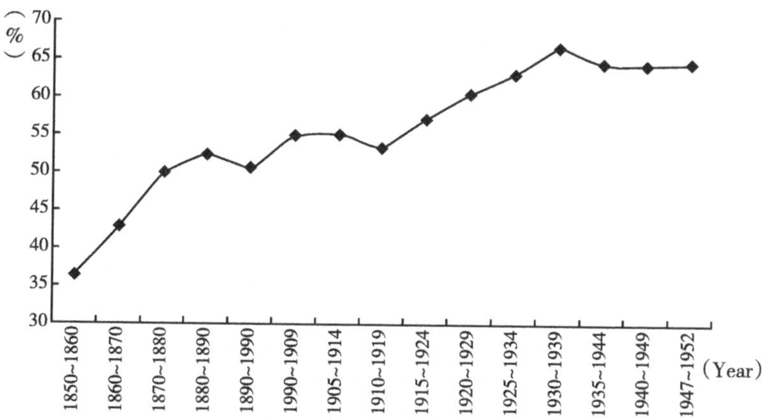

Fig. 2 Proportion of employee wages in US GDP

Figure 5 shows the changes in the proportion of self-employed sectors in China's GDP, which has averaged around 20% from 1978 to 2010. In terms of economic structure and output composition, the gap between China and developed economies is no longer all that significant. At present, only about 20% of China's GDP is attributed to non-formal or self-employed sectors, the biggest part of which comes from the agricultural sector. That being said, large-sized farms must be classified under the employment sectors, so we must exclude their income from that of the agricultural sector. As a result, both the rural and urban self-employed sectors still account for the largest shares of that 20% of China's GDP.

In order to analyze the reasons for such changes in the shares of China's GDP, we have not only estimated the outputs, but also accounted the production factors, the most important of which are labor and capital. Figure 6 shows the working population in China's employment and self-employed sectors. In terms of quantity,

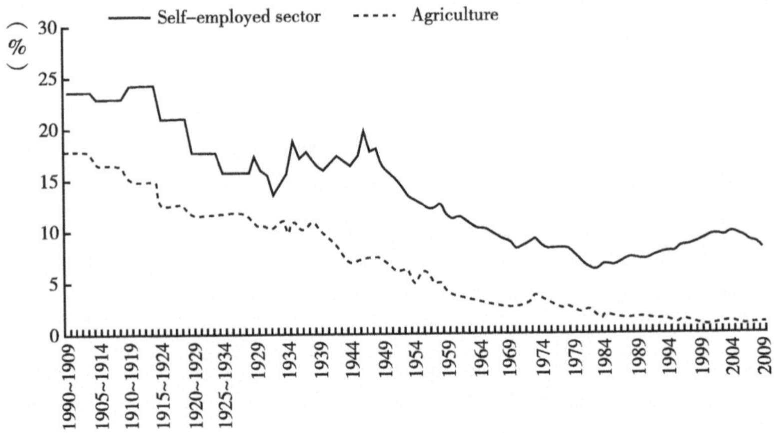

Fig. 3 Proportions of mixed economy and agriculture in US GDP

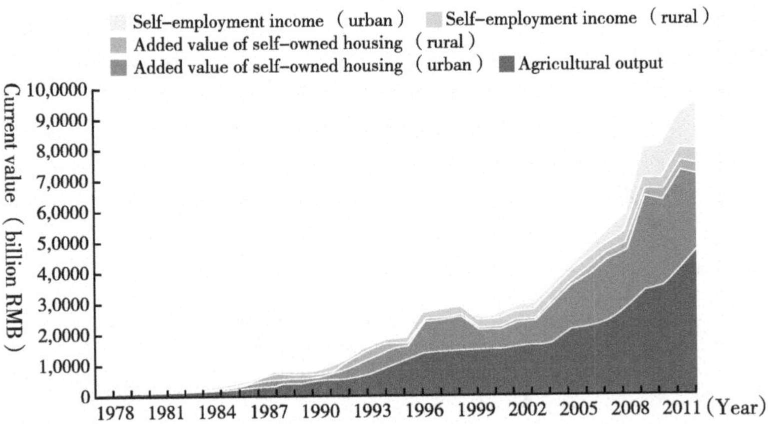

Fig. 4 The output structure of China's self-employed sector

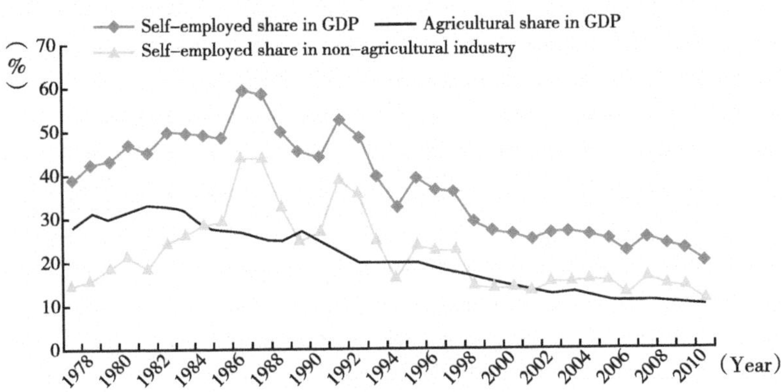

Fig. 5 Proportion of self-employed sectors in China's GDP

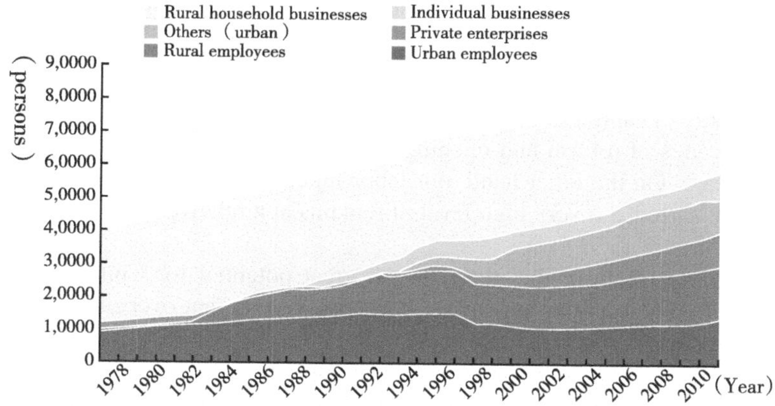

Fig. 6 Working population in China's employment and self-employed sectors

employees now account for over 50% of China's workforce. Since 2002, the number of domestic employees has been growing by 1% annually, indicating an enormous achievement for China in terms of boosting employment over the past decade or so. In the mid-1990s, however, the labor market was oriented toward the informal sector. Consequently, the proportion of formal employees declined slightly in the period spanning from the late 1990s to 2002, but it has been increasing rapidly over the past two years.

At the same time, we have also recalculated China's capital stock and thereby concluded certain structural changes in the output value and production factors, as seen in Fig. 7. We shall dig more deeply into such changes, because they reflect major structural issues for the Chinese economy. Figure 7 shows the changes in the output and factor structures of both the formal and informal sectors of the Chinese economy. It also conveys the important message that, from an output point of view, China has

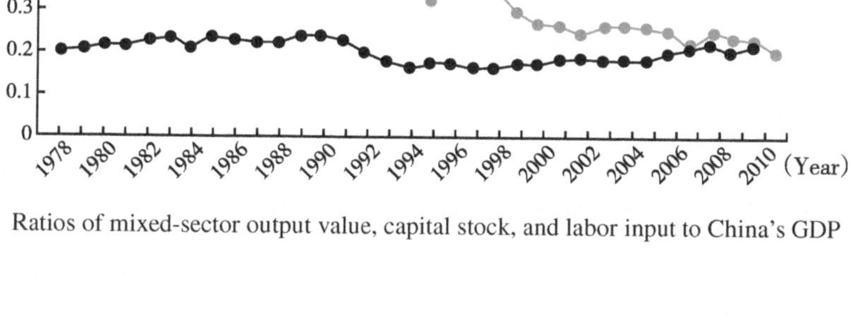

Fig. 7 Ratios of mixed-sector output value, capital stock, and labor input to China's GDP

realized the formalization of its economy. In China, capital always concentrates in the formal sector. By contrast, there is not much capital stock in the informal sector, as in rural household businesses or urban individual businesses. As we can see in Fig. 7, the ratio of capital stock in the mixed-sector to China's GDP has not declined over the decades of reform and opening-up. In fact, it has even increased slightly in recent years. On the other hand, our labor input has declined considerably; yet given that it started at a very high level, it remains at a relatively high level despite its declines.

Some scholars believe that there is still great potential for China's economic development. Where is that potential? It lies in the fact that over one-third of the national labor force is still in rural areas or the informal sector, which accounts for a very small part of its GDP. If we look back, in the years between 1978 to 2010, nearly 50% of China's labor force has created less than 20% of its GDP. That is to say, China has the capacity to constantly improve its economic efficiency through the further formalization, organization, and corporatization of its economic sectors, because there is a world of difference between the efficiency of individual businesses and that of an organized, corporatized economy.

Figure 8 is our estimate of changes in the labor share of China's employment sector, which is generally on a downward trend.

As we can see in Fig. 8, the labor share exceeded 80% in the early period of China's reform and opening-up in the 1980s. In the early 1990s, however, the profit erosion of wages was so serious that the Chinese economy was on the verge of collapse.

Is this downward trend justified or unjustified? Correct or incorrect? We have also probed into it using production functions. We have simulated changes in the labor share using the production functions, hoping to find out whether they are consistent with the previously-released statistics. Although we know that the Cobb-Douglas production function is not quite appropriate in this case because it implies constant returns to labor, we still use it for a general simulation, the result of which can be seen in Fig. 9.

Fig. 8 Estimated real changes in the labor share of China's employment sector

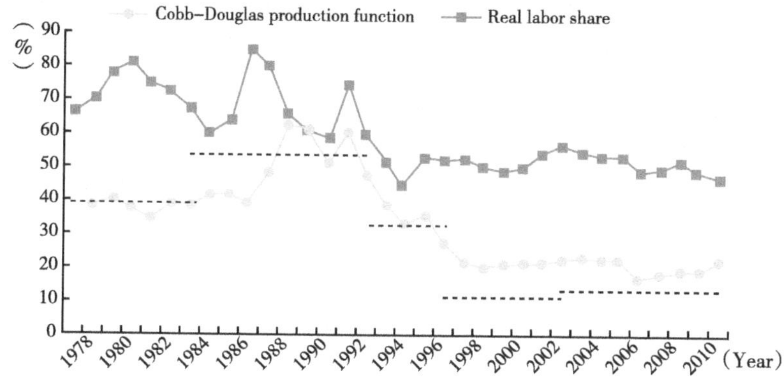

Fig. 9 Cobb-Douglas production function estimates and the real labor share

Besides, in its broadest sense, the Cobb-Douglas production function is meant to loosen the hypothesis of the elasticity of substitution. Further simulations reflect a consistent trend of theoretical and real changes in the labor share (see Figs. 10 and 11, for example). What follows is that the decline in China's labor share is not entirely due to income distribution, but is, to some degree, inherent to or endogenous in our model of economic development. Given the above, does the decline in our labor share make any sense at all? We have also estimated the current elasticity of substitution in China. When the elasticity of substitution is exactly one, the labor share is constant. When the elasticity of substitution is less than one, the labor share is on the rise. When the elasticity of substitution is greater than one, the labor share falls. If China's elasticity of substitution is greater than one, the current problem in its income distribution would more likely be a developmental issue. We estimate the elasticity of substitution between the labor and capital of China's employment and self-employed sectors, as well as within the overall Chinese economy. It is

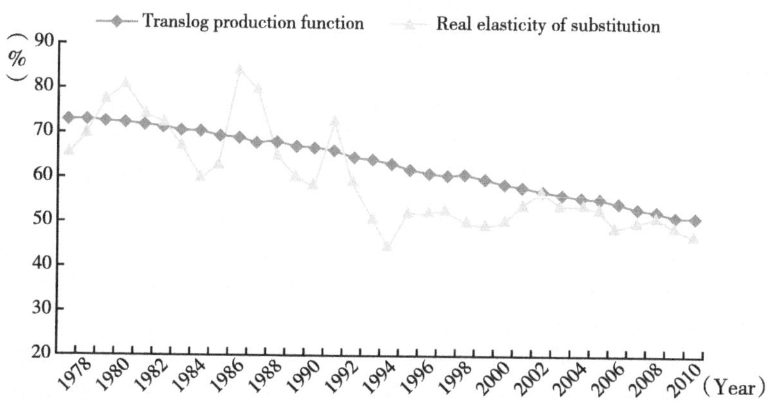

Fig. 10 Translog production function estimates and real elasticity of substitution of China's employment sector

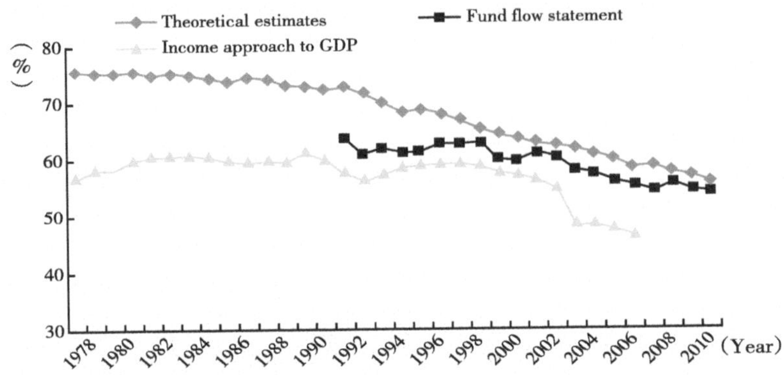

Fig. 11 Theoretical and statistical labor shares of China

between 0.88 and 0.95 in the employment sector and between 0.85 and 0.87 in the self-employed sector. There is some contradiction between our estimates and the theoretical and real elasticity of substitution, but there is something in common between them, too, which is that China's elasticity of substitution must be less than one at the current stage of development, because it has an abundant (infinite) labor supply.

According to our estimates, the decline in China's labor share must not be completely attributed to its model of development. To some degree, it also results from the current income distribution. If the Chinese economy has not yet reached the Lewis Turning Point, the result of our modeling is a decline of the labor share in itself. For a long time, our laborers or employees have merely been paid a living wage in the rural areas instead of a formal sector wage. That is why the labor share has declined in our simulation.

Yet we have all noticed that wages are soaring in many places and are, in fact, approximating or determined by the marginal product in the formal sector. If this is the fact, we should have also seen a slight increase in the labor share at the beginning of an uptrend. But this has not materialized. Is there, then, something wrong with our labor market after all?

In my eyes, China has basically accomplished the reforms of its labor market, achieving a very high degree of marketization. If the problem does not lie in the labor market, we will naturally think of the capital market. Although it is not the theme of this chapter, our analysis does point us to the capital market.

If the prices of factors are not determined by the marginal product—whereas wage (or the price of labor) *is* determined by it—we can only justify the decline in China's labor share by the fact that capital is not priced by the marginal product. How, then, is capital priced?

The answer is, according to our regulations and financial will. Consequently, capital has gained excess profits and a far higher value. As capital cost is brought under artificial control, capital gains are shared between financial institutions and real enterprises. When the cost of capital is kept artificially low, its market price (or the price that it deserves) turns into enterprise profits. Under such circumstances, it is only natural for there to be strong profit growth.

Of course, the profits of financial institutions are also from capital gains. Therefore, the lower the cost of capital, the more money they make. Based on our analysis, to solve the problems with China's income distribution, we must focus more on the financial market, rather than the labor market, and make it more flexible and more market-oriented. I think it is probably an entry point for improving the pattern of income distribution in our country.

3 Conclusion

The decline in China's labor share is a complex issue, around which there are still many misunderstandings.

The decline in the labor share must be true. Both the NBS statistics and our production function estimates have reflected a consistent downward trend amongst labor shares, which indicates that such a decline is not merely a problem of income distribution, but is, in a way, related to our model of economic growth.

According to our estimates, China's elasticity of substitution is less than one, which means an upward trend for the labor share in theory. Yet this has never occurred in reality. Why? The only answer is that something must be wrong with our labor market, our capital market, or both. The problem with our labor and capital markets is that, on the one hand, wages are lower than the marginal product of laborers and, on the other hand, capital gains are greater than its marginal product.

Chapter 13
Reform the Distribution System to Boost the Growth of Consumption

Shi Li

This chapter focuses on how to boost consumption growth by reforming the distribution system. It consists of four sections. Section 1 reviews the changes in the share of consumption of China's national income, as well as the proportion of household consumption expenditures in the final consumption expenditure, and deduces from them the current share of consumption of China. Section 2 analyzes the correlation between the income gap among Chinese residents and the corresponding changes in their shares of consumption. As we all know, the income gap affects consumption. In Keynesian economics, the marginal propensity to consume for lower-income groups is always higher than that of higher-income groups. This suggests that it is possible to increase the aggregate consumption-income ratio using income redistribution measures that increase the income of lower-income groups and transfer income from the rich to the poor. Yet it is only theoretically feasible. Whether or not there is statistical support for it in practice requires further probing. Section 3 summarizes the changes in China's income and wealth gaps and predicts further changes in the future. As our economic growth slows down, how will our income gap change in the following years? Certainly, predicting the future is always risky. My prediction is cautiously made based on my personal experience and is for reference only. Section 4 gives some suggestions to boost consumption growth through income distribution reforms in response to the declining share of consumption in China's national income.

1 Changes in China's Share of Consumption

We have concluded the following characteristics of the changes in the share of consumption in China's national income. First of all, the share of final consumption expenditures (i.e., the sum of household and government consumption expenditures)

S. Li (✉)
Institute for Income Distribution, Beijing Normal University, Beijing, China
e-mail: lishi@bnu.edu.cn

F. Cai (ed.), *China's Economic New Normal*, Research Series on the Chinese Dream and China's Development Path, https://doi.org/10.1007/978-981-15-3227-6_13

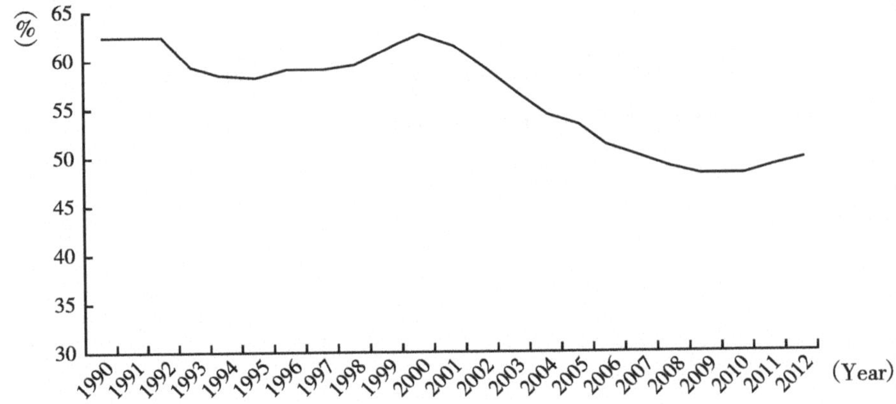

Fig. 1 Proportion of final consumption expenditures in China's national income

in the national income and that of household consumption expenditures in the final consumption expenditure decreased both sharply and significantly in the first decade of the 21st century. Secondly, the share of consumption has stabilized, relatively speaking, and even risen again over the past two years, but anything resembling a significant improvement to the downward trend is still absent. Finally, the share of consumption is likely to decline again under the current pattern of income distribution. In spite of its recent stabilization, ongoing decline remains a possibility in the years to come.

First we must consider the share of final consumption expenditures in the national income from 1990 to 2012. As we can see in Fig. 1, there was a sharp decline in the share of consumption from 2002 to 2012. The proportion was around 62% in 1990, but has declined ever since, reaching its lowest point of around 48% in 2010. In recent years, it has increased slightly, to approximately 50%. In Fig. 1, we can see a significant decline since 2002.

Likewise, the proportion of household consumption expenditures in the national income has also declined over this period, yet more significantly (see Fig. 2). From 2002 to 2010, it dropped by over ten percentage points. The declining share of final consumption expenditures in the national income is mainly attributable to the ever-increasing share of capital, which reflects a process of capital deepening in China; whereas the fall in the proportion of household consumption expenditures in the national income is not only related to the increasing share of capital in the national income, but also to the increasing share of government consumption expenditures.

Figure 3 shows the changes in the proportion of household consumption expenditures within China's final consumption expenditure. In terms of national income accounting, the final consumption expenditure equals the sum of household consumption expenditure and government consumption expenditure. In Fig. 3, we can also see a decline in the proportion of China's household consumption expenditures. It was not a very sharp decline, but it started earlier and developed into a downward trend in the mid-1990s, when household consumption accounted for about 77% of

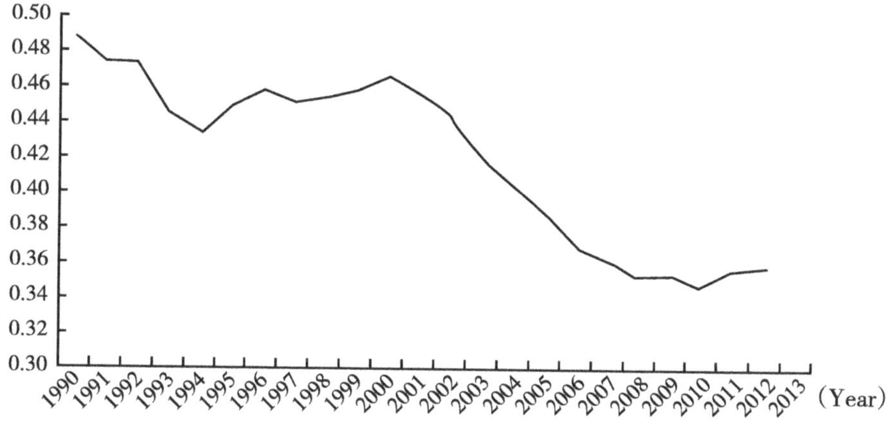

Fig. 2 Proportion of household consumption expenditures in China's national income

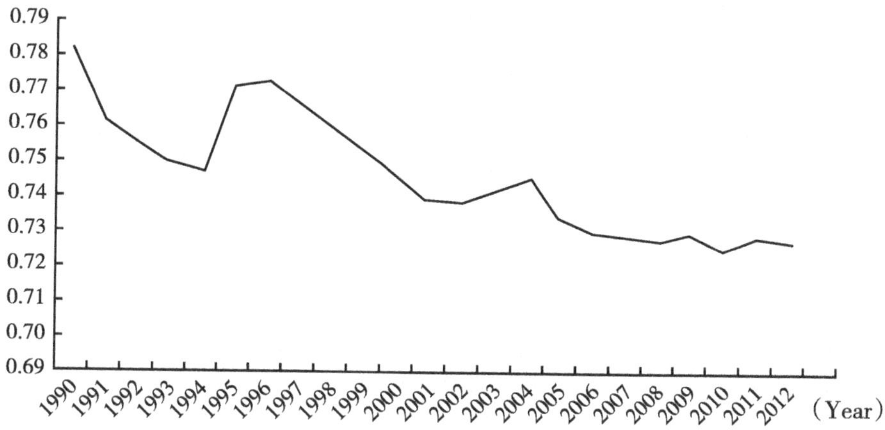

Fig. 3 Proportion of household consumption in final consumption

the final consumption. In the years that followed, this proportion kept decreasing, down by three percentage points to 74% in 2000 and slipping further, to below 73%, in 2010. On the other hand, the decrease in the proportion of household consumption means an increase in that of government consumption in the final consumption.

Next, let's look at the proportions of urban and rural household consumption expenditures in the final consumption expenditure. We divide the final consumption into three parts: urban household consumption, rural household consumption, and government consumption. In the early 1990s, urban and rural household consumption expenditures were almost equivalent in China. Although the population was far larger in the rural areas than in the cities at that time, the shares of urban and rural household consumption expenditures were basically identical as a result of the rural-urban income gap, with each accounting for around 40% of the final consumption

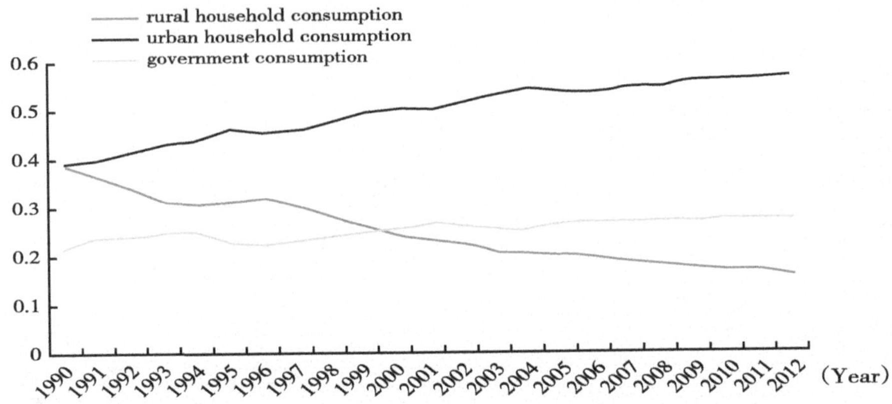

Fig. 4 Ratios of urban and rural household consumption and government consumption to final consumption

expenditure. Nonetheless, they shortly went through a dramatic process of differentiation. By 2012, the proportion of rural household consumption expenditures had dropped to below 20%, while the urban proportion had exceeded 50% and was heading toward 60%, with the latter approximately three times higher than the former or roughly equivalent to the rural-urban income gap at that time. Meanwhile, there has been a steady increase in the proportion of government consumption, which has been quite significant in certain years (see Fig. 4).

2 Correlation Between the Income Gap and Changes in the Shares of Consumption

In this section, we will discuss the correlation between the income gap and changes in the shares of consumption using empirical analysis results. We will look into it from four perspectives: (1) the urban-rural income gap and changes in the propensity to consume—according to empirical analysis, a large income gap between urban and rural residents results in a significant difference in their propensity to consume; (2) the relationship between the income gap of urban residents and their propensity to consume; (3) the relationship between the income gap of rural residents and their propensity to consume; and (4) the income level and income gap of migrant workers and their propensity to consume.

The first is the urban-rural income gap and corresponding changes in the propensity to consume. Figure 5 is based on statistics of NBS household surveys, showing the changes in the propensity to consume of China's urban and rural residents from 1990 to 2012. Interestingly, the average propensity to consume was almost the same among urban and rural residents in 1990. Even given the income gap in between, the propensity to consume was high, around 85% in both urban and rural areas.

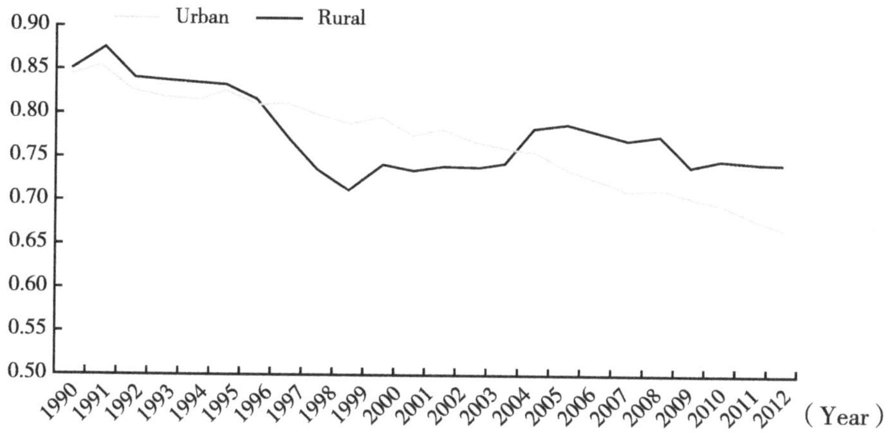

Fig. 5 Propensity to consume of China's urban and rural residents

From 1990 on, however, there has been a steady decrease in the average propensity to consume of urban residents. This certainly results from the average increase in income—as their income increases, their propensity to consume decreases. In contrast, greater changes have taken place in the propensity to consume of rural residents, marked by a significant decline in the late 1990s. This was, to a large extent, due to the social and economic changes in rural areas in addition to concurrent social and tax policies. In particular, the constant increase in taxes and levies and the marketization of public services affected rural residents' consumption. Under such circumstances, there was a sharp decline in the average propensity to consume of rural residents in the late 1990s. Moreover, their level of consumption was much lower than that of urban residents in the same time period, because the per capita income of rural residents was far lower than that of urban residents. That is to say, the propensity to consume is not only subject to income level, but also affected by a good many other factors, such as social security coverage and the prices of public services.

It was not until 2004 that rural residents' propensity to consume started to rise significantly, a fact that was closely related to the implementation in the same year of a series of policies benefitting farmer interests. For example, the abolition of the agricultural tax, the establishment of the rural subsistence allowance system alongside a preliminary rural social security system, and the introduction of a variety of agricultural subsidies have not only raised farmers' incomes, but also had the effect of encouraging consumption and increasing the average propensity to consume of rural residents. More interestingly, while the urban propensity to consume has continued its steady decline, since 2000 there has been no such change in the rural propensity to consume. In other words, the income of rural residents has been on the rise, but their propensity to consume has remained quite stable. As a result, rural residents' propensity to consume exceeded that of urban residents in this period, with the increase in income playing a major role.

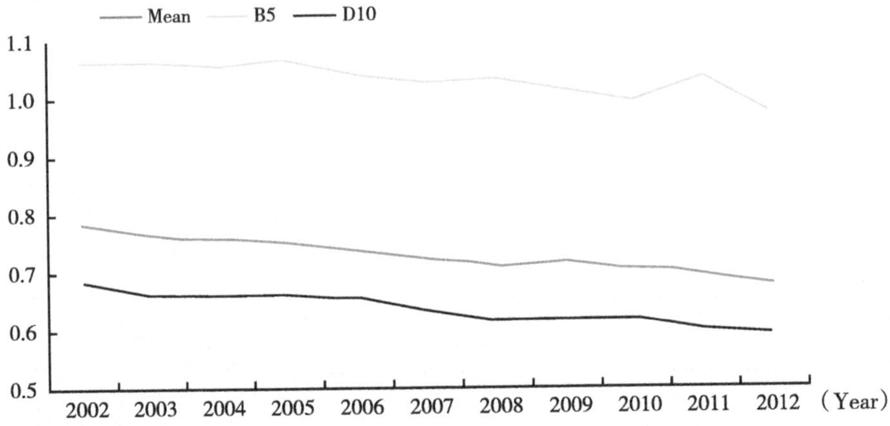

Fig. 6 Propensity to consume of urban income groups

Based upon the above analysis, it would be even more instructive to look at the propensity to consume of different income groups among urban and rural residents. While the increase in income has had an effect on the propensity to consume of both the higher- and lower-income groups—that is, the marginal propensity to consume of both groups has decreased with the increase in their income—there are distinct differences between them in their average propensity to consume. Figure 6 shows the average propensity to consume (Mean) of urban residents, and those of the bottom 5% (B5) and top 10% (D10) of urban income earners. As we can see, the average propensity to consume of the bottom 5% of urban residents was greater than one in most years, indicating that the majority of them were unable to make ends meet. In contrast, the figure of the top 10% of income earners was not only much lower than that of low-income residents, but also lower than that of all urban residents. Moreover, it had declined over the course of the decade, down from 70% in 2002 to 60% in 2012 (see Fig. 6).

In terms of the variation among different income groups in the marginal propensity to consume, there were both similarities and differences between rural and urban residents. As we can see in Fig. 7, the propensity to consume of the higher- or lower-income group did not change significantly with a corresponding increase in their income. For example, the average propensity to consume of the bottom 20% of rural income earners (Q1) was greater than one throughout this period. This is not hard to understand, as many low-income farmers would borrow to get by, spending more than they earned. Meanwhile, there was almost no change in the figure of the top 20% of rural income earners (Q5), which had stabilized at around 60% since 2002. This has, to some extent, provided a sound basis for our policy-making—any further increase of farmers' income will not significantly pull down the average propensity to consume, but will improve the overall consumption capacity.

Now let's look at the propensity to consume of migrant workers. While migrant workers are influenced by urban ways of life, they are also not completely free from

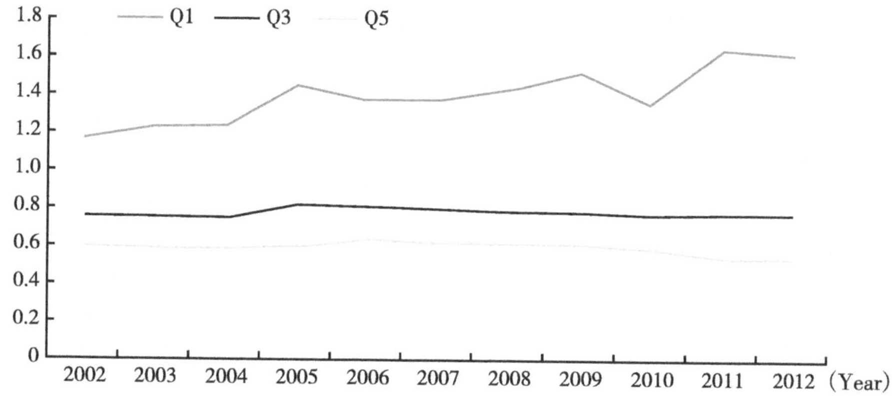

Fig. 7 Propensity to consume of rural income groups

the rural ways of consumption. In terms of the relationship between income and the propensity to consume, they are similar to urban residents, with distinct differences between income groups in the average propensity to consume, which is lower in the higher-income group and higher in the lower-income group (see Fig. 8).

From a policymaker's point of view, we must pay more attention to the consumption of migrant workers, because they are a very large group of people whose expenditure-income ratio is not only lower than that of urban residents, but also far below that of rural residents. According to our estimates, their average propensity to consume is no more than 50%, whereas that of urban residents is 68% and that of rural residents is 78%. Obviously, there is a wide gap between migrant workers and urban and rural residents in the propensity to consume. Therefore, we must pay

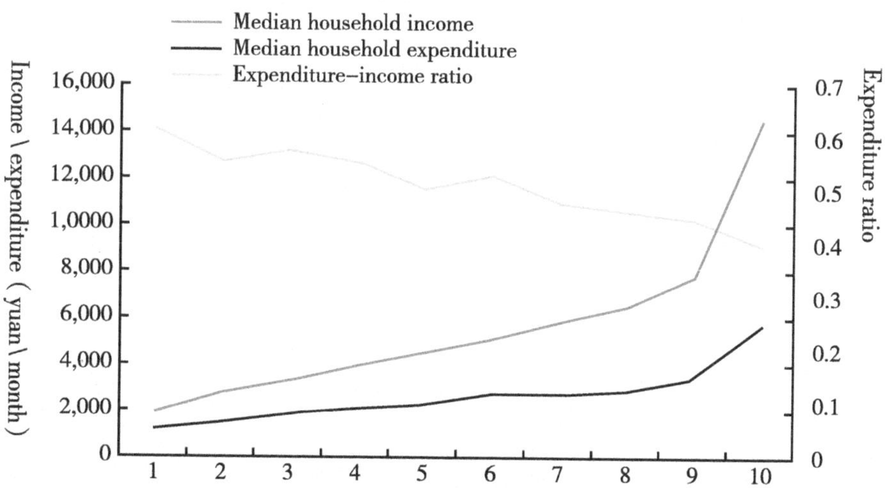

Fig. 8 Propensity to consume of migrant workers (2013)

special attention to this group in policymaking, and consider how to increase their capacity and propensity to consume as a major policy issue.

To this end, we must dig into the relatively low propensity to consume of migrant workers. If migrant workers are underpaid, it will not only affect their consumption, but also influence a series of related issues, such as their housing, social security, and access to public services, all of which have a significant effect on their propensity to consume. On the other hand, migrant workers' propensity to consume is also subject to their expectations for the future, i.e., whether they would continue to live in cities or return to the countryside in the future. According to our statistical description in this regard, migrant workers with stable housing in a city rate higher in their propensity to consume. As Fig. 9 shows, migrant workers in possession of a purchased or owner-built property have a higher propensity to consume than those who live in rental housing or staff quarters.

Furthermore, the propensity to consume of migrant workers is significantly associated with their long-term settlement intentions in their current places of residence. When asked "Are you willing to be a long-term resident in this place?" in a questionnaire, 57% of the surveyed migrant workers said yes, 14% said no, and the rest remained uncertain. Yet there is an obvious difference in the propensity to consume between those who said yes and those who said no.

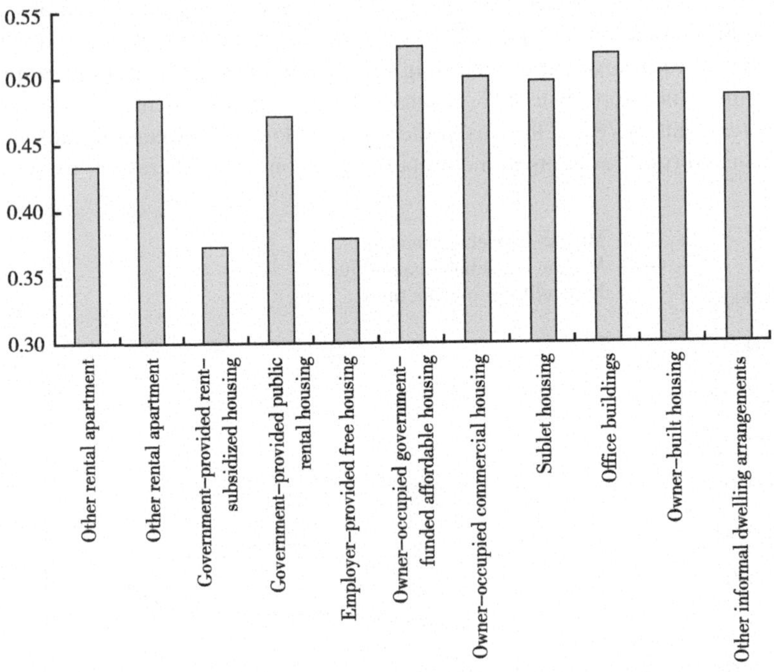

Fig. 9 Housing types and propensity to consume of migrant workers (2013)

Admittedly, the above is but a simple correlation analysis, without the support of complex modeling to describe the causal relationships. Nonetheless, based on our common sense, if migrant workers have stable housing in cities, they would certainly be freed from the so-called "precautionary" ways of consumption and have the confidence to spend more.

3 China's Income and Wealth Gaps: A Predictive Point of View

Now that we have established that income distribution influences consumer behavior and the share of consumption in the national income, what will become of China's income gap?

Figure 10 shows the long-term trends of China's income gap that we have drawn by piecing together its Gini coefficients across different years as estimated by the World Bank, China National Bureau of Statistics, and our income distribution research group. As we see it, China has entered a critical period for its income gap, as a significant change is taking place—the ever-rising Gini coefficient has plateaued, and even started to decline. Of course, some people would argue that our Gini coefficient has been underestimated. If there is any underestimation, I think, it is probably not as great as we imagine—and either way, the trend is quite obvious.

Besides, judging by the policies implemented in recent years, China's income gap is likely to linger on in the short run. Nevertheless, when full allowance is given to underestimation, we must admit that China's income gap is still at a very high level, and China must therefore be regarded as a country with a high level of income inequality. That being the case, it is natural for us to be concerned about further changes in our income gap. With our economic growth slowing down, will

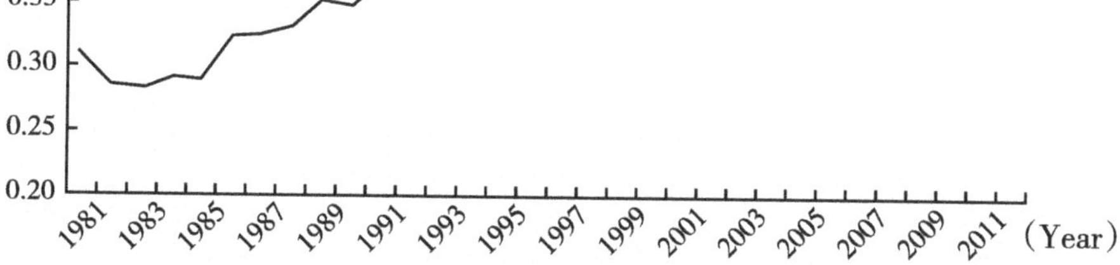

Fig. 10 Long-term trend of China's gini coefficient

our income gap narrow or, conversely, widen further? This is a question we have to consider.

In addition to the trend of the overall income gap, the urban-rural income gap is another public concern. As previously mentioned, the urban-rural income gap has some effect on the propensity to consume of both urban and rural residents. According to NBS statistics, China's urban-rural income gap has narrowed since 2009, quite modestly, but remains high at present.

Even worse, our wealth gap has widened much more than our income gap over the same period. In my recent paper, co-authored with Wan Haiyuan and Xie Yu, we estimated the changes in China's wealth gap from 2002 to 2010. Our estimate shows that China's wealth gap widened significantly over this period, with the rural wealth gap up from 0.45 to 0.69, the urban wealth gap from 0.40 to 0.67, and the overall wealth gap from 0.54 to 0.73, as measured by the Gini coefficient.

Does the wealth gap have a positive or negative effect on the propensity to consume? I am not quite certain about that. As we analyzed earlier, an increase in income tends to decrease the marginal propensity to consume, while a widening income gap lowers the average propensity to consume of a community. Then what about the growth of wealth and the widening of the wealth gap? This absolutely depends on the type of wealth gap in question. In China, for example, real estate is the major form of wealth. So what effect will the rise in real estate prices have on the propensity to consume? In my view, it has both direct and indirect impacts. By direct impacts, we refer to the sharp decline in urban residents' propensity to consume since 2000, which is largely due to the influences of the real estate market, including the direct influence of real estate prices. In China's national accounting, residents' expenses on housing purchase are not accounted for in terms of consumption, but rather in the accumulation of wealth. In other words, their spending on the purchase of a house is not regarded as a consumptive expenditure, but a type of wealth transformation—from a savings deposit into real estate. From this point of view, it is a form of capital accumulation. Yet the increase in the expenses of a housing purchase will put the squeeze on other expenditures. For example, when a resident spends more on a housing purchase, he or she will have to reduce his or her consumption expenditures correspondingly. This is a direct impact of real estate prices.

On the other hand, there are also indirect impacts of real estate prices, mainly on those given to housing purchases—those who have a plan to buy a house or who are inclined to save for it. For such residents, it is only natural to reduce their consumption expenditures and save more money to realize that dream as soon as possible. It is in this light that we attribute the widening of the wealth gap to the rise in real estate prices, which, in turn, is likely to reduce the propensity to consume. Yet we still need further empirical studies on the real conditions in China.

Wealth is a stock-oriented concept, while consumption and capital are flow-oriented in terms of national income accounting. Over the next few years, we may be faced with the further slowdown of our economic growth. The question is: will such a slowdown narrow or widen China's income gap? Based on existing literatures, we have not yet found a significant correlation between the growth rate and the income gap, either in China or in other countries.

When we say that economic growth affects the income gap, it is the model of growth that matters, rather than the growth rate itself. That is, any variation in the income gap rests with the model of growth, or, more exactly, with whether it is inclusive or non-inclusive growth. Under the current growth model, we believe, the acceleration of China's economic growth will narrow its income gap. Why? A glance at the changes in both its growth rate and income gap over the past five years tells us why. The past five years was probably one of the fastest periods of economic growth in Chinese history, yet during these years the income gap did not widen further. Instead, it narrowed over this period. Of course, we must not deny the effects of policy and other factors on its making. But there is also no denying that high-speed economic growth does improve the pay level in the lower-end labor market.

With substantial increases in government investments, massive funds are constantly poured into infrastructure construction. The result is a huge demand for less-skilled and lower-educated workers, which brings about a rise in the wages of migrant workers and improves the pay level in the lower-end labor market. To a certain degree, this narrows the income gap. There are therefore two reasons why high-speed economic growth narrows the income gap in China. On the one hand, under the current circumstances, any substantial growth in investments increases the number of various construction projects, and thus increases both employment and wages. This is what we call the effect of economic growth on employment. On the other hand, economic growth also has an effect on fiscal expenditures. It goes something like this: at times of high-speed economic growth, government revenue usually grows faster than the economy, and therefore the government has the capacity to increase expenditures on people's livelihood, e.g., improving social security.

When jointly brought into play, these effects will be fairly conducive to narrowing the income gap. In the coming years, if our economic growth slows down further, we must speed up the modal transformation of our economic growth and shift to the projected model—from extensive to intensive, from labor-intensive to capital-intensive, and from emulation-based to innovation-driven development. To some degree, such a broad-ranging transformation may not be favorable to the lower-end laborers, as it tends to slow down their wage growth. In that case, I predict that the income gap is likely to widen again.

4 Suggestions for Adjusting Income Distribution to Boost Consumption

Under such circumstances, how should we adjust income distribution in order to boost consumption? In the years to come, the share of consumption in China's national income may decline further. And as we know, income distribution is closely related to the proportion of consumption. Therefore, adjusting income distribution in order to boost consumption must be counted as an important issue in our policy considerations for the next period.

Above all, we must narrow the urban-rural income gap by speeding up the income growth of farmers so as to increase the overall average consumption ratio. As mentioned previously, farmers' average propensity to consume is much higher than that of urban residents and is quite stable across different income groups. Moreover, it has not declined significantly with the increase in farmers' income in recent years. In this sense, if farmers' incomes grow faster than those of urban residents, it will play a significant role in mitigating the declining share of consumption in the national income.

Next, we must narrow the intra-urban and intra-rural income gaps, particularly the former, which will contribute to raising the share of consumption. As the propensity to consume differs significantly across different urban income groups, it will boost consumption if we increase the income of the lower-income groups.

Finally, we must bring out the potential for consumption in migrant workers by integrating them into urban life and entitling them to the same welfare and benefits enjoyed by urban residents, as a breakthrough point aimed at boosting consumption. That is, we must make greater efforts to improve migrant workers' income, social security, housing, and the education of their children. In my estimates, the average wage of migrant workers is around RMB 30,000 per year, and their average propensity to consume is approximately 20% points lower than that of urban residents. Should their average propensity to consume reach the level of urban residents, it would translate into an increase of one to two percentage points in the overall share of consumption. On the other hand, as a medium-to-low income group in cities, we would expect migrant workers to be higher than urban residents in terms of the average propensity to consume. Therefore, the localization of migrant workers is of profound significance for increasing the overall share of consumption of the national income.

Chapter 14
Income Distribution and Economic Transformation

Li Gan

1 An Introduction to the China Household Finance Survey

The China Household Finance Survey (CHFS) is a nationwide survey, conducted in 1,048 communities across the 262 districts/counties of 29 provincial divisions. It is a province-specific assessment using representative samples. In 2013, we collected the information of 28,141 households consisting of 97,916 individuals.

In 2014, we launched the quarterly follow-up Computer-Assisted Telephone Interviewing (CATI). So far we have publicized part of our studies on the data of the first three quarters, and will soon complete our fourth-quarter report.

2 The Status Quo of Income Distribution in China

As Table 1 shows, the Gini coefficient of Chinese household income is fairly high and has been relatively stable in recent years.

The NBS statistics are 0.481, 0.474, and 0.473, respectively, for the three years from 2010 to 2012. How come our figures are higher than those released by the

Table 1 The Gini coefficient of Chinese household income

	National	Urban	Rural
2010 (CHFS 2011)	0.61	0.58	0.61
2012 (CHFS 2013 follow-up)	0.60	0.58	0.58
2012 (CHFS 2013 sampling expansion)	0.61	0.59	0.59

L. Gan (✉)
Research Institute of Economics and Management, Southwestern (China) University of Finance and Economics, Chengdu, China
e-mail: ganl@swufe.edu.cn

F. Cai (ed.), *China's Economic New Normal*, Research Series on the Chinese Dream and China's Development Path, https://doi.org/10.1007/978-981-15-3227-6_14

NBS? There are two reasons for this. On the one hand, household income derived from industry, business, and property is much higher in our sample than in the NBS statistics. On the other hand, the income of high-income groups is much higher in our statistics than in theirs. For example, the per capita net income for operational purposes and per capita property income in our statistics are, respectively, 2.3 and 2.5 times the size of the figures released by the NBS. Yet this is only true of urban statistics. When it comes to rural statistics, the inverse is true. Meanwhile, household wage income is slightly lower in our figures than in the NBS statistics. Therefore, we can conclude that the income gap mainly derives from the distribution of property income and income for operational purposes. According to our estimates, micro, small, and individual businesses account for 23% of the Chinese economy, and income for operational purposes accounts for 29.7% of the Gini coefficient, both of which are much higher than the NBS statistics (Table 2).

As we can see in Tables 3 and 4, the CHFS figures are much higher than the NBS statistics in terms of the per capita disposable income of the top 10% of urban households and the top 20% of rural households.

According to the CHFS statistics in Table 5, if the per capita income of an urban household exceeds RMB 228,600, they are part of China's richest 1% of urban residents. The NBS has not released this figure, but we have managed to get it by fitting the available data. The fitted data shows that if the per capita income of an urban household exceeds RMB 86,819, they are part of China's richest 1% of

Table 2 Property income and the income for operational purposes of urban residents (2012)

	CHFS (RMB)	NBS (RMB)	CHFS/NBS	Contribution to Gini coefficient (%)
Per capita wage income	14,473	17,336	0.8	45.8
Per capita net income for operational purposes	5,929	2,548	2.3	29.7
Per capita property income	1,746	707	2.5	9.3
Per capita transfer income	6,566	6,368	1.0	15.2

Table 3 Per capita disposable income of urban households (2012, by income group)

Income group	CHFS (RMB)	NBS (RMB)	CHFS/NBS
Lowest 20%	3,457	10,352	0.3
20–40%	10,781	16,761	0.6
40–60%	17,307	22,419	0.8
60–80%	27,742	29,814	0.9
80–90%	43,399	39,605	1.1
Top 10%	128,910	63,824	2.0

Table 4 Per capita disposable income of rural households (2012, by income group)

Income group	CHFS (RMB)	NBS (RMB)	CHFS/NBS
Lowest 20%	988	2,316	0.4
20–40%	3,270	4,808	0.7
40–60%	6,483	7,041	0.9
60–80%	10,589	10,142	1.0
Top 20%	28,716	19,009	1.5

Table 5 Quantiles of urban-rural per capita income (2012)

Income group	Urban		Rural	
	CHFS (RMB)	NBS (RMB)	CHFS (RMB)	NBS (RMB)
Lowest 25%	8,055	14,824	2,462	4,330
50%	17,400	21,948	6,240	6,868
75%	32,660	32,332	12,330	10,830
90%	57,125	46,548	20,900	16,308
95%	86,895	57,054	29,018	21,037
99%	228,600	86,819	63,125	35,773

urban residents. Our findings based on rural statistics are similar. Why is there such a difference between the CHFS and NBS statistics? The difference lies in income from industry, business, and property, and the income of high-income groups.

The current income distribution in China is a natural result of effective, market-based resource allocation.

First of all, we find the Gini coefficient higher in the developed eastern region (0.60) than in the central (0.56) and the western (0.54) regions.

Secondly, civil servants in monopoly industries are not one of the main causes of the income distribution gap, as their contribution to the Gini coefficient is limited. Excluding households involved in monopoly industries, the Gini coefficient is 0.57; excluding public servant households, it is 0.58.

Thirdly, the Gini coefficients are very low (around 0.3) in OECD countries, but in the primary distribution stage they are generally around 0.5, e.g., 0.49 in the US, 0.53 in Italy, and 0.50 in Germany (see Fig. 1). Considering the social differences in China, I believe we would all agree that the Gini coefficient is much higher in China than it is in OECD countries—and we all know that our secondary distribution has little effect on the income gap. Therefore, I suspect it is almost impossible for China's Gini coefficient to be lower than 0.5.

Furthermore, by reference to a fair number of literatures, we find that the so-called international warning line of 0.40 or 0.60 is without academic support. Moreover, it is inequality of opportunity—rather than of income—that affects social stability, a consensus we also find in mainstream journals.

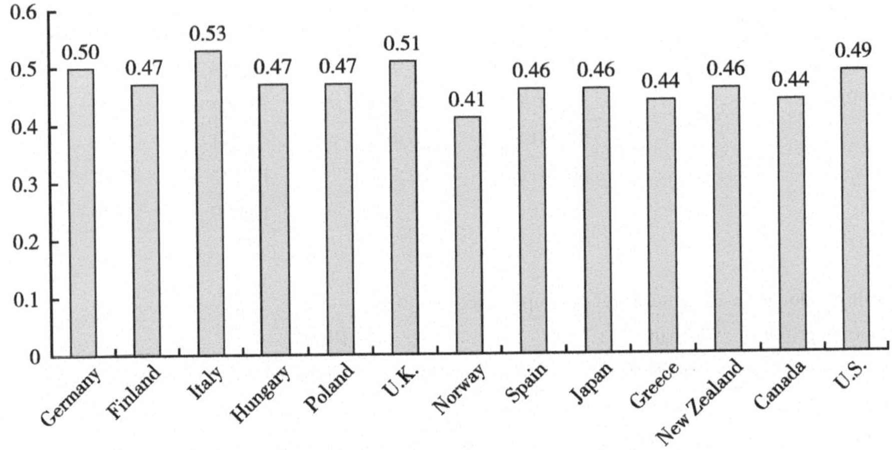

Fig. 1 The Gini coefficients of major OECD countries

3 Uneven Income Distribution: The Fundamental Reason for Sluggish Consumption

As we can see in Table 6, the household savings rate was very high in China over the past years. According to our statistics, the national savings rate increased from 29.2% in 2010 to 31.8% in 2012. According to the NBS, it rose from 28.7 to 30.6% over the same period of time.

As Table 7 shows, the higher-income groups are the major source of household savings in China. For example, the top 5% of households account for 49.1% of all aggregate household savings, with a savings rate of 69.9%. Likewise, the savings

Table 6 Household savings rates in China

		2010			2012		
		Urban	Rural	National	Urban	Rural	National
CHFS	Per capita income (RMB)	24,687	9,373	16,990	28,714	10,473	20,659
	Per capita consumption expenditure (RMB)	16,878	7,236	12,031	19,167	7,693	14,100
	Savings rate (%)	31.6	22.8	29.2	33.3	26.5	31.8
NBS	Per capita income (RMB)	19,109	5,919	12,472	24,565	7,917	16,669
	Per capita consumption expenditure (RMB)	13,472	4,382	8,898	16,674	5,908	11,568
	Savings rate (%)	29.5	26.0	28.7	32.1	25.4	30.6

Table 7 Higher-income groups as the major source of household savings

	Savings rate (%)	Proportion in aggregate savings (%)	Proportion of financial assets (%)
Highest 20%	57.2	76.6	60.5
Highest 10%	64.3	61.9	44.8
Top 5%	69.9	49.1	32.8

rates of the highest 10% and 20% of households have reached 64.3% and 57.2%, respectively.

The highest 20% of households account for three quarters of China's aggregate savings. Consequently, the aggregate household savings rate is very high, with the major driving force being the higher-income groups. Not all families are saving, however. In 2012, only 60.6% of Chinese households spent less than they earned. That means many families still could not make both ends meet (see Table 8).

Which types of households are living beyond their means, then? Our study suggests that it is primarily low-income households with fewer assets. Underconsumption against a high savings rate: this is characteristic of China. The main reason is that savings are concentrated among the rich, while the poor spend more than they earn.

Then what supports the consumption of households with a negative savings rate? Table 9 shows the consumption-related liabilities of Chinese households. As we can see, both the debt ratio and debt-to-income ratio of households with a positive

Table 8 Proportion of Chinese households with savings (annual income > annual consumption expenditures)

Year	2012
Urban (%)	64.1
Rural (%)	55.6
National (%)	60.6

Table 9 Consumption-related liabilities of Chinese households

	Urban			Rural		
	Debt ratio (%)	Amount of debt (RMB)	Debt-income ratio (%)	Debt ratio (%)	Amount of debt (RMB)	Debt-income ratio (%)
Households with a positive savings rate	15.3	8,087	5.7	13.4	5.080	7.6
Households with a negative savings rate	17.5	4,788	14.6	19.8	4,977	35.9

savings rate are lower than those with a negative savings rate. It follows that the latter depend on incurring debts for their consumption expenditures. Where do they borrow from, then? According to our study, private lending is the major source of funding, especially for the poor, whereas the rich mainly resort to formal loans.

Over the course of many years, our policies aimed at boosting consumption have produced very little effect. The fundamental reason is that, on the one hand, under liquidity constraints, the poor have little money to consume, and on the other hand, the rich have already been spending as necessary. Therefore, it does not make sense to merely stimulate consumption. Based on that, we are convinced that the country's insufficient domestic demand is rooted in the uneven distribution of income and that improvement in income distribution would therefore facilitate economic transformation. Meanwhile, it is also our view that income distribution reform is by far the best policy to boost China's economic growth and transformation.

4 Transfer Payments and Economic Transformation

There are many ways to reduce income inequality. A frequently used method by governments is to raise the minimum wage. Nonetheless, according to one of our studies, any increase in the minimum wage has a very limited effect in terms of narrowing the income gap. On the contrary, excessive increases in minimum wages can have an adverse effect on lower-income groups. By our estimates, a 10% increase in the minimum wage translates into a 0.4% rise in per capita wage in enterprises but a 0.6% decrease in the number of enterprise employees. As a matter of fact, the minimum wage makes little difference to the income gap. When it increases by 50%, the Gini coefficient will be 0.59; when it increases by 100%, the Gini coefficient will be 0.58.

Likewise, the current individual income taxation also has little effect on income distribution, as we see little change in the Gini coefficient before and after taxes. As another of our studies shows, the size of real taxpayers is far smaller than the taxable population, and the amount of tax paid is also much smaller than that of tax payable. For what it's worth, our statistics outlining tax paid are very close to those released by the NBS.

By contrast, many OECD countries have effectively narrowed their income gaps through transfer payments. Figure 2 is an important chart for an international comparison of the Gini coefficient, where the gray bars stand for the current Gini coefficients of OECD countries after transfers, and the white bars for the figures after the primary distribution but before transfers. By our calculation, taxes and transfer payments have contributed 25% and 75%, respectively, to lowering the Gini coefficients for OECD countries. It is precisely because of transfer payments that the Gini coefficients for developed countries have declined from around 0.5 to around 0.3.

Figure 3 is the case of Brazil. The Gini coefficient in Brazil was 0.61 around the year 1990, slightly lower than its peak of 0.63. This figure dropped to 0.55,

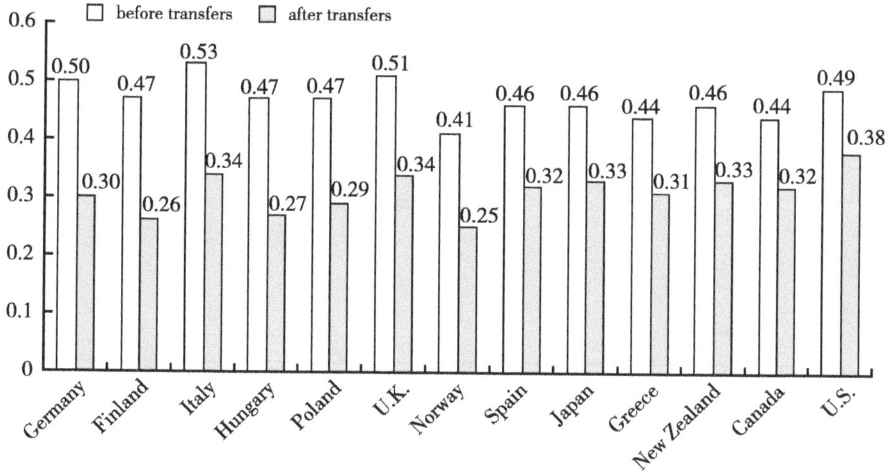

Fig. 2 The Gini coefficients of major developed countries

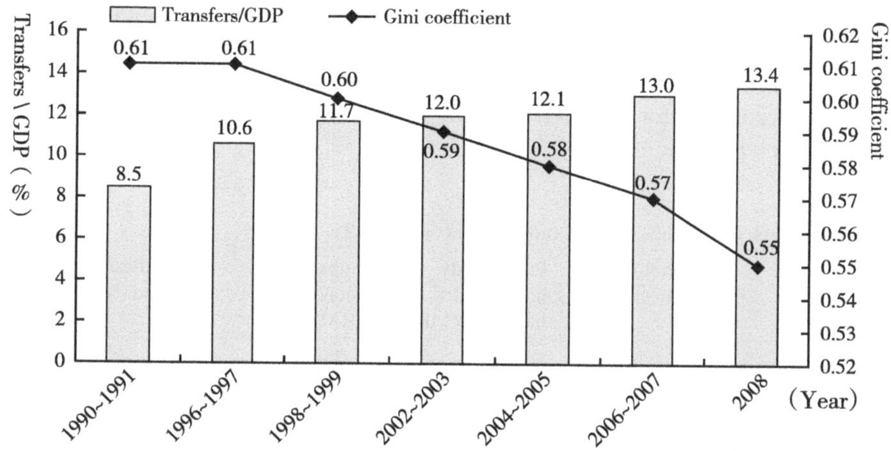

Fig. 3 Brazil's Gini coefficient lowered through increased transfer payments

however, when the proportion of transfers in Brazil's GDP increased from 8.5 to 13.4%. Obviously, it was transfer payments that had precipitated such a decline.

As we can see in Fig. 4, the proportion of social security expenditures—an important form of transferred payments—in GDP has a significant effect on the consumption rate. The larger this proportion, the higher the consumption rate. It is 12.3% in China, which means our social security expenditures are at a very low level, compared with the 36.6% seen in the US. In the US, the per capita income of the poorest 20% of households is USD 7,500 per year before transfers, but it soars to USD 30,000 after transfers.

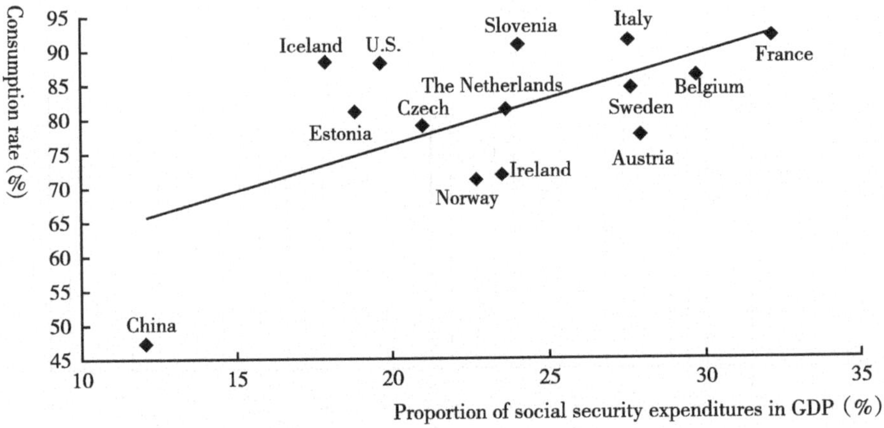

Fig. 4 Proportion of social security expenditures in GDP and the consumption rate

Another form of transferred payments is government subsidies. Tables 10, 11, 12 and 13 are a summary of government subsidies for Chinese households in 2012. Nationally, 18.4% of households had received government subsidies in 2012, which was not considered a low number. Yet for this subset of households, government subsidies accounted for only 3.6% of the household income overall, which was obviously too low.

Table 10 Government subsidies in household income (2012)

	Households subsidized (%)	Pre-subsidy household income (RMB)	Subsidies received (RMB)	Subsidies/household income (%)
National	18.4	50,072	1,750	3.6
Urban	13.7	71,889	2,195	3.1
Rural	24.6	33,831	1,419	4.4

Table 11 Non-productive government subsidies in household income (2012, by income group)

Pre-subsidy income group	Households subsidized (%)	Pre-subsidy household income (RMB)	Government subsidies received (RMB)	Subsidies/household income (%)
Lowest 20%	29.5	3,279	1,568	47.8
20–40%	20.8	16,886	1,682	10.0
40–60%	16.6	36,568	1,814	5.0
60–80%	13.5	63,031	1,456	2.3
Highest 20%	11.4	222,247	2,595	1.2

Table 12 Non-productive government subsidies in urban household income (2012, by income group)

Pre-subsidy income group	Households subsidized (%)	Pre-subsidy household income (RMB)	Government subsidies received (RMB)	Subsidies/household income (%)
Lowest 20%	22.7	5,865	2,348	40.0
20–40%	14.2	27,450	2,204	8.0
40–60%	12.2	49,814	1,486	3.0
60–80%	10.0	80,622	1,914	2.4
Highest 20%	9.6	297,247	3,016	1.0

Table 13 Non-productive government subsidies in rural household income (2012, by income group)

Pre-subsidy income group	Households subsidized (%)	Pre-subsidy household income (RMB)	Government subsidies received (RMB)	Subsidies/household income (%)
Lowest 20%	31.1	2,060	1,147	55.7
20–40%	29.7	8,512	1,457	17.1
40–60%	22.9	21,920	1,281	5.8
60–80%	20.7	41,863	1,624	3.9
Highest 20%	18.6	123,920	1,753	1.4

For lower-income groups, government subsidies are an important aspect of their income and are typically used for consumption, rather than saved up. As our statistics reveal, 91.6% of the lowest 20% of households spent the money after they received their government subsidies. Nationally, however, only 54% of households receiving subsidies spent the money. In other words, 46% had saved those government subsidies they received. Separately speaking, 50% of urban households and 58.6% of urban households spent the government subsidies they received. Indeed, this is a low rate of conversion from subsidies to consumption. The reason lies in the fact that the government not only subsidizes the lower-income groups, but also the higher-income groups. As we can see in Table 11, 11.4% of the highest 20% of households still received subsidies. Nonetheless, as previously mentioned, the higher-income groups have already been spending as necessary. As a result, they would naturally treat these government subsidies as extra money and save them up.

If we are to increase transfer payments, where would this money come from? We have confidence in the government's fiscal capacity for large-scale transfer payments. In 2012, China's national fiscal revenue was over RMB 11.7 trillion, up by RMB 1.35 trillion since 2011 (and by RMB 1.62 trillion annually from 2010 to 2012). The total profit of China's state-owned enterprises was RMB 1.98 trillion in 2010 and, in 2011, exceeded RMB 2 trillion. Currently, China's deficit is only 1.6% of its GDP and 8% of its tax revenue. Therefore, we recommend increasing the deficit for redistribution. If we increase our deficit by 2% of our GDP, and pool it together with 70% of the annual profit of the country's state-owned enterprises and 50% of our annual fiscal revenue, it will add up to RMB 3.8 trillion, accounting for 36% of China's annual fiscal expenditure. If we spend this sum of money on redistribution, we are convinced that the 3.8 trillion in transfer payments will significantly narrow the income gap.

Then the question becomes, how shall we make these payments? While few studies have been conducted in this respect in China, across the world there are already fairly mature systems of transfer payments fully integrated with incentive mechanisms. For instance, school lunch programs provide free lunch meals to school-age children on the condition that they go to school. Such conditional cash transfer programs are being implemented in almost all major developing countries to encourage schooling and investment in education and healthcare. Yet little of this sort has been done in China so far. Besides conditional cash transfers, there are very few government transfer programs. If there are experimental programs, they are invariably carried out by a very few scholars in a very few places. As far as we know, there is a cash-transfer program in Liangshan Prefecture of Sichuan Province, which encourages hospitalized childbirth by pregnant women of the Yi ethnic minority. It reduces health risks and is therefore not only good for women, but also for the whole country.

Besides, many developed countries have enacted an earned income tax credit (EITC). Likewise, China has also implemented a policy characterized as the "replacement of subsidies with rewards." Moreover, developed countries have increased their income tax rates. In the US, for example, the federal income tax rate can be as high as (or even more than) 30% of taxable income; yet low-income groups not only enjoy exemptions, but also receive proportional subsidies, and are thus better motivated to work hard. Such practices have proven highly effective in many developed countries. For the same purpose, we in the China Household Finance Survey and Research Center are conducting our own experiments in income distribution reforms.

In Leshan of Sichuan Province, for example, we have launched a Household Rejuvenation Program, subsidizing low-income families with our research funding in the hopes that it will somehow improve their lives. For a household with a per capita income of less than RMB 1,200 per month, as long as their labor-based income increases, we will provide a subsidy, which is a per capita subsidy multiplied by the number of household members. In July 2014, the initial diagnostic survey was completed, and at present the project is well under way, with 28 households in the observation group and 32 in the control group. We have benchmarked 808 households and issued new bank cards for them. In January 2015, we will provide eligible households with subsidies for the first time. The program has won strong support from both the local government and the people. We have made up our mind to start small, but will raise more funds and expand the project, from Leshan to other localities, in a year or so when we have accumulated enough experience. We will develop specific procedures and rules for the program, which is projected to last for five years, and will soon put forward our proposals on income distribution reforms to the state.

Table 14 Government expenditures per student of China and OECD countries (in USD)

Economy (year)	Elementary school	Junior high school	Senior high school	Higher education
Japan (2009)	7,729	8,985	9,527	15,957
South Korea (2009)	6,658	7,536	11,300	9,513
US (2009)	11,109	12,247	12,873	29,201
OECD average (2009)	7,719	8,854	9,755	13,728
China (2011)	801	1,055	968	1,547

In the short run, however, China's income distribution reform will have to count on a substantial increase in the proportion of transferred payments—not by three or five percentage points, but ten and even 20% points.

Finally, there is the matter of educational expenditures. China has spent too little per student. Its per capita income is about 1/6 that of OECD countries, but its government spending per student is only 1/10, or even less, of theirs (see Table 14). China's fiscal investment in education is far too small.

5 Conclusions

China has a very high degree of income inequality at present. Yet a high Gini coefficient is not terrible in and of itself—it is a common phenomenon during high-speed economic development as well as a natural result of effective, market-based resource allocation. The so-called warning line of the Gini coefficient is without any academic support. Nonetheless, uneven income distribution is indeed the fundamental reason for sluggish consumption in China. Income distribution reform is the best policy for boosting China's economic growth and transformation. In the short term, the Chinese government has a large enough fiscal capacity to increase transfer payments and narrow the income gap. As a matter of fact, there are successful policies of transfer payments around the world that are already integrated with incentive mechanisms. In the long run, it is advisable for China to increase its education input and simultaneously reduce its inequality of opportunity so as to narrow its extant income gap.

Chapter 15
The Potential Growth Rate of the Chinese Economy

Fang Cai and Yang Lu

The reason why we have chosen to predict the potential growth rate, rather than the real growth rate, is that a country's long-term economic growth primarily depends on its growth potential, which is determined by such factors as capital, the labor force, human capital, and total factor productivity. A potential growth rate is the highest possible level of economic growth when such input or supply-side factors are brought into full play. To some degree, it is a probabilistic concept. Therefore, it is possible for the real growth rate to be either higher or lower than the potential growth rate. When the real growth rate is higher than the potential growth rate, the result is overcapacity or inflation; when it is lower than the potential growth rate, unemployment or deflation occurs. In the long run, the real growth rate fluctuates along with and tends to approximate the potential growth rate.

In this chapter, we will analyze three possibilities for China's potential growth, namely, the lower-, medium-, and higher-speed potential growth rates of the Chinese economy. We first estimate the medium-speed potential growth, a result of the disappearance of the demographic dividend with which we were much concerned in the past. More specifically, it refers to, all things being equal, the highest level of economic growth possible given demographic changes. It is the baseline scenario of our estimates. On that basis, we assume that return on capital (ROC) falls below the baseline level and, consequently, the potential growth rate would thereby decline further. This is what we define as a "lower potential growth rate." Finally, we assume a high potential growth rate as inevitably resulting from the dividends of China's reform. In this section, we will estimate the highest possible speed of China's economic growth through policy simulation.

F. Cai (✉)
Chinese Academy of Social Sciences, Beijing, China
e-mail: caifang@cass.org.cn

Y. Lu
CASS Institute of Population and Labor Economics, Beijing, China
e-mail: luyang@cass.org.cn

F. Cai (ed.), *China's Economic New Normal*, Research Series on the Chinese Dream and China's Development Path, https://doi.org/10.1007/978-981-15-3227-6_15

The country's medium-speed potential growth is related to its demographic dividend, which essentially refers to a country's population structure, with no connection to its population size. There are two constituent parts necessary for a demographic dividend. One is a working-age population that is on the rise, which increases the supply of labor force and thus favors economic growth. The other is a dependency ratio that is in decline, which reduces government expenditures, increases savings, and thus favors capital formation. In economics, a country's economic growth mainly depends on improvements in its total factor productivity (TFP) over the long run. But the demographic dividend tells a different story: based on the aforementioned favorable demographic structure, a country has the chance to achieve a higher growth rate without the necessity of improving its TFP. This is the most important characteristic of the demographic dividend.

As we readily admit, the high-speed growth of the Chinese economy over the past 30 years would not have been possible without the contribution of its demographic dividend. At the same time, however, China's population structure has also been changing over time. Figure 1 is a review of China's demographic transition. Figure 1a reveals the changes in China's working-age population (which peaked in 2013); Fig. 1b shows the variation in China's dependency ratio (which started rising in 2010). That is to say, both components of the demographic dividend have turned against China's economic growth since 2010.

In fact, the demographic dividend is not a uniquely Chinese phenomenon. Let's look at the Japanese case. As we can see in Fig. 2a, Japan's working-age population peaked in 1995; in Fig. 2b, Japan's dependency ratio started rising in 1993. If the demographic dividend started to fade away in China in around 2010, it was in the early 1990s that the same thing had happened in Japan.

Having conducted a comparative study of the changes in the Chinese and Japanese potential growth rates in corresponding periods, we have concluded that similar trends of changes over time are due to the disappearance of the demographic dividend. Therefore, as an explicit policy recommendation, we should not resort to "artificial" stimulus measures for a higher real GDP growth and thus pull it off the potential growth rate. We have to instead draw lessons from Japan's experience.

Our estimates in this chapter are based on the standard form of the Cobb-Douglas production function. In the first step, we will begin by estimating total factor productivity. Next, we will estimate potential employment, which refers to the highest possible employment rate under full employment, subject to the population structure, the labor force participation rate, and the natural rate of unemployment. Finally, we will estimate the potential growth rate using the derived formula. A basic assumption in our modeling is a constant rate of TFP. Referencing estimates of China's population provided by Professor Guo Zhigang in 2013, our population estimates herein are mainly based on the total fertility rate (TFR), which, at different levels, is used to predict the population by gender and age.

To calculate the potential growth rate, we must first estimate the potential capital stock. This is the capital stock of the base period multiplied by the depreciation rate and added to new capital in the current period. At the same time, we establish a relation between the fixed capital formation and the dependency ratio. In fact, when

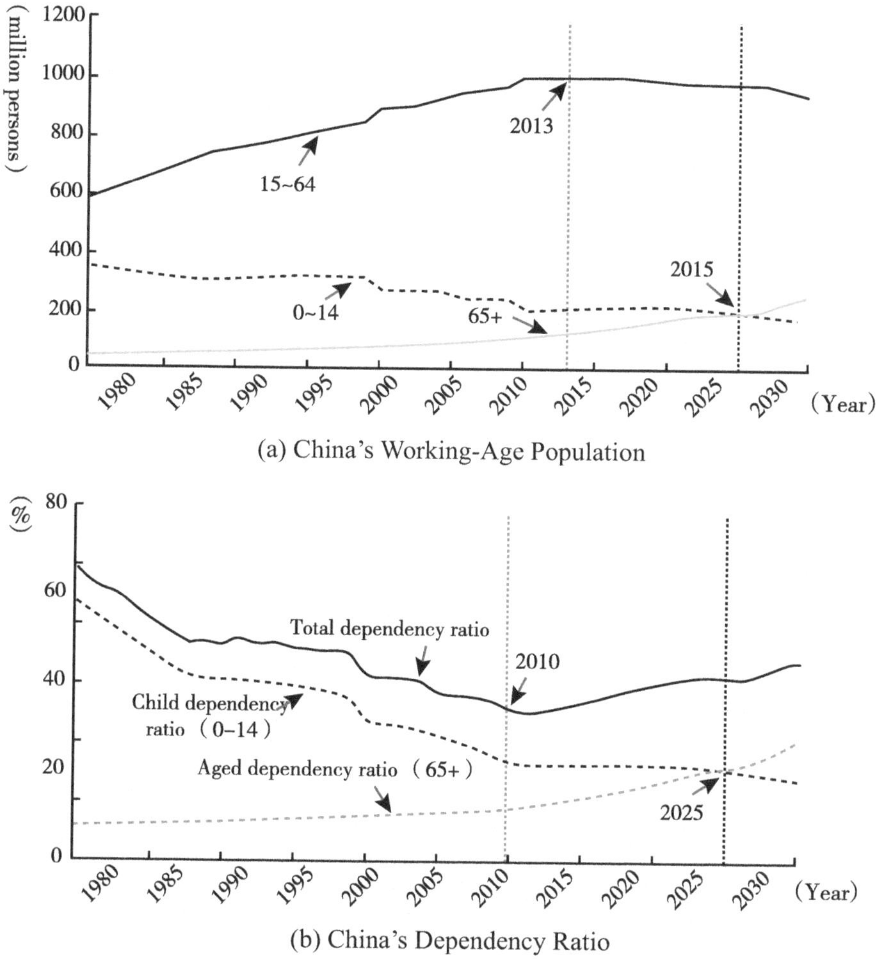

Fig. 1 Changes in China's population structure, 1980–2030. *Source* Lu and Cai (2014)

a country's demographic dividend disappears, the major consequence is a rise in its dependency ratio, which will increase its consumption expenditures and reduce its savings and capital formation. Therefore, we have determined a negative correlation between capital formation and the dependency ratio. Another determining factor for capital formation is the rate of return on capital. We have adopted the real return on capital invested in enterprises on a tax-exclusive basis. The real return on capital in enterprises consists of two parts: one is the real impact of the invested capital on an enterprise—namely, the after-tax ROC—and the other is the amount taxed away. When we incorporate both these variables into our model, we will be able to estimate the determining factors of the fixed capital formation using historical data.

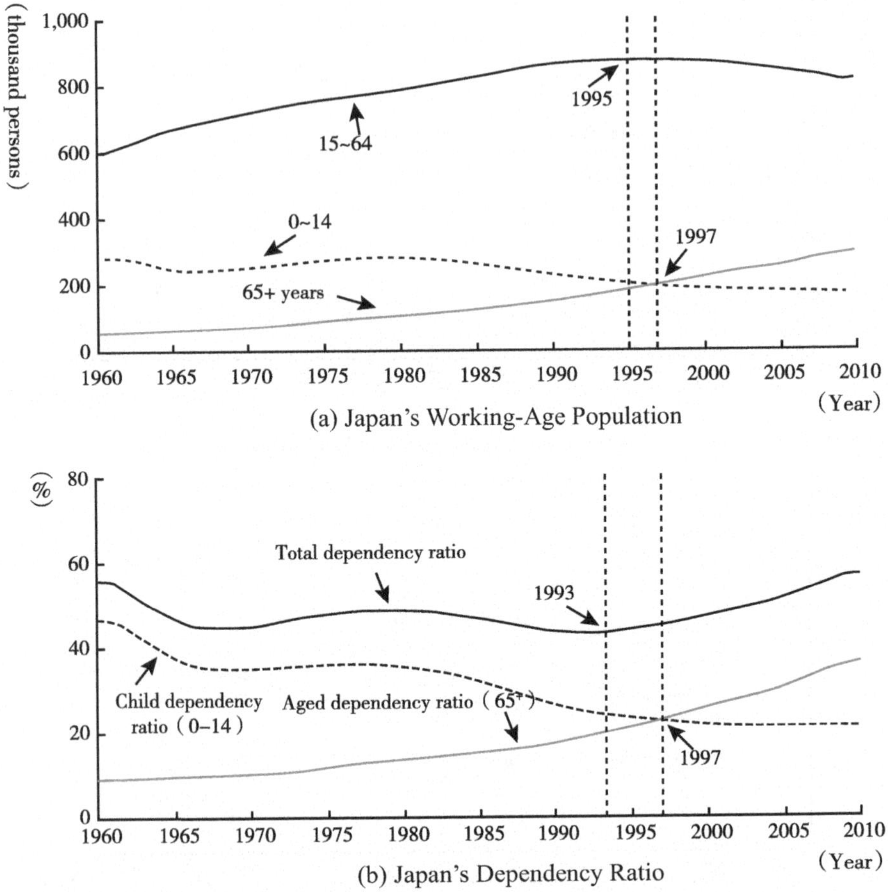

Fig. 2 Changes in Japan's population structure, 1960–2010. *Source* Lu and Cai (2014)

Table 1 shows our estimates of a medium-speed potential growth rate for the Chinese economy. Over the past three decades, China's potential growth rate averaged between 9 and 10%. It dropped to 7.49% during the 12th Five-Year Plan Period due to changes in the population structure, and will decline further to 6.65% during the 13th Five-Year Plan Period. If we set China's GDP growth target accordingly, it should range between 7.0 and 7.2% for 2015. Despite its declining potential growth rate, China is very likely to grow into a high-income economy in or around 2020.

Next, we estimate the lower potential growth rate of the Chinese economy. This is the potential growth rate predicated on the assumption that ROC declines further from the year 2013 onward, e.g., by 1/2, 1/3, 1/4, and 1/5, respectively, from its baseline level. For instance, on the condition of a medium-speed potential growth of 6.65% during the 13th Five-Year Plan Period, if we assume that ROC declines by

Table 1 Estimates of a medium-speed potential growth rate

Indicator (%)	China: 1980–2030						
	1980–1990	1991–2000	2001–2010	2011–2015	2016–2020	2021–2025	2026–2030
Real GDP growth rate	9.20	10.46	10.48				
Potential GDP growth rate	9.92	10.37	10.55	7.49	6.65	5.77	5.17
Potential employment growth rate	3.37	1.67	1.10	0.51	−0.14	−0.46	−0.62
TFP growth rate	4.01	3.66	3.72	2.37	2.37	2.37	2.37
China: GDP per capita 1980–2030 (USD 2005, at constant price)							
GDP per capita (USD)	1,012	2,414	5,764	10,739	14,740	19,687	25,709

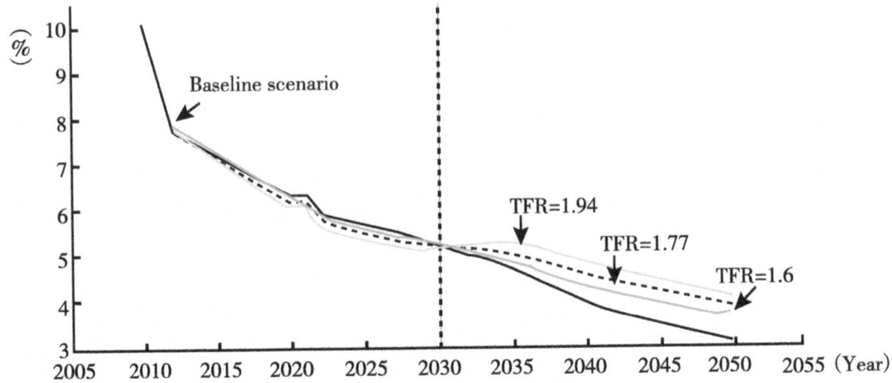

Fig. 3 Potential growth rates of China's GDP at different TFR levels. *Source* Lu and Cai (2014)

1/2 thereafter, the lower-speed potential growth would be 0.25% points below the medium-speed growth.

Finally, we estimate the higher potential growth as a dividend of China's reform. In this context, the reform dividend refers to an increase in China's potential growth rate with the break-down of its institutional barriers and the promotion of its factor supply through reforms. To begin with, we simulate the realization of a higher potential growth rate by cutting taxes to boost capital formation. We assume a reduction in taxes by 1/3, 1/4, and 1/5, respectively, from the 2013 level. The VAT rate is 17% in China at present. If we cut it by 1/5, it becomes 13.6%. In that case and on the condition of a medium-speed potential growth of 6.65% during the 13th Five-Year Plan Period, a reform-boosted higher potential growth rate would be 7.41% over the same period, including a reform dividend of about 0.8% points.

Secondly, we simulate the potential growth rate under a loosened fertility and population policy, so as to estimate the impacts of population policy reform on China's potential growth. With the country's economic development and the implementation of the one-child policy, the total fertility rate (TFR) in China has dropped to 1.4 at present. Even though China has practiced the "two-child policy for an only-child parent" since 2013, under which families could have two children if one parent—rather than both parents—was an only child, there has been no significant effect on TFR (the average number of children born to a woman). When we simulated the medium-speed potential growth rate, we assumed a constant TFR of 1.4. In this step, we assume that China's TFR rises to 1.6, 1.77, and 1.94, respectively, and estimate its corresponding potential growth rates (Fig. 3).

Raising the total fertility rate would result in both short-term and long-term effects. In the short run, it will have an adverse effect on economic growth, because more babies and children would mean a higher dependency ratio and a lower rate of capital formation—that is, until they grow up into a working-age population. In the long run, however, when these little citizens grow up (roughly 15–20 years later), the working-age population will increase and the dependency ratio will decline.

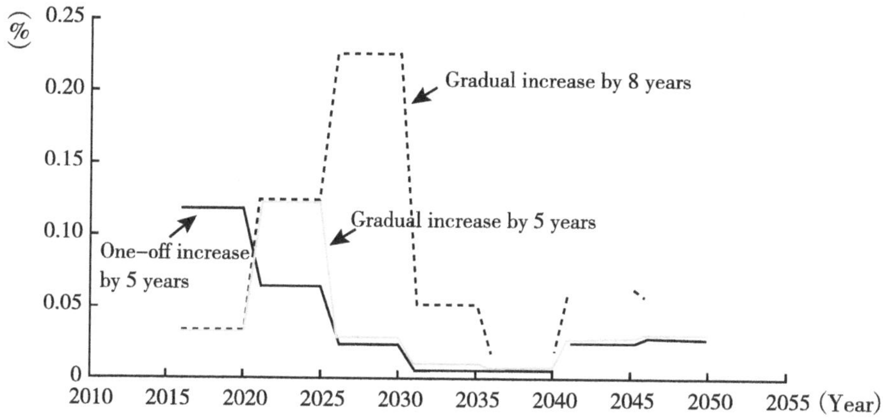

Fig. 4 Weak effects of a retirement-age increase on China's potential growth

Therefore, a higher total fertility rate is conducive to increasing the potential growth rate in the long term. The short-term negative effect is less than 0.2% points, but the long-term dividend of such reform can reach as much as 0.4–0.5% points.

Thirdly, we estimate the impacts of increases to the retirement age on China's potential growth. In this part, we assume that the retirement age in China is currently 58 for men and 52 for women. On that basis, we simulate and compare three schemas for reform. The first option is to increase the retirement age by five years, once and for all, in 2016. The second possibility is a progressive increase of the retirement age by one year every three years for a total of five years. The third option is similar to the second one, but will gradually increase the retirement age by a total of eight years.

According to our simulations, such an increase in the retirement age will have an insignificant impact on China's potential growth. For example, if we adopt the first option and increase the retirement age by five years all at once, we will see a short-term positive effect ranging between 0.1 and 0.15% points, but it will vanish shortly afterwards. If we gradually increase the retirement age by five years, we will see a bigger dividend of reform from 2020 to 2025, which will also range between 0.1 and 0.15% points. Even if we choose the third option and gradually increase the retirement age by eight years, the positive dividend of such a reform would be no more than 0.2–0.25% points. These measures may have a positive effect on China's potential growth in the short term, but that effect will soon disappear. From this simulation, it follows that we should not merely rely on any further increase in our labor input, because it is no longer a dividend that we can count on for the long term (Fig. 4).

Fourthly, we simulate the effect of a higher level of education or a higher quality of human capital achieved through reforms. We simulate two approaches in pursuit of this goal: one of which is to increase enrollments and the other is to increase training. Comparison shows that increased training is more conducive to improving the potential growth rate because it can cover all individuals in the labor market,

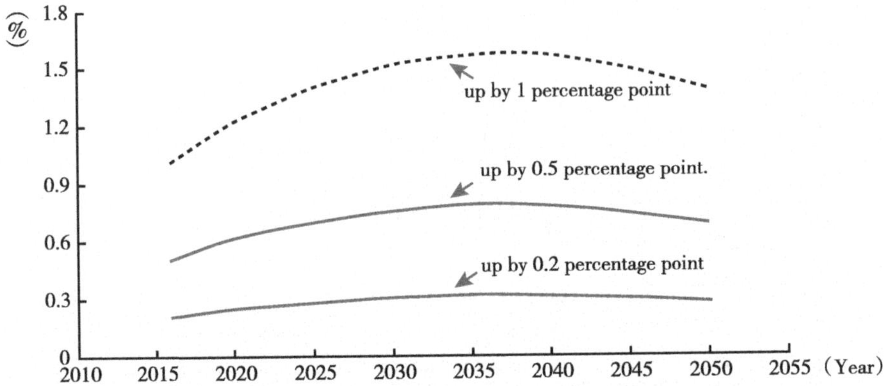

Fig. 5 Significant effects of TFP improvement on China's potential growth rate

whereas it will take a very long time for increased enrollments to have any kind of effect on human capital.

Fifthly, we simulate the effect of higher total factor productivity on China's potential growth rate. In our simulation of the medium-speed growth, we assumed a constant rate of China's TFP. In this part, we assume that China's TFP increases by 0.2, 0.5, and 1 p.p., respectively. Figure 5 is our simulation of the three scenarios, in which the long-term perspective allows us to see a 0.2% point rise in the TFP that directly translates into a 0.23 point increase in the potential growth rate. Obviously, increasing the total factor productivity can yield a significant and long-lasting dividend on China's potential growth. Hence, higher production efficiency is the very dividend of reform that we should count on in the long run (Fig. 5).

Finally, we simulate the dividend of a comprehensive policy adjustment. As we analyzed previously, a single policy instrument tends to have an insignificant effect on the potential growth rate, but a policy mix is likely to pay generous dividends. Based on the estimated medium-speed 6.65% growth, if we bring into play a diverse mix of policy instruments concurrently, we will be able to raise China's potential growth rate to 7.4% during the 13th Five-Year Plan Period. This, then, is what we define as the higher-speed potential growth rate of the Chinese economy. By means of a comprehensive mix of reform measures, China will be entitled to a future reform dividend averaging one to two percentage points (Fig. 6).

At the end of this chapter, we can draw two conclusions from our simulations. On the one hand, China's potential growth rate has begun to decline just as its demographic dividend fades away. On the other hand, it is feasible for China to increase its potential growth rate by implementing a series of reforms in the following fields. First of all, it is absolutely necessary for China to adjust its family planning policy and gradually loosen its fertility and population control, and make the transition from the "two-child policy for an only-child parent" to a "general two-child policy." Next, it must steadily deepen its reformation of the financial and household registration systems while simultaneously improving its production efficiency and

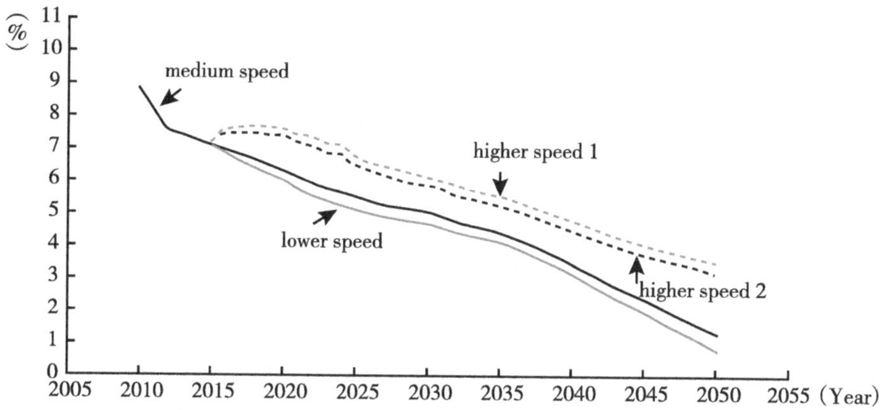

Fig. 6 China's potential growth rate: from lower to higher speeds

further increasing its factor supply. Finally, we also highlight the significance of tax cuts (e.g., the VAT rate reduction) as an effective measure to increase real ROC in enterprises and facilitate capital formation, which will eventually support a higher potential growth rate for the Chinese economy.

Reference

Lu, Y., & Cai, F. (2014). Changes in the population structure and the impacts on the potential growth rate: A comparison between China and Japan. *Journal of World Economy, 37*(1), 3–29.

The manufacturer's authorised representative in the EU is Springer Nature Customer Service Centre GmbH, Europaplatz 3, 69115 Heidelberg, Germany. If you have any concerns regarding our products, please contact ProductSafety@springernature.com

Printed and bound by CPI Group (UK) Ltd, Croydon, CR0 4YY
25/09/2026
02222903-0010